D1566169

Globalizing Taipei:
The Political Economy
of Spatial Development

Planning, History and the Environment Series

Editor:
Professor Dennis Hardy, Middlesex University, UK

Editorial Board:
Professor Arturo Almandoz, Universidad Simón Bolivar, Caracas, Venezuela
Professor Nezar AlSayyad, University of California, Berkeley, USA
Professor Eugenie L. Birch, University of Pennsylvania, Philadelphia, USA
Professor Robert Bruegmann, University of Illinois at Chicago, USA
Professor Jeffrey W. Cody, Chinese University of Hong Kong, Hong Kong
Professor Robert Freestone, University of New South Wales, Sydney, Australia
Professor David Gordon, Queen's University, Kingston, Ontario, Canada
Professor Sir Peter Hall, University College London, UK
Dr Peter Larkham, University of Central England, Birmingham, UK
Professor Anthony Sutcliffe, Nottingham, UK

Technical Editor
Ann Rudkin, Alexandrine Press, Marcham, Oxon, UK

Published titles

Globalizing Taipei: The Political Economy of Spatial Development

edited by

Reginald Yin-Wang Kwok

Routledge
Taylor & Francis Group

NEW YORK AND LONDON

First published by Routledge,
270 Madison Ave, New York, NY 10016

Simultaneously published in the UK
by Routledge
2 Park Square, Milton Park,
Abingdon, Oxfordshire OX14 4RN

Routledge is an imprint of the Taylor & Francis Group

Typeset in Palatino and Humanist by PNR Design, Didcot, Oxfordshire
Printed and bound in Great Britain by MPG Books Ltd., Bodmin, Cornwall

This book was commissioned and edited by Alexandrine Press, Marcham, Oxfordshire

The publisher makes no representation, express or implied, with regard to the accuracy of the information contained in this book and cannot accept any legal responsibility or liability for any errors or omissions that may be made.

British Library Cataloguing in Publication Data

A catalogue record for this book is available from the British Library

Library of Congress Cataloging in Publication Data

Globalizing Taipei : the political economy of spatial development / edited by Reginald Yin-Wang Kwok.
    p. cm.
  Includes bibliographical references and index.
  ISBN 0–415–35451–X (hb : alk. paper)
  1. City planning—Taiwan—Taipei. I. Kwok, R. Yin-Wang.
  HT169.C62T354 2005
  307.1′216′0951249--dc22

                                                 2004023538

ISBN 0–415–35451–X

Contents

Part 3. Social Differentiation

Part 4. Cultural Reorientation

Acknowledgements

There are many people who helped to make this book a reality, and it is quite impossible to thank them all. We would like to mention a few key people without whose contribution it would never have been published. The Department of Geography at the National Taiwan University provided the venue for the continuous discussions amongst the contributors, and an intellectual home. Hsin-Huang Michael Hsiao and Lucie Cheng discussed with us the concept and encouraged us to pursue the project. Kong Chong Ho gave practical and critical comments in reviewing the first draft. Bruce Hung-Jen Tan and Chu-Joe Hsia participated in all our forum and made substantive suggestions. Sir Peter Hall, in addition to supporting the project, guided us in publication.

In the production of the book, Ann Rudkin gave us continuous advice in the preparation of the manuscript and gave it the final polish. James Yao spent countless hours on the thankless tasks of proofing and formatting. Ruby I-Te Yang chased up references and footnotes effectively and seemingly effortlessly. To all, we owe our thanks.

Finally, the editor, contributors and publisher would like to thank all those who have granted permission to reproduce illustrations. We have made every effort to contact and acknowledge copyright holders, but if any errors have been made we would be happy to correct them at a later printing.

Glossary

This glossary is based on how the term appears in the text, and Chinese characters, in *Fantizi*, 繁体字 , consistent with the convention in Taiwan, are given as the reference. In the text, all names of key places and persons are given in the commonly used and conventional spelling (e.g. Chiang Kai-shek, Taipei), generally based on the Wade-Giles system. All other terms are given in the Pinyin system. In this list, Pinyin romanization is given in (), Wade-Giles romanization is given in [], and English equivalent is given in {}.

A
Aiqing wansui {Vive L'amour}   愛情萬歲

B
Banqiao [pan-ch'iao]   板橋
Beiqing Chengshi {City of Sadness}   悲情城市
Beitou [Pei-tou]   北投
Beitou Knowledge Park   北投知識園
   Also known as Beitou Knowledge-Based Economic Park   北投知識經濟園

C
Cai shichang   菜市場
Cankun 3C   燦坤 3C
Changhua (Zhanghua)   彰化
Chen Shui-Bian   陳水扁
Chengshi dianying {City film}   城市電影
Chiang Ching-kuo   蔣經國
Chiang Kai-shek   蔣介石
Chiayi (Jiayi)   嘉義
Chientan (Jiantan)   劍潭
Chongqing South Road   重慶南路
Chung-yuan University (Zhongyuan)
   Also known as Chung-yuan Christian University   中原大學

D
Da'an [Ta-an]   大安
Da'an senlin gongyuan {Ta-an Forest Park also known as No.7 Park}   大安森林公園
Dadaocheng [Ta-tao-cheng]   大稻埕
Dafo de tongkong {The Eyes of the Buddha}   大佛的瞳孔
Dali [Ta-li]   大里
Damaichang   大賣場

Datong Corporation	大同公司
Daya [Ta-ya]	大雅
Dinghao Supermarket	頂好超級市場
Dinghao shichang [Ting-hao shih chang]	頂好市場
Dong {The Hole}	洞
Dunhua North Road	敦化北路
Dunhua South Road	敦化南路

E
Erzi de dawanou {Sandwich Man}	兒子的玩偶

F
Fengqun Group	豐群集團
Fujian	福建

G
Guangyin de gushi {In Our Time}	光陰的故事

H
Heliu {The River}	河流
Hemei [Ho-mei}	和美
Hou Hsiao-hsien (Hou Xiaoxian)	侯孝賢
Huanghun shichang	黃昏市場
Hsieh Tung-min (Xie Dongmin)	謝東閔
Hsinchu Industrial Park	新竹工業園
Also known as Hsinchu Science Park	新竹科學園
or Hsinchu Science Industrial Park	新竹科學工業園
or Hsinehu Science-Based Industrial Park	
Huangmei diao	黃梅調

I
Ilan [Yi-lan]	宜蘭

J
Jiankang xieshi pian {Healthy and Realistic melodramas}	健康寫實片

K
Kaohsiung (Gaoxiong)	高雄
Keelung (Jilong)	基隆
Kinmen (Jinmen)	金門
KMT [Kuomintang]; (Guomindang)	國民黨
Kuo Mao-Lin (Guo Maolin)	郭茂林

L
Lee Kang-sheng (Li Kangsheng)	李康生
Lee Teng-hui	李登輝

Liangfandian 量販店
Linkou 林口
Lin Yang-kang (Lin Yanggang) 林洋港
Liu Xiyang [Liu Hsi-yang] 劉喜陽
Luzhou [Lu-chou] 蘆洲

M
Ma Ying-Jeou (Ma Yingjiu) 馬英九
Mazu 媽祖
Mengjia [Meng-chia] 艋舺
Miaoli 苗栗
Miao Tian [Miao Tien] 苗天
Mingde [Ming-te] 明德
Minsheng East Road 民生東路
Muzha [Mu-cha] 木柵

N
Nangang [Nan-kang] 南港
Nangang Software Industrial Park 南港軟體工業園
   Also known as Nangang Software Park
   or   Nangang Industrial Park 南港工業園
   or   Nangang Science Park 南港科學園
Nangang Trade Park 南港經貿園
Nantou 南投
Nanzi [Nan-tzu] 南梓
Neihu 內湖
Neihu Science Park 內湖科學園
   Also known as Neihu Industrial Park 內湖工業園
Nezha 哪吒
Ni nabian jidianzhong? {What Time Is It There?} 你那邊幾點鐘

P
Penghu 澎湖
Pingtung (pingdong) 屏東

Q
Qingshaonian Nezha {Rebels of the Neon God, or, Rebels} 青少年哪吒

R
Renai Road 仁愛路
Roosevelt Road 羅斯福路

S
Sanchong [San-chung] 三重
Shantou 汕頭
Shanghai 上海

Shetou	社頭
Shenzhen	深圳
Shichang	市場
Shin Kong Life Tower	新光人壽摩天大樓
Songshan [Sung-shan]	松山
T	
Tainan	台南
Taichung (Taizhong)	台中
Tamsui River (Danshui)	淡水河
Taoyuan	桃園
Tsai Ming-liang (Cai Mingliang)	蔡明亮
Tucheng	土城
W	
Wanhua	萬華
Wenshan	文山
Wuxiao pian (Gongfu pian); [Kung fu pien]	武俠片; 功夫片
X	
Xiamen	廈門
Xiao Kang	小康
Xiao Nanmen [Hsiao Nan-men]	小南門
Ximen [Hsi-men]	西門
Ximending [Hsi-men-ting]	西門町
Xindian [Hsin-tien]	新店
Xinyi [Hsin-i]	信義
Xinyi Fubang	信義富邦
Xinyi International Trade Center	信義國際金融中心
Xinzhuang [Hsin-chuang]	新莊
Xizhi [Hsi-chih]	汐址
Xinxindazhong (Hsin-hsin-ta-chung)	欣欣大眾
Y	
Yang Dechang {Edward Yang}	楊德昌
Yang Ming Shan National Park	陽明山國家公園
Yanji Supermarket	延吉超級市場
Yonghe [Yung-ho]	永和
Yongkang [Yung-kang]	永康
Yunlin	雲林
Z	
Zhonghe [Chung-ho]	中和
Zhongshan [Chung-shan]	中山
Zhongxiao [Chung-hsiao]	忠孝
Zhongzheng [Chung-cheng]	中正
Zhuhai	珠海

Contributors

Yi-Ling Chen is an Assistant Professor in the Department of Social Studies Education at the National Hualien Teachers College. She received her PhD in urban planning and policy development at Rutgers University. Her research interests are housing, gender, and urban development.

Chia-Ho Ching is the Director of the Department of Land Economies and Administration, National Taipei University. He holds a PhD from the Department of Civic Design, Town and Country Planning, Liverpool University. His teaching and research topics include urban regeneration, globalization and local development, transborder production networks, and the spatial and institutional restructuring in Taiwanese regions and cities.

Tsu-Lung Chou is a Professor in the Graduate Institute of Urban Planning, National Taipei University. He holds a PhD from the Department of Civic Design, Town and Country Planning, Liverpool University. He teaches planning theory and planning system, local economics and urban development, and regional development policy and planning. His recent research is primarily concentrated on globalization, local transformation and planning in Asian countries, especially Taiwan and China.

Jinn-Yuh Hsu is an Associate Professor of Geography at National Taiwan University. He received his PhD from the University of California at Berkeley. He specializes in high-technology industries and regional development in late-industrializing countries, particularly Taiwan; labour markets, technology learning, industrial organization and dynamic institutionalism.

Li-Ling Huang is an Assistant Professor in the Architecture Department and the Graduate Institute of Media Space Design, Ming Chuan University. She holds a PhD from the Graduate Institute of Building and Planning, National Taiwan University. Her research interests include participatory design, historical preservation, and city and regional development.

Sue-Ching Jou is a Professor of Geography at National Taiwan University. She received her PhD from the Department of Geography, University of Minnesota. Her research interests focus on urban policy and politics, and cross border investment of Taiwan capital. She is currently working on a project of new corporate landscapes with regard to the production and representation of high-rise buildings in Chinese global cities.

Reginald Yin-Wang Kwok is a Professor of Asian Studies and a Professor of Urban and Regional Planning, University of Hawaii at Manoa. He received his PhD from the Graduate School of Architecture and Planning, Columbia University. He previously taught at the Architectural Association, London and Columbia University, and was the founding Director of the Centre of Urban Planning and Urban Studies (now Centre of Urban Planning and Environmental Management), University of Hong Kong. His research interests include the political economy of Chinese development and urbanization, globalization in East Asia, urban economic and spatial development, and the impact of culture on urban design.

Po-Fen Tai is an Assistant Professor in the Department of Landscape Architecture at Chung Hua University. She received her PhD from the Graduate Institute of Building and Planning, National Taiwan University. Her research interests include environmental planning and design, urban sociology, cultural landscapes, and community planning.

Chih-Hung Wang is an Assistant Professor at the Graduate Institute for Social Transformation Studies at the Shih Hsin University. He received his PhD from the Graduate Institute of Building and Planning, National Taiwan University. He has written articles on the cultural governance of Taipei City, cultural geography, and politics of translation, and he currently undertaking research on the consumption of organic foods and migrant workers identity formation through food practices.

Peter Cheng-Chong Wu is an Assistant Professor in the Department of Geography, National Taiwan Normal University. He received his PhD from the Department of Geography at the London School of Economics and Political Science. His research interests include urban and social geographies and, in particular, the geography of everyday life.

Kuang-Tien Yao is a Cataloging Librarian at University of Hawaii Library at Manoa. She received an MLS from Simmons College Graduate School of Library and Information Science, Boston, and an MA in Asian Studies from the School of Hawaiian, Asian, and Pacific Studies, University of Hawaii at Manoa.

Introduction

Asian Dragons, South China Growth Triangle, Developmental Governance and Globalizing Taipei

Reginald Yin-Wang Kwok with Jinn-Yuh Hsu

Compared to the other capitals of the Asian Dragons – Seoul, Hong Kong and Singapore – little has been written about Taipei. To remedy this, this volume is a study of contemporary Taipei, from the post-World War II period, with emphasis on the most recent events. It reviews and analyzes the current political economy of Taipei's development from the globalization perspective – assessing the economic and social impacts of globalization on urban development, and identifying the local factors, which impact the city's global development.

This volume examines the key aspects of Taipei's developmental process towards a global city, thus 'Globalizing Taipei'. The working frame for analyzing the city's current development is based on a combination of global city theories which have been developed from Hall's original 'world cities' idea (Hall, 1966). Friedmann's 'world city formation' proposes that the world city network is based on the spatial connection of transnational production and the international division of labour (Friedmann and Wulff, 1982; Friedmann, 1986)), with a fast growth of transnational professionals congregating in the city centres (Clark, 1996). Spatial division of labour causes the postindustrial cities to become centres of commercial and professional services. Sassen's 'global city' finds that cross-border transactions are located in cities, restructuring their economies with a dominance of producer services.[1] The dynamics of power, centrality and inequality are the new urban organizational elements created by global economic activities (Sassen, 2001a). Knox (1994) asserts that global cities are the nodal points for production, and they display distinctive characteristics – control over production, news, information and culture. They are the locales of economic and social inequality and spatial segregation, new immigration, and class and political conflicts (Knox, 1994; Held and McGrew, 2002). Friedmann further argues that the fluctuations of the urban global ranking are dependent on the city's response to exogenous political and economic changes, intercity competition, and social and environmental sustainability (Friedmann, 1998). These are the components by which we define the global city, and which guide our investigations.

National wealth resides in the economic activities of cities (Jacobs, 1984), and large cities are sites of innovation and civilization (Hall, 1998). Within a state of self-enclosed 'container of socio-economic and political-cultural relations', cities serve the primary national or subnational economic roles (Brenner, 1999). Taiwan is no exception. Its political economy has been opened to globalization for almost half a century. Taiwan's urban centre for the continuous globalization process is Taipei, and the capital is the spatial concentration of transnational production, foreign investment and international trade. The city has ascended to the primary city of the urban hierarchy since the turn of the twentieth century. Taipei's primacy has been well studied by many urban scholars (e.g. Ching, 2003; Jou, 2001; Liu and Tung, 2003). Taiwan's urbanization was initially based on agricultural production, and started in the south. Since Japanese colonization in the late 1800s, the introduction of industrialization steadily shifted urbanization to the coastal cities in the north. From the 1950s, urbanization accelerated and migration began to concentrate in the large cities. Taipei took the lion's share of urban expansion. By 2001, 32 per cent of all industrial, commercial and service firms were concentrated in the Taipei metropolitan region, providing 40 per cent of employment in these sectors, and producing 43 per cent of Taiwan's total production value (Ching, 2003). It is the location where economic, political and cultural activities concentrate. Of the three major city-regions, all on the western coast, Taipei city-region, relative to Taichung and Kaohsiung city-regions, is by far the most powerful (see figure 0.1). Domestically, Taipei is the primary economic, political and cultural centre of the urban hierarchy, dominating the northern Taiwan city-region, and controlling Taiwan's economy.

The high speed rail system in the western Taiwan corridor, connecting Taipei and Kaohsiung, was proposed by the Executive Yuan in 1987, and 2005 sees its completion. This inter-regional infrastructure project will connect the three city-regions and some 30 smaller cities into a combined economic and production area. The objectives are to link and integrate these cities and their hinterlands, improve access to all the science and industrial parks, expand production, commerce and community, and to improve technology and innovation in order to pave the way for Taiwan's transnational development (BOTHSR, 2004). With the agglomeration

Figure 0.1 Map of Taiwan.

effect and inter-regional infrastructure support, Taipei's function as the primary centre of this conurbation will be strengthened, and the city will be in the position to provide the producer services needed for the entire western coastal region for global production. Taipei's primacy and future development as the economic, political and cultural urban centre will have a dispersal effect on the two other city-regions, Taichung and Kaohsiung. With its role reinforced, Taipei will lead and facilitate Taiwan's globalization project.

Asian Dragons: Asia-Pacific Mode of Globalization

As Taiwan is one of the Asian Dragons, Taipei's development naturally follows the Asian Dragons model of development, which, therefore, provides the global context for the city's recent growth. As the Asian Dragons have turned from receivers into exporters of foreign investment, Taiwan, Hong Kong and the south China coast were brought together, and formed a regional growth triangle with the three metropolises – Taipei, Hong Kong and Shanghai – as the nodes of transnational capital, production, and entrepreneurial flows. In the last two decades, Taipei's growth has been closely tied to the South China Growth Triangle. Taiwan's industrialization has been guided and managed by the state. Spatially, the developmental state has concentrated its political and economic power in the capital. Taipei's growth has been shaped by its particular administrative and spatial position in Taiwan's political economy. The Asian Dragons, South China Growth Triangle, and Developmental Governance, which shape the capital's recent development, provide the overall frame in reviewing globalizing Taipei.

The phenomenal Asia-Pacific growth in the post-World War II era is a familiar story well told by many scholars (e.g. Bello and Rosenfeld, 1990; Berger and Hsiao, 1993; Chan, 1990; Chowdhury and Islam; 1993; de Bary, 1988; Woronoff, 1986). Here, a synoptic reminder of the formation and growth path of the Asian Newly Industrializing Economies will serve as the global context for Taiwan's development. South Korea, Taiwan, Hong Kong and Singapore started their independent growth out of a series of economic and political crises – the Korean War in South Korea, the Kuomintang government's flight to Taiwan, the UN embargo on the *entrepôt* economy of Hong Kong, and the separation of Singapore from Malaysia. All four economies had to rely on their own resources and efforts in order to survive. All had little or no natural resources, small domestic markets, small industrial bases, but abundant low-skilled labour. The only path to development was labour intensive industrialization for export, though both South Korea and Taiwan initially took the import substitution route to strengthen their economic bases, but they too, soon reverted to export oriented industrialization.

Most industrial enterprises were family-run small-scale industries with a low-cost, hard working, quick learning and skill escalating labour force. These firms operated with a network of sub-contractors to compete for foreign contracts (Sit, 1980; Sit and Wong, 1989; Hamilton and Kao, 1990). The governments took a development state mode in directing and managing the economy. Most scholars excluded Hong Kong as a developmental state, because the colonial state adopted a *laissez faire* economy. The colonial government, in reality, intervened indirectly and discretely through subsidizing collective consumption in order to reduce the labour costs (Taylor and Kwok, 1989; Castells, Goh and Kwok, 1990; Kwok, 1999). It also took a supporting and facilitating role by providing business friendly institutions, and infrastructure conducive to industrial production. All four economies initially benefited from the United States market, which was opened for their low-technology inexpensive industrial products. Without exception, the low-cost, efficient and productive industrial labour, the only economic assets, produced the initial and rapid economic growth. The Asian Dragons' economic successes are attributed to the free market and the high performance export activities. The international economy introduced and allowed these economies into the globalization process.

The success of the Asian Dragons was often credited to their Confucian ethics (Goldstein, 1991; Vogel, 1991), in particular, family frugality and commitment to education. After one generation of economic growth, production profits were transferred into a significant accumulation of family savings, now looking for investment opportunities. The family commitment to investing in education for the second generation propelled a dramatic structural change in the labour force. The blue collar labour pool was converted into a white collar labour pool in one generation. By the 1970s, there was a blue collar labour shortage amongst the Asian Dragons. In its place, a pool of domestic educated white collar workers emerged, and a new reserve of investment funds was ready. The industrial entrepreneurs began to explore abroad for lower cost locations, investing first in ASEAN Four (except Singapore), concentrated in Bangkok, Thailand, and Jakarta, Indonesia where low-cost industrial labour and land were available.

By late 1978, China adopted the Open Policy under Economic Reform, and in the following year, four Special Economic Zones – Shenzhen, Zhuhai, Xiamen and Shantou, were set up in south China, and later, Hainan was added to the list. Offering the lowest factor costs in the region, and cultural affinity, China has become the most advantageous production location for Hong Kong and Taiwan entrepreneurs. Leapfrogging the Asian Flying Geese hierarchy,[2] the Asia-Pacific ranking system of globalization, the two newly industrializing economies diverted their investment to China. Hong Kong investors immediately dominated all foreign investments in China, and have maintained the top position from the onset, with Taiwan's investment rising prominently in recent years. Because of Taiwan's impasse on the Chinese proposed 'Three Links' policy,[3] direct economic links between Taiwan and China are prohibited, and all cross-strait investment, trade, personnel and production flows have to go through a third country. Hong Kong, because of its geographic location, international producer services, cultural affinity and China connections, has become the crucial transition point for all kinds of transactions between Taiwan and China. Consequently, the international producer services in the *de facto* city-state have expanded and the economy has restructured accordingly. The transnational flows between Taiwan, Hong Kong and the south China coast formed a global economic, social and cultural network – the foundation of the South China Growth Triangle.

The Asian Dragons mode of development, which propels Taiwan's development, is the key to its globalization process. But it was the opening of China, which provided the vital condition and opportunity for regional economic integration for these three economies. Because of the necessity for industrial restructuring and production relocation, Taiwan's entrepreneurs, technology and capital have been drawn into China through Hong Kong. This transnational production network is the economic and institutional base for the formation of the South China Growth Triangle, now one of the most notable Asia-Pacific regions for global production and marketing.[4] The growth triangle is the regional extension of the globalization process into an East Asian cultural, political and economic space.

South China Growth Triangle: Partnership and Competition

The South China Growth Triangle is a topic that has attracted much academic attention. Many studies of these three economies have been published (e.g. Cartier, 2001; Naughton, 1997; Ng and Tuan, 1996; Van Kemenade, 1998; Wang, 1998). A brief summary of these findings will provide a regional context and condition for Taipei's global city formation. Present globalization trends induce city-regions in national political economies to connect with other city-regions in other national political economies, and breaks up the nationally bounded rural-urban interlinked relation. City-regions within the same nations and between nations compete with each other in the cross-border economic networking (Scott, 1988; 2000). The core of global economy resides not in nations, but concentrates in major cities (Sassen, 2001*b*). In the new economic network, cities become the nodes of knowledge, capital and talent flows (Castells, 1996). In the case of the South China Growth Triangle, the core cities are Taipei, Hong Kong and Shanghai. The convergence of these three metropolises occurs when they engage in the global production process and information networking. Global market competition and pragmatic adjustment direct the three metropolises into different but complementary roles.

Historically, these cities found their modern origins in Western colonization of China between the 1840s and 1870s. Forced open by Western powers, and led by international development, Shanghai blossomed into an industrial, business and social centre, giving the city its international prominence and glamorous sheen. Taipei, a small remote provincial town, started as a Japanese colonial capital functioning as a military and administrative centre for the island colony. It was a political command post for commercial control to advance the expanding imperial power. In contrast, Hong Kong, the small fishing village under British rule, started as a struggling Cantonese trade town. Gradually the city developed as an international *entrepôt* specializing in import/export and finance, attracting migration from its adjacent province. With disparate beginnings, these cities witnessed, after the World War II, socialism in China, the UN embargo, and the cross-strait separation in the early 1950s. These international events further segregated and diverted the development of the three cities. Up to the late 1970s, they developed almost entirely independent of and isolated from each other. From the early 1980s, the three converged, as the South China Growth Triangle began to connect. They all adopted the transnational developmental mode and were brought into direct link and competition through globalization. Even with very diverse growth paths, all now are cosmopolitan metropolises of commerce, trade, finance, professional service, and migration.

For the last two and a half decades, international investment, enterprises and professionals flooded into Hong Kong. They are now converging into Shanghai. Hong Kong's building boom in the 1970s to 1990s is also now echoed in Shanghai. Taipei, developing through export-oriented industrialization, prospered as a major production and political centre. Following Hong Kong's lead, Taiwan's production plants were steadily transferred to south China, first to the Pearl River Delta adjacent to Hong Kong but now targeting the Shanghai region as their investment destination. Taipei and Hong Kong have developed their respective global roles in technological development and financial professional services. The awakening of Shanghai, the Pearl of the Orient of the 1920s and 1930s, attracted global investment and has transformed its immediate region, the Yangtze River Delta, as the one of the world's major industrial production sites. Though under different political economic systems, the three urban economies intertwine and adjust, exploiting each other's comparative advantages for its own benefits. Presently, the three cities complement each other within the sub-global production network, and all benefit economically. Transnational production integrates and coordinates these three cities into an interlocking global network system.

The South China Growth Triangle is not static or stable, but subject to indigenous and exogenous disturbances. The Asian Financial Crisis, which affected both Taipei and Hong Kong, shook their confidence and swagger. In contrast, Shanghai regains its prominence as China's undisputed economic and production centre and is poised for global challenges. The confident newcomer, with the largest population of the three cities, now seems to be ready to take over its southern and eastern counterparts. In the midst of cooperative and complementary networking, an intensive competition for the top regional commanding post is brewing between the three fragile partners. Hong Kong and Shanghai are now Taipei's most immediate competitive rival cities.

Developmental Governance: Developmental State and Civil Society

The role of the state in formulating and managing economic policies to enhance the competitive advantages has been attributed to the success of the Asian Dragons (Amsden, 1991; Douglass, 1994; Wade, 1990). The rapid growth of Taiwan's export industrialization was accompanied by strong state intervention in key and selected struggling sectors, allowing these industrial firms to exploit comparative advantages, and to insert themselves into the global production chains (Gereffi, 1992). Once Taiwan's economy deepened its transnational connection, state intervention became controversial as globalization brings with it political democratization and social liberalization. The state, under global pressure, cannot but follow the international norm and deregulate the economic institutions. Otherwise, the economy would be left behind by the world system. Even with global forces so overwhelming and omnipotent, local institutions still matter in determining the consequences of external linkage (Storper, 1997; Scott, 2002). How the global space affects national state territory is not a deterritorialization process, but a process of rescaling and reconfiguring territory (Brenner, 1998). What the nation state is doing is to change its nature and identity in the global world. The role of the state in a global economic system is concentrated increasingly in the coordination and regulation of the institutional environment for business, the enhancement of human capital in knowledge-based economy but with decreasing attention to welfare (O'Neill, 1997). In reality, the state still functions firmly in global development. The state, at both the central and city level, plays critical roles in managing the articulation of national economy in relation to global trade and investment.

Globalization has been Taiwan's developmental mode since it adopted an export oriented industrialization strategy in the 1960s. Taipei, since the 1970s, has entered the global city race and has been pursuing urban development strategies towards that goal. With the central government in the same urban locality, and with a shared developmental goal, Taipei should be receiving policy support and preferential treatment for its urban development from the central government, as Taipei's global success will be mutually beneficial to both levels of the state. Taipei's road of development should be smooth, paved by a cooperative central government. The negotiation and collaboration of centre-city inter-agency politics is one of the main factors, which influence Taipei's development.

With the state being redefined, it actively relaxes the regulatory and institutional barriers to facilitate free trade and market economy, in order to comply with the global trend of neo-liberalism. The timely growth of the middle class has exerted a new domestic pressure demanding the state to be more responsive and responsible to the society. Consequently, there is a greater operational space for enterprises to engage in international business and trade. There is also a greater space for society in policy formation and social expression. Taiwan in the 1980s witnessed the convergence of these external and internal political forces. In combination, they pushed forth the development and expansion of the civil society and the transformation of the state. The globalization process has brought forth the state–society relations as a key political, social and cultural factor in development. With the introduction of democracy, multi-party debates, identity politics, and cross-strait links have emerged as the intermingling ideological and developmental topics, dominating Taiwan's state society discourse.

Globalizing Taipei: Theme and Organization

Against this global, regional and domestic background, Taipei's development is examined as a unique phenomenon responding to the global economy, but conditioned by international politics and regional competition. Globalization as the free market mode of development under neoliberalism, and the developmental state are the primary keys in decoding Taipei's development (see figures 0.2 and 0.3). The specific domestic factors – the cross-strait relationship, identity politics, and centre-city inter-agency politics, which are particular to Taiwan – significantly influence the city's development towards its global goal. These provide a secondary frame for analyzing specific issues. Within the two levels of contextual specificities, the theme of this volume is to investigate the crucial urban changes brought on by

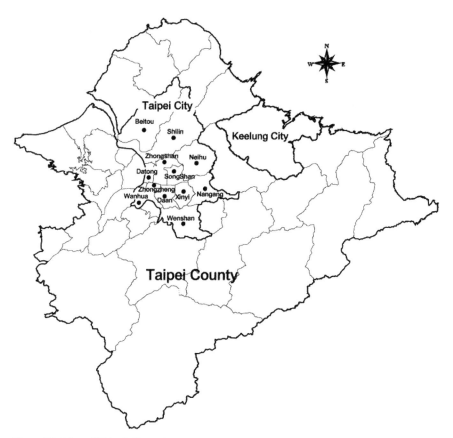

Figure 0.2. Map of Taipei city-region.

Figure 0.3. Map of Taipei City.

globalization in Taipei's economy, polity, society, and culture. Structurally, this book analyzes these prominent global effects on contemporary Taipei in four parts.

The first part, Economic and Spatial Restructuring, investigates Taipei's role in Taiwan's postwar economic transformation and the historical evolution of the city's spatial structure. The first three chapters establish how globalization determines the current level of the city's development, economic position and current global functions. Jinn-Yuh Hsu's chapter reviews the major changes in the city's development since the end of World War II in relation to Taiwan's economic and industrial polices. His chapter demonstrates the transformation of the economic base from manufacturing, through trading service, to the present high-technology headquarters and producer services. The key factors of the urban evolution are global economy, developmental state, and industrial decentralization.

Chia-Ho Ching's chapter assesses the current level of globalization, and the limited growth of the producer services due to the city's role as a transnational sub-contractor and the cross-strait policies. In spite of the dispersal of the manufacturing sector to the periphery and the growing services sectors, the city's economic development takes a different trajectory from other global cities, leading Taipei to the second-tier, rather than the advanced, producer services. In the next chapter, Tsu-Lung Chou reviews Taipei's urban spatial diversification process generated by globalization, causing a spatial shift of the city centre. Induced by party political rivalries between the city and central government, there was an intensive competition for economic development between the capital city and its surrounding regions. Responding to the globalization process and centre-city politics, a fragmented spatial reorganization has taken place. The capital has grown from a mono-centric to a poly-centric pattern.

The second part, 'State and Society Realignment', reviews the actions taken by the developmental state, and the subsequent changes in the state–society relationship. Different areas of planning are introduced to illustrate a variety of state–society configurations in three urban developmental sectors. Li-Ling Huang's chapter explains the radical shift of urban planning practice towards community development and participation. Reflecting the new political environment brought on by globalization, the process of transplanting a Western planning ideology loosens the authority of the state and opens up to middle-class activism. Next, Yi-Ling Chen's chapter examines the urban housing sector. The dominant state ideology, neo-liberalism, practically excludes the state from providing social housing. Left to the private sector, housing construction creates rampant land speculation and rising housing costs. With the market in total command, the society is separated into two housing consumer segments, with the lower income groups reduced to a marginal status. Sue-Ching Jou's chapter investigates the developmental process of the newly designated Central Business District (CBD), Xinyi, which is planned to attract and accommodate global economy. An intensive political negotiation and confrontation between the city and the central government on resources and spatial image weakens the state, and the planning of the district totally excludes the local community. With a weakened state and society, the project is dominated by the corporate power of real estate. With the developers' special interests, which often deviate from those of the state, the development projects a global image but significantly changes the spatial functions.

The third part, 'Social Differentiation', examines the key social consequences generated by globalization. At this transitional stage, the urban labour market and consumption patterns are selected in order to reflect two major social responses to globalization – the level of social polarization and diversification. Po-Fen Tai's chapter discusses how the domestic labour structure change and globalization of production have caused a mild social polarization but a marked income inequity. Through labour policy and international labour movement, an uneven labour market and a sizable social group excluded from the labour market have arisen in Taipei. The findings both confirm and deviate from the norms of other global cities. Peter Cheng-Chong Wu's chapter reviews how the globalization of consumption divides Taipei's current food markets into four different types, mirroring the pattern of the current social differentiation process. The diversification of the market allows for specific class consumption as well as intermixed social consumption. The variety of food markets, which is a temporal phenomenon, indicates that Taipei is at a stage of social transition towards a more homogenous global society.

The fourth part, 'Cultural Reorientation', reviews the urban cultural changes resulting from globalization. The two chapters demonstrate how urban culture is being managed in order to set a new mode of behaviour conducive to globalization, and the cultural consequence for those left out of global economy. The state's authoritarian role in preparing a global culture and the cultural effect of globalization on a passive society are discussed. Chih-Hung Wang's examines Taipei's recently completed rapid transit system, which is not only an urban infrastructure necessary for a globalizing city, but also a new cultural landscape, instructing and conditioning the urban residents into global citizens. The utilitarian transportation mode and the architectural imagery provide a clear visual manifestation of modernity and a social discipline for acceptable conduct in a public space. Kuang-Tien Yao's chapter summarizes Tsai Ming-liang's work – a set of his five major films on the new urban culture – which have been internationally recognized as an important cultural commentary on modern Taipei. The marginalized underclass, which is either on the edge of, or excluded by, the global economy, is graphically illustrated and studied. The visual narrative documents the disintegration of individual aspiration and cultural disorientation of the citizen, who does not identify with the global developmental process.

The volume concludes with Reginald Yin-Wang Kwok's postscript, which extracts the key elements from the inter-relations of the chapters, providing a summary on how globalization, developmental state and politics interact in Taipei's global development.

The eleven contributors to this edited volume, except the editor, are Taiwan scholars, presenting critical insiders' views from Taiwan. Based on each author's specialization and research interest, each chapter provides an in-depth analysis of one of Taipei's developmental issues generated by globalization. Collectively, they provide a broad, insightful and coherent coverage of this crucial era of Taipei's global transition.

Notes

1. Producer services include banking and finance, legal services, advertising, accounting and consultancy.
2. This is the theory that the East Asian economies form a pyramidal hierarchy with Japan at the summit, with sequential lower layers of the Asian Newly Industrializing Economies, the ASEAN four (Indonesia, Malaysia, Philippines, and Thailand), and China, Vietnam, and North Korea at its base. The growth effects are postulated to filter downward through a descending flow of transnational capital – the 'Flying Geese' pattern (Kwok, 1995).
3. China proposed the 'Three Links' policy in the 1980s, opening up direct links between China and Taiwan on personal travel, mail and trade, which Taiwan rejected. All these flows therefore have to go through a third country. Since 1997 when Hong Kong was returned to China, Taiwan has allowed that Hong Kong has a 'third country' status.
4. The other working growth triangle in the Asia-Pacific region is the Johor-Singapore-Riau Growth Triangle.

References

Amsden, A. (1991) Big business and urban congestion in Taiwan: the origins of small enterprise and regional decentralized industry (respectively). *World Development*, **19**(9), pp. 1121–1135.
Bello, W. and S. Rosenfeld (1990) *Dragon in Distress: Asia's Miracle Economies in Crisis*. San Francisco: Institute for Food and Development Policy.
Berger, P. L. and Hsiao, H. M. (eds.) (1993) *In Search of an East Asian Development Model*. New Brunswick, NJ: Transaction Publishers.
BOTHSR (Bureau of Taiwan High Speed Rail) (2004) <http://www.hsr.gov.tw>.
Brenner, N. (1998) Between fixity and motion: accumulation, territorial organization and historical geography of spatial scale. *Environment and Planning D*, **16**(4), pp. 459–481.
Brenner, N. (1999) Beyond state-centrism? Space, territoriality, and geographical scale of globalization studies. *Theory and Society*, **28**(1), pp. 39–78.
Cartier, Carolyn (2001) *Globalizing South China*. Oxford: Blackwell.
Chan, S. (1990) *East Asian Dynamism*. Boulder: Westview Press.
Castells M. (1996) *The Rise of Network Society*. Oxford: Blackwell.
Castells, M., Goh, L. and Kwok, R.Y. (1990) *The Shek Kip Mei Syndrome: Economic Development and Public Housing in Hong Kong and Singapore*. London: Pion.
Ching, C.H. (2003) Taibei chanye jiegou bianqian yu shijie chengshi gongnang fazhan zhi Xianzhi. (Taipei's economic restructuring and constraints of developing world city functions). *Dili Xuebao* (Journal of Geographical Science), No. 34, pp. 19–39.
Chowdhury, A. and Islam, I. (1993) *The Newly Industrializing Economies of East Asia*. London: Routledge.
Clark, D. (1996) *Urban World/Global City*. London: Routledge.
de Bary, W. T. (1988) *East Asian Civilization: A Dialogue in Five Stages*. Cambridge, MA: Harvard University Press.
Douglass, M. (1994) The 'development state' and the newly industrialized economies in Asia. *Environment and Planning A*, **26**(4), pp. 543–566.
Friedmann, J. (1986) The world cities hypothesis. *Development and Change*, **17**(1), pp. 69–74.
Friedmann, J. (1998) World city futures: the role of urban and regional policies in the Asia-

Pacific Region, in Yeung, Y.M. (ed.) *Urban Development in Asia*. Hong Kong: Chinese University of Hong Kong Press.

Friedmann, J. and Wulff, R. (1982) World city formation: an agenda for research and action. *International Journal of Urban and Regional Research*, **6**(3), pp. 309–344.

Gereffi, G. (1992) New realities of industrial development in East Asia and Latin America: global, regional, and national trends, in Appelbaum, R. (ed.) *States and Development in the Asian Pacific Rim*. Thousand Oaks, CA: Sage, pp. 85–112.

Goldstein, S.M. (ed.) (1991), *Mini Dragons: Fragile Economic Miracles in the Pacific*. New York: Westview Press.

Hall, P.G. (1966) *The World Cities*. London: Weidenfeld and Nicolson.

Hall, P.G. (1998) *Cities in Civilization*. New York: Weidenfeld and Nicolson.

Hamilton, G. and Kao, C.S. (1990) The institutional foundations of Chinese business: the family firm in Taiwan. *Comparative Social Research*, **12**, pp. 135–151.

Held, D. and McGrew, A. (2002). *Globalization/Anti-Globalization*. Cambridge: Polity Press.

Jacobs, J. (1984) *Cities and Wealth of Nations: Principles of Economic Life*. New York: Random House.

Jou, S.C. (2001) Taiwan de doushi yu juelue (Cities and settlements in Taiwan), in San-Hsin Chiang (ed.) *Cikaifuermosha de miansha: Taiwan de renwen dili* (*Revealing Formosa's Veil: HumanGeography in Taiwan*). Taichung: National Taichung Library, pp. 195–200.

Knox, P. (1994) Economic crisis and urban restructuring 1972–1983, in Knox, Paul (ed.) *Introduction to Urban Geography*, New York: Prentice-Hall, pp. 52–75.

Kwok, R.Y. (1995) Hong Kong investment in South China, in Sumner, J. La Croix, Plummer, Michael and Lee, Keun (eds.) *The Emerging Patterns of East Asian Investment in China*. Armonk NY: M.E. Sharpe, pp. 69–93.

Kwok, R.Y. (1999) Last colonial spatial plans for Hong Kong: global economy and domestic politics. *European Planning Studies*, **7**(2), pp. 207–229.

Liu, P.K.C. and Tung, A.C. (2003) Taiwan doushi fachan de yianjin – Lishi de huigu yu Zhanwang (Urban development in Taiwan: retrospect and prospect). *Renkou xuekan* (*Journal of Population Studies*), No. 26, pp. 1–25.

Naughton, B. (ed.) (1997) *The China Circle: Economics and Technology in the PRC, Taiwan, and Hong Kong*. Washington, DC: Brookings Institute Press.

Ng, L.F. and Tuan, C. (1996) *Three Chinese Economies: China, Hong Kong and Taiwan: Challenges and Opportunities*. Hong Kong: The Chinese University Press.

O'Neill, P. (1997) Bringing the qualitative state into economic geography, in Lee, R. and Wills, J. (eds.) *Geographies and Economics*. London: Arnold, pp. 290–301.

Sassen, S. (2001*a*) Global cities and global city-regions: a comparison, in Scott, Allen J. (ed.) *Global City-Region: Trends, Theory, Policy*. Oxford: Oxford University Press, pp. 78–95.

Sassen, S. (2001*b*) *The Global City: New York, London, Tokyo*. Princeton: Princeton University Press.

Scott A. (1998) *Regions and the World Economy*. Oxford: Oxford University Press.

Scott A. (2000) *Global City-Regions: Trends, Theory, Policy*. Oxford: Oxford University Press.

Scott A. (2002) Regional push: towards a geography of development and growth in low- and middle-income countries. *Third World Quarterly*, **23**(1), pp. 137–161.

Sit, V. (1980) *Hong Kong's Small Scale Industry*. Hong Kong: Centre of Asian Studies, University of Hong Kong.

Sit, V. and Wong, S. (1989) *Small and Medium Industries in an Export-Oriented Economy: The Case of Hong Kong*. Hong Kong: Centre of Asian Studies, University of Hong Kong.

Storper, M. (1997) *The Regional World: Territorial Development in a Global Economy*. New York: Guilford.

Taylor, B. and Kwok, R.Y. (1989) From export center to world city: planning for the transformation of Hong Kong. *American Planning Association Journal*, **55**(3), pp. 309–321.

Van Kemenade, W. (1998) *China, Hong Kong, Taiwan, Inc.* New York: Vintage Books.

Vogel, E.F. (1991), *The Four Little Dragons: The Spread of Industrialization in East Asia*. Cambridge, MA: Harvard University Press.

Wade, R. (1990) *Governing the Market: Economic Theory and the Role of Government in East Asian Industrialization.*, Princeton: Princeton University Press.

Wang, H. (1998) Economic relations between China, Taiwan and Hong Kong, in Fouquin, Michel and Lemoine, Francoise (eds.) *The Chinese Economy: Highlights and Opportunities*. London: Economica, pp. 121–135.

Woronoff, J. (1986) *Asia's 'Miracle' Economies*. Seoul: Se-sa-yong-o-sa, Inc.

Chapter One

The Evolution of Economic Base: From Industrial City, Post-Industrial City to Interface City

Jinn-Yuh Hsu

In the current global economy, cities have become the key locations which connect a country's national economic activities with the broader world economy. Scott (1998; 2000) dubbed the major cities and their neighbouring region, or city-regions, as the engine of the mosaic global economy. Sassen (2001) even claimed that it is the global cities, not the national economy, that should be the focus in the discussion of the global system. Taipei, the capital city of Taiwan, is no exception.

Little of the literature dealing with the development of postwar Taiwan economy has taken the city's role seriously. Most focused on the national development caused by the interplay between state intervention and market formation (see Wade, 1990; World Bank, 1993). However, as recognized by Short (1996) Lo and Marcotullio (2000) and Byrne (2001) the urban and the economic worlds would co-evolve and create divergent roles played by the cities in the economic transformation process. In light of such understandings, this chapter aims to explore Taipei City's economic base in the globalization process.

This chapter will demonstrate that the economic base of Taipei has evolved from the manufacturing centre around the 1960s, the trading service centre in the 1970s, and gradually to knowledge-based activities after the 1980s. The key to the evolution lies in the interaction between the global economy, developmental state and local industrial system. In the following three sections, the periodization of the economic evolution will be tackled sequentially in accordance with the theoretical context. The conclusion and summary remarks will summarize the findings.

Industrial City and Rapid Industrialization before the 1970s

According to Liu (1992*a*) Taiwan's economy entered a stage of import substitution after a series of land reforms and exploitative transfers of surplus from the agricultural sector to manufacturing sector by government grain price-depreciation policies in the 1950s.[1] With aid from the US, the Kuomintang (KMT) government engaged in industrial recovery from the war, and had stipulated economic plans from 1953. The first and second 4-year plans (1953–1960) targeted the growth of light industries, such as textiles, footwear, agro-processing, and fertilizers, and transportation and electricity infrastructure to improve industrial performance. To protect these infant industries, the government raised import tariffs and appreciated the currency value. Most of the industries grew up and targeted the domestic market in the late 1950s. As industrialization proceeded, the share of the manufacturing sector in GDP rose from 12.9 per cent in 1952 to 19.1 per cent in 1960. Most of the manufacturing activities were concentrated in the urban regions, where the high population density was most suitable for the domestically-oriented firms to locate (Li, 1986).

The situation changed in the early 1960s, as two events emerged to derail the dominant industrial trajectory from import substitution to export promotion. First, the domestic market was too small to absorb the output of the rapidly growing industries, and was saturated by late the 1950s (Li, 1980). New outlets were explored to fix the crisis of over-accumulation. Second, the paradoxical shortage of foreign exchange induced by the import substitution, with increasing demand for equipment and capital goods imported in order to establish and upgrade light industries, generation of foreign exchange became imperative to sustain the economic system (Li, 1980). Under these circumstances, export activities turned out to be the logical option. Third, the opening of the massive market in the advanced industrial countries, mainly the US, rendered export possible and allowed for an industrial restructuring (Massey, 1984). Finally, a new pattern of international division of labour emerged and some of the developing countries became the platform for outsourcing by making use of their cheap labour and land (Frobel *et al.*, 1980). Taiwan took advantage of this production opportunity and transformed itself into an export-oriented economy.

A number of key factors characterized Taiwan's export industrialization process in the 1960s. First, it was the state, rather than the market itself, that initiated the transformation process (Wade, 1990). The government adopted numerous measures to change the terms of trade to attract foreign capital by depreciating currency and reducing tax. To improve the business climate, the government also set up Export Processing Zones (EPZs) to host subsidiaries of the multinationals (Li, 1980). In addition, industrial policies to encourage new firm entry were introduced by the government. These policies were incentive oriented rather than picking the winner. As a result, the proliferation of small firms took effect.

Second, in the social context, the key agents of export were not the conglomerates (mostly state owned) but a wide array of small and medium sized enterprises (SMEs) in labour intensive industries such as plastics, textiles, foods and footwear (Levy and Kuo, 1991; Mody, 1990).[2] As shown in table 1.1, over 99 per cent of the industrial establishments were in the category of SMEs, each employing less than 100 people. According to the Ministry of Economic Affairs, the SMEs generated more than 65 per cent of the export value from the 1960s onward. It was no exaggeration that the SMEs were the pillars of Taiwan's postwar economic miracle (Orru, 1991; Zhou, 1999).[3]

Table 1.1. The percentage of Small and Medium Enterprises (SMEs) in Taiwan.

	Number of establishments (% of total)	Product value (% of total)	Employees (% of total)	Average number of employees
1961	99.57	–	64.28	5.98
1966	99.28	–	57.30	7.04
1971	98.96	37.09	52.52	8.72
1976	98.90	32.27	53.00	8.79
1986	99.00	34.46	57.89	8.49
1991	99.24	41.23	63.82	7.94

Source: The Industrial and Commercial Census data for Taiwan-Fukien District.

Third, the concentration of manufacturing plants in the big cities, particularly Taipei Metropolis, which comprises Taipei City and the surrounding Taipei County, continued and even expanded up to the 1960s, as shown in table 1.2. The reason behind the agglomeration in the key metropolises came from the huge demand for labour by the labour-intensive industries, together with the poor infrastructure in the non-urban areas (Lai, 1986). At the same time, the decline of the agricultural sector as a result of the grain price-depreciation policy gradually led to an impasse of employment opportunities in the rural regions, which, in turn, induced a rural-urban migration after 1964. As estimated by Liu (1992*b*) more than one million of the agricultural population migrated to urban areas after the 1960s. Consequently, both the rural exodus and industrial agglomeration contributed to the rapid urbanization of Taipei Metropolis in the 1960s, and consolidated the primacy of the capital city, which was subsequently granted a special city status in 1969.

In sum, the Taiwan economy before the end of the 1960s relied on the export of labour-intensive goods, which were produced by SMEs agglomerated in the urban areas. The rural-urban migration increased the polarization effect across the island. Taipei City played the role of industrial base in facilitating Taiwan's economic

Table 1.2. The location quotient of industrial sectors in Taipei City and Metropolis, 1966–1996.

		Agri-culture	Mining	Manu-facturing	Utilities	Con-struction	Com-merce	Service	Trans-portation
1966	Taipei City	17	53	132	568	191	232	206	363
	Taipei Metropolis	32	143	175	364	134	170	159	239
1971	Taipei City	12	50	98	215	215	302	NA	NA
	Taipei Metropolis	24	188	160	144	149	201	NA	NA
1976	Taipei City	10	209	74	166	212	274	238	214
	Taipei Metropolis	20	174	128	123	154	192	168	157
1981	Taipei City	11	34	58	139	186	254	265	219
	Taipei Metropolis	18	80	114	113	141	150	187	163
1986	Taipei City	10	33	49	117	186	268	239	217
	Taipei Metropolis	16	72	105	102	136	186	167	162
1991	Taipei City	4	23	81	323	128	186	220	217
	Taipei Metropolis	17	49	114	239	130	168	180	189
1996	Taipei City	3	16	81	323	102	157	211	207
	Taipei Metropolis	16	27	110	226	113	145	173	167

Source: Calculation from Industrial and Commercial Census data for Taiwan-Fukien District.

growth. Because of Taipei's contribution, an average of over 10 per cent in the annual growth of GNP was achieved during the period of 1964–1973 in Taiwan.

Rural Industrialization and the Rise of the Post-industrial City in the 1970s

Export activities were the major driving force behind Taiwan's economic development since the 1960s. They not only increased in economic scale, but also expanded in geographical scope in the 1970s. Kuo (1983) found that the contribution of export to the growth was 35 per cent during 1961–1966, 45.9 per cent during 1966–1971, and 68.7 per cent in 1971–1976. Taiwan's economy was clearly export oriented as were most newly industrializing economies such as South Korea, Hong Kong and Singapore. However, more impressive than the rapid growth was that industrialization spread to the rural areas and formed an urban-rural network of production, which was distinctive from other developing economies (Gilbert and Gugler, 1992; Gugler, 1996).

The global economic recession caused by the first oil crisis hit Taiwan in 1973, as a result of a series of protectionist policies in the US, the major outlet for Taiwan's products. At the same time, the ruling party, the KMT, encountered the double political predicaments of retreating from the international community by the forced withdrawal from the United Nations in 1971, and a leadership succession problem as the strongman was old and ill. The new leader, then-premier Chiang Ching-Kuo, declared 'The Great Construction Plan' to upgrade the industrial structure and strengthen his control in the political power struggle. The plan consisted of two major programmes; one concentrated on the introduction of heavy industries, such as, petrochemical, steel, and shipbuilding plants to substitute the intermediate production for the export industries and deepen the industrial structure, while the other clustered around improving transportation and infrastructure, such as, by the construction of an expressway, port and nuclear plant, and broadening the industrial structure (Liu, 1992b).

Worst of all, the decline of the agricultural sector became a thorny problem in the early 1970s, as the rate of growth in agricultural value turned from positive to negative in 1971, and continued to decline thereafter. According to Liaw et al. (1986) the agricultural crisis would have exploded if there had been no appropriate intervention. As more young and skilled workers migrated to the urban regions, the rural area had a labour shortage in agricultural production, innovation deficiency and productivity decay, under the unfavourable and unequal exchange with industry. The government was forced to change its grain price-depreciation policy and replace it with a policy of subsidizing grain production. In addition, the government attempted to draw the embryonic industries into rural areas to create job opportunities to alleviate the stress of transformation and balance the rural-urban disparity (Sun, 1988).[4] The government persuaded manufacturing firms to move from urban areas to the rural regions, at the same time extolling the virtues of hard work and encouraging rural households to take part-time jobs with these manufacturing firms.[5] Pitch roads were paved, and new industrial parks were constructed in the rural areas with the policy goal of moving these areas forward by the introduction of manufacturing industries (Xu, 1986). From the 1970s the countryside became the site of a mixture of agricultural and manufacturing activities. As illustrated in table 1.3, the sources of income for agricultural households steadily moved to the non-agricultural sector, particularly wages from manufacturing sectors, which became the chief source of rural household income.

From the perspective industrial development, the concentration of manufacturing firms in urban areas led to spiralling land prices, traffic congestion and a shortage of unskilled labour (Tang, 1981). Urban diseconomies of agglomeration occurred. As a result, labour-intensive industrial firms started to disperse to the hinterland of the core city, and even the rural areas after 1971. As shown in table 1.2, the location quotient of manufacturing industries in Taipei City declined dramatically in the early 1970s, and decreased slightly continuously in the metropolitan area. However, the overall pattern of development reflected deindustrialization in the

Table 1.3. The structure of agricultural household income.

| | The source of income (% of total) | | |
	Agriculture	Wage	Others
1966	66.0	20.1	13.9
1968	52.6	32.2	15.2
1970	48.7	36.0	15.3
1971	45.2	35.5	19.3
1972	42.3	42.3	15.4
1973	45.6	40.7	13.7
1974	48.1	37.3	14.6
1975	46.3	38.9	14.8
1976	41.4	40.4	18.2
1977	40.5	42.1	17.4
1978	33.4	47.8	18.8
1979	27.3	52.8	19.9
1980	26.4	52.2	21.4

Source: Taiwan Statistical Data Book, Council for Economic Planning and Development, Executive Yuan.

capital city, and service industries emerging as the dominant sector (see Chapter 2). How would the replacement occur? The industrial restructuring was caused by the process of rural industrialization and the rural-urban spatially networked production system.

As illustrated above, Taiwan's economic structure consisted of a wide array of SMEs. Small size and flexibility were regarded as the significant features of Taiwanese industries. Most of Taiwan's labour-intensive industries had a unique feature not found in any other country in the world apart from newly industrialized Asian economies; that is, Taiwan's industry was not led by a few big corporations but created by various small firms producing all kinds of industrial parts, which composed the critical element of the export-oriented industry. Industrial goods were not developed and produced within a factory or a company, but through a network of production service – a subcontracting production network. This was another critical element, which provided strong support for those who made business deals with foreign companies or buyers. The backbone firms concentrated on production. Usually, they did not contact foreign buyers unless they had other products or parts, which could be sold independently in the market. Many such firms simply stayed backstage and provided production services to other local companies, the 'upstage' coordinators, which made business contacts and business deals with foreign buyers, developing products, and coordinating productions. The production activities were basically driven by those out front service firms (Hsia, 1988; Shieh, 1992).

To support the production of these products, hundreds of satellite factories were in place making various components or parts. Most of the firms in the same industrial group were located in the same township, village, community and even avenue. Jobs subcontracted to the household would mobilize the labour reserve army, such as housewives, the elderly, children, and particularly, those men who still engaged in farming (Shieh, 1992). In most cases, each township produced just one product, and transformed the locality into a specialized district, for example, shoes in Dali (Hsu and Cheng, 2002) stockings in Shetou (Liu, 2000) bicycles in Daya (Chen, 2002) and umbrellas in Homei (Hsia, 1988) all in central Taiwan's rural areas. Geographical concentration saved the subcontracting firms' costs in delivery and transactions enhanced the diffusion of business information, and even technical skill in the local labour market.[6]

How could the Taiwanese SMEs get orders from overseas firms, and export to foreign markets? The key players here were the hundreds of trading companies which were initially dominated by the Japanese, and gradually replaced by Taiwanese companies located in Taipei. The role of the trading companies could only be understood in the context of the arrangement of Original Equipment Manufacturing (OEM) production chains (Hsing, 1998; Hoesel, 1999). Many key foreign retailers such as Wal-Mart, JC Penny, and others were placing OEM orders with Taiwanese firms. In 1983, there were around 36,000 domestic trading companies in Taiwan, and most of them were located in Taipei City (Chen, 1991; Ching, 2001). It was reported that over 72 per cent of Taiwanese shoe manufacturers sold more than half of their products through these trading companies. According to Hsing (1998) the trading companies not only took charge of the import-export transactions, but also, more importantly, engaged in quality control and on-time delivery, product design and development, risk sharing, and coordination of inter-firm scale and scope economies.[7] The production network is depicted in figure 1.1. Occasionally, the traders would extend their business to supervising the manufacturing process, and the manufactures would expand forward to the trading business. Job hopping between these two interlinked businesses was quite frequent, and firm boundaries became blurred (Chen, 1991). The interpersonal ties lubricated the interaction process, and led to the underdevelopment of other producer services, such as legal, financial and consulting business in the management of rural-urban production networks (Daniels, 1998).

It was clear that in Taipei City in the 1970s, economic restructuring acted as the 'dragon head' of the extended rural OEM networks to connect with the international buyers. The post-industrial role played by the city was closely associated with relocation of manufacturing activities to the rural areas. A new pattern of rural-urban division of labour replaced the old one, characterized by urban industrialization and rural out-migration. This pattern did not disappear until the outflow of industries occurred in the late 1980s.

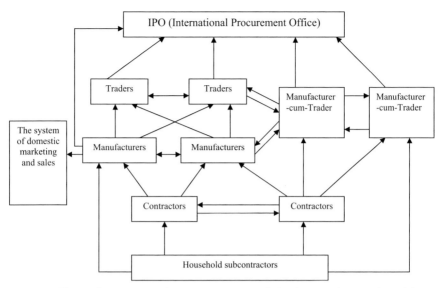

Figure 1.1. The production networks in Taiwan's export-led industries. *Source:* Adapted from Hsing (1998).

Production Globalization and the 1980s Emergence of the City-Region

At the beginning of the 1980s, an acute shortage of cheap labour and land occurred, and more importantly, the rise of the late-latecomers such as the Southeast Asian industrializing countries and mainland China, changed the patterns of industrial development in Taiwan (Chung, 1997). The change evolved in two ways: on the one hand, the government initiated the industrial upgrading process by promoting high-technology industries such as personal computer and integrated circuit industries in the Northern Region with the core in Taipei; on the other hand, it triggered the emigration of Taiwanese capital in search of new cheap production in terms of land and labour, and broke down the rural-urban division of labour that had existed in the 1970s.

In the 1980s, the government decided to transfer to high-technology industries, and upgrade the industrial structure from labour-intensive to technology-intensive. As the SMEs constituted the pillar of the economy, the government had to support the start up of these risky industries, as most of the private firms, both small and relatively large ones, such as Formosa Plastics hesitated participating in investment-intensive business. The government set up key research institutions such as the Industrial Technology Research Institute to bridge technology transfer, and constructed the Hsinchu Science-based Industrial Park to subsidize and host new firms. The Industrial Park and its neighbouring corridor extending to Taipei was praised as one of the most successful technopoles around the world (Castells and Hall, 1994; Mathews, 1997). The area is now the home to Taiwan's most rapidly growing microelectronics industries such as integrated circuit and personal computer manufacturers. These firms, mostly small and medium sized, collectively build up a vertically disintegrated industrial system. Local companies dominate the market for a large and growing range of computer-related products, from notebook computers, motherboards and monitors, to optical scanners, keyboards and power supplies.

At present, Taiwan's state-of-the-art semiconductor foundries account for two-thirds of global output. Not surprisingly, the industry has grown dramatically in the past two decades. Taiwan's information technology sector now ranks third in the world, with total output of US$78 billion in 2003, ahead of larger nations such as South Korea, and only behind the US and Japan. The emergence of these high-tech industries demonstrated that the state could lead in the creation of industrial upgrading in Taiwan. As a result, the Taipei-Hsinchu corridor re-industrialized in the early 1980s, and became a high-technology city-region in the global market. Taipei Metropolis regained industrial power in the restructuring process with the simultaneous development of the role of producer services (Ching, 2001).

Another starkly different story unfolded in the rural industrial areas, as the state was forced to allow the outflows of rural industries. At the same time, Taiwan transformed from foreign capital recipient to outward investor in economic development. With the price increase in domestic labour and land, industrial investment initially went to ASEAN countries. With even less costly production inputs and cultural familiarity, Taiwan's foreign direct investment (FDI) soon took off to mainland China after 1987, and quickly overshadowed its FDI to Southeast Asia. According to Kao (2000) during the early phase (1987–1991) most of Taiwanese FDI on mainland China was carried out by SMEs in labour-intensive sectors such as the plastics, footwear, toy, and garment industries. Most of the trans-border firms remained connected with their suppliers and customers in Taiwan, and reproduced the whole production networks in the host countries (Chen, 1998; Hsing, 1998). The hollowing out of the labour-intensive industries from the countryside led to the restructuring of the rural-urban division of labour. Searching new connection with emigrated business became the imperative for the 'dragon head', Taipei City, in order to reposition itself in the rearrangement of the trans-border production chain.

Rise of the Interface City after the 1990s

The 1990s marked the emerging new trend of cross-border investment to mainland China and global competition for Taipei. For one thing, the battle for position at the strategic nodes in the global space of flows resulted in direct and fierce rivalry between the cities, even those within the same national boundary (Sassen, 2001; Castells, 1996). Taiwan was no exception. Each city had to build up linkages with other nodes, even beyond the national boundaries, in the global web of business in order to tap into resources and maintain growth. For another, Taiwanese FDI to China has shifted from labour-intensive and small-scale to technology-intensive and large scale, including those personal computer firms in the Taipei-Hsinchu corridor, as the opening of China's market was expected after China's entry to the World Trade Organization (WTO).[8] This situation raised concern about the possibility of the hollowing out of the high value-added activities out of Taiwan. Most Taiwanese investors (in China) imported inputs from Taiwan to China for processing in the 1980s, but gradually more and more materials were locally sourced and the ratio of import from Taiwan declined to about 30 per cent by 1998.

In response to the new situation, Taipei City had to manage the connections with other nodes and, at the same time, extend high value-added activities to the cross-border production chain. On the one hand, the Taipei-Hsinchu corridor benefited from the interdependencies between it and California's Silicon Valley, the world technology hub, by virtue of a community of US-educated Taiwanese engineers. They coordinated a decentralized process of reciprocal industrial upgrading by transferring capital, skill, and know-how to Taiwan and by facilitating collaboration between specialist producers in the two regions (Saxenian and Hsu, 2001). This bilateral connection underscored the role of regional motor played by the Taipei-Hsinchu corridor in worldwide economic competition. The Taipei city-region, to a certain degree, aligned itself more with international nodes in global capitalism than other domestic nodes. It was a process of territorial realignment and rescaling. Taipei became the leading location in handling the economic growth of the city-region, and the headquarters for over 70 per cent of Taiwan's top 100 informatics firms (see figure 1.2).

Furthermore, to meet the challenge of the transnational high-technology firms, Taipei City had to upgrade its producer service provision. As shown by Ching (2001) the share of product value of producer service industries, such as marketing, logistics, advertising, insurance, legal service and trading service, in the total value produced in Taipei increased from 19.8 per cent in 1981 to 29 per cent in 1996. It demonstrated that the expansion of informatics FDI in China enhanced, rather than weakened, the connection with the parent firms in Taipei. As more Taiwanese investors (in China) upgraded from Original Equipment Manufacturing to Original Design Manufacturing[9] and imported critical parts from Taiwan to China for processing (Hobday, 2001) the service activities supporting the cross-border manufacturing chains created more business opportunities for the headquarters in the Taipei city-region.

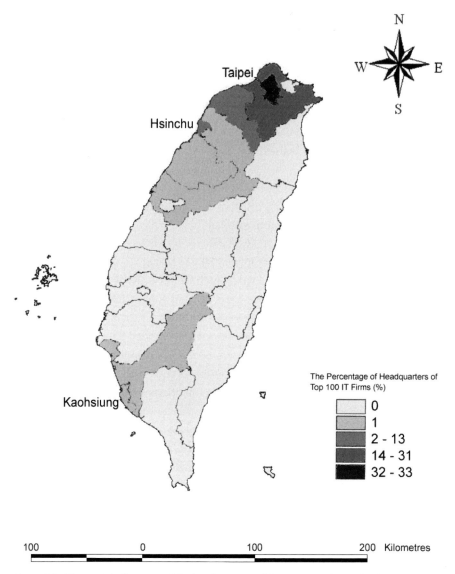

Figure 1.2. The spatial allocation of the headquarters of the top 100 informatics firms. *Source: Business Next Magazine* (2002) pp. 24–31.

A new character was emerging for Taipei City in the global economy: an interface city, which acted as a node to connect with the technology hub in Silicon Valley, and extended the high technology investment across the strait, characterized the city's role in the global space of flow. It exploited the advantage of dense technical communities, the industrial structure which complemented Silicon Valley, and the knowledge base accumulated over more than two decades of technological learning (Hsu and Saxenian, 2000).[10] In addition, the ethnic ties and cultural affinity between

Taiwan and China enabled cross-border investment and exploration of the China market with relative ease (Hsing, 1998; Hsu, 2002). Both connections were mutually imperative, as the technology advantage rendered Taiwanese high-technology FDI profitable, and the cultural advantage attracted more Silicon Valley firms to collaborate with the Taiwanese to enter China's market. Taipei City could grow as a city of knowledge and producer services in the transformation after the 1990s. However, the new industries had greater freedom of location choice, and were able to locate beyond the Taipei City boundary. As a result, the Taipei-Hsinchu corridor, rather than Taipei City itself, became a localized industrial district to articulate with other economic nodes in the world economy. Taipei struggled to maintain the segment of high value-added in the new industrial linkage.

The role of the interface city should be understood within the context of the social embeddedness of the global placeless economic flow. It has been argued that a transnational ethnic community usually bridged the dispersed regional economies and enhanced the flows of information, capital, people and the knowledge they held within the worldwide ethnic economic network (Ong and Nonini, 1997). Each locality was re-bounded in the ethnic network, and recombined to create new business firms, new industrial practices, and new economic geographies. The process of interlinking among the nodes of the ethnic web created organizational and geographical forms of the particular trans-nationalism. Some cities and regions gained growth momentum, while others failed and declined in the interconnection. However, it did not mean that the destinies of each city or region would be determined by its external connections. In contrast, this chapter argues that the current globalization process provided both challenges and opportunities. The result would depend on how each locality took advantage of its strategic nodal position in the territorial division of labour and production process, whether the city countered the challenge with pro-active policies or passively withdrew from the opportunities. Therefore, the city had, on the one hand, to build up close connections with other nodes in the global network, and on the other, enhance its own competitive advantages in absorbing external resources. The 'ungrounded empire' became re-grounded in particular cities (Zhou and Tseng, 2001). These cities, such as Hong Kong and Taipei, or part of the cities, such as the 'Little Taipei' in Los Angeles (Zhou and Tseng, 2001) played the nodal roles in worldwide ethnic business networks. In this sense, they were interface cities.

However, a number of governance contradictions hindered the China connection around which the city needed to steer carefully.

Ways Ahead: the Governance of the Interface City

As urban competitiveness in the global knowledge economy resided in the hard (physical) and especially the soft (social interaction) networks (Malecki, 2002) the key to enhancing Taipei's advantages would hinge on preparing infrastructure and more importantly, operating networks at the global, national, regional and local scales, gathering knowledge via social interaction. The difficulty arose in the process of building up a collective order in the networking (Scott, 1998).

First, production globalization and the consequent break up of the rural-urban industrialization mode led the different localities to face direct competition with hardly any supportive intervention from other cities. As a result, the race for infrastructure construction became fierce, and often brought about repeated infrastructure investments. For example, the contest for high-technology parks (for knowledge industries) and international airports (for cross-Strait investment) among different cities occurred after the mid-1990s. Consequently the fight for budget allocation between Taipei and other cities cost the former millions of dollars.[11] In addition, the political conflict between the central and Taipei government, which were led by opposition parties, caused delay in new infrastructure construction in Taipei[12] and thus a shortage of hard infrastructure in the city. According to a report by the municipal government, the availability of sewerage in Taipei only reached 46 per cent, lower than that of Bangkok.

Second, the inward looking of the developmental state created barriers for the cross-border connection. In contrast to the picture of the Singaporean state painted by Yeung and Olds (2001) the Taiwanese state was reluctant to allow the direct flow of capital and people. In particular, the political tension between Taiwan and mainland China brought about interference from the central government in cross-Strait investments. Most official policies towards mainland China aimed to hinder, rather than promote direct flows. Taiwanese investors, especially high-technology firms, were forced to register in a third country, such as the Cayman Islands, as foreign companies in order to make investments in China, rather than report to the government. There were policies which did not allow direct transportation between Taiwan and mainland China. Consequently, to serve these 'sneaky' investments, the added costs to the producer service providers did not enhance the interface city's advantage in the global economic competition (Ching, 2001).

Finally, the lack of the frequent and open flow of talented people would reduce the long-term competitiveness of the interface city. In fact, in the new economy, technical communities were usually the major source of tacit knowledge, which was the critical ingredient of innovation (Maskell and Malmberg, 1999). The social network of talented people constituted the competitive advantage of regions (Saxenian, 1994; Storper, 1997). Furthermore, the networks have to keep open without the peril of lock-in, and the social milieu must be tolerant and facilitate the connections to maintain diversification and innovation (Florida, 2002; Amin and Thrift, 2002). In light of these arguments, Taipei possessed the potential advantages in their connections with Silicon Valley and China. The work of the professional networks in Silicon Valley and the Taipei-Hsinchu corridor had demonstrated the cross-fertilization between the two city-regions.[13] However, due to political contention, the connection between Taiwan and China was always thorny. In fact, in addition to the flows of goods and services across the Strait, information talent flow had followed suit and strengthened the cross-Strait connection between Taipei and China's prominent global cities, particularly Shanghai (Hsu, 2002; Leng, 2002; Sum, 2002). The central government still attempted to restrict the flow of engineers from Taiwan to China and *vice versa*. Only 730 mainland Chinese high-technology workers had gone to Taiwan by the end of September 2000. The difficulty in the free exchange of talented people would hurt Taipei as an interface city and restrict the opportunity of taking advantage of brokering the connection.

Summary and Conclusion

This chapter explored dynamics of the economic development of Taipei City in the post-World War II era. It has shown that the economic base of the capital city evolved from the manufacturing centre before the 1960s, the trading service centre in the 1970s, and gradually to knowledge-based activities after the 1980s. The key to the role of evolution lies in the interaction of the global economy, the state (both central and local levels) and local industrial systems in Taipei. In the 1960s, Taipei and its surrounding areas took advantage of the new international division of labour to become one of the major industrial sites and attracted huge rural exodus. In the meantime, Taipei grew rapidly and enlarged the rural-urban gap. It forced the government to encourage industrial dispersal and make rural industrialization possible in the 1970s. The major economic role of Taipei shifted from a manufacturing site to an agglomeration of producer services, particularly trading companies, which connected the rural subcontractors with the global buyers. However, the situation changed dramatically after the 1980s. On the one hand, more industrial firms moved part of their operations overseas to mainland China, some to Southeast Asia, and reshuffled the transnational production networks. On the other, the core competitive advantage of the city and region came not from traditional service sectors, but from the knowledge activities in the global knowledge economy. In consequence, Taipei raised the agenda of transforming from a post-industrial city to an interface city. It tried to position itself as a node in the cross-border flows of capital and people. Under such conditions, the city engaged in the process of decoupling with the rural hinterland, simultaneously coupling with the trans-border economies. This raised tension between Taipei and the other areas of Taiwan, particularly the central government. It needed new governance mechanisms to handle the situation. This chapter demonstrates that rather than being treated as a bounded space on a map, Taipei connotes different territorialities and spatial articulation with divergent geographic scales of economic activities in the process of organizational decoupling and re-coupling in the global production chains (cf. Allen, Massey and Cochrane, 1998).

As the global networks of goods, capital, and talents became the norm in current world economies, the connections between divergent socio-economic spaces created the nodal sites to hold down the global flow. The interface region emerged in the intertwined extension of global spaces of flow. It was an interface in that it possessed part of the connecting but contrasting regions, thus was able to assimilate, transmit, and expand the assets of these regions. Taipei City, in light of the concept, gained its momentum from the close links, in capital and talent flow, with the different economic spaces in Silicon Valley and China's coastal cities, particularly the Shanghai region. In brief, Taipei's key advantage hinges on the role it can play well as an interface city in the high-technology industries, and it has to broaden its scope of business networks to enhance the advantage. However, Taiwan's current conservative policies, particularly those towards China, seriously hampered Taipei City in becoming a global city to link with heterogeneous socio-economic spaces. In the long run, these may further hinder the city's position to continue as the interface city for the worldwide business networks.

Notes

1. As estimated by Lee (1971) the surplus being transferred from the agricultural sector to the manufacturing sector reached 22 per cent of the aggregate product value of the former from 1950 to 1955. In other words, around one billion NT dollars per annum were transferred from agriculture to subsidize the manufacturing sector during the 1950s.
2. In most cases, the conglomerates monopolized the production of intermediates for the downstream SMEs, which had to procure inputs from the former and exported the final goods overseas. In some cases, the improvement in the production efficiency of the conglomerates benefited from the comparative advantage of the exporting SMEs (Amsden, 1985).
3. This is not an argument that the SMEs matched the rosy picture of flexible specialization and craft democracy. In reality there was exploitation and labour abuse in the labour-intensive SMEs, as reported by Shieh (1992).
4. As suggested by McGee (1998) one of the main goals of state policies was to achieve a more balanced spatial distribution of productive activities, employment, and population, influenced by such researchers as Hirschmann and Myrdal. However, only a few developing countries could meet the mission, as the economic structure tended to polarize in favour of urban regions, and the states did not possess the power to reverse the trend.
5. The key slogans were proclaimed by the then-provincial governor, Hsieh Dong-Min, who promoted 'the living room as the factory', 'the community as the workplace' and 'hardwork as a virtue'.
6. Orru (1991) observed the similarity between Taiwan and Italy in the SMEs' social institutions, such as, familism, entrepreneurship and independency, personal ties and business networks, and the reliance on personal savings. Also the geographical patterns between these two countries were quite similar, with existing industrial clusters of traditional sectors in an industrial district, as in the Third Italy. However, a key distinction

should be made here: that while most of Italy's industrial sectors possessed their own brand name and controlled the whole production chain, their Taiwanese counterparts usually occupied one or a few segments of the chains as OEM makers without the power to drive the industrial development.

7. In the phenomena of the 'third Taiwan', the trading companies were the key institution in governing the production networks, as the Mark II district classified by Asheim (1997).

8. The average size of investment in China rose sharply from US$ 735,000 in 1991 to 2.78 million in 1995 (Chung, 1997).

9. As manufacturing matured, the Original Equipment Manufacturing firms themselves would learn and verify their technological knowledge as they moved into production, and became Original Design Manufacturing partners.

10. Taiwan's technological achievements are reflected in international comparisons of patenting. While all the Asian newly industrializing economies ranked low in the 1980s, Taiwan received US patents at an accelerating rate in the 1990s and surpassed not only Singapore but also Korea and Hong Kong in the number of patents granted per capita. In fact Taiwan, along with Israel, now ranks ahead of all of the G7 except the US and Japan in patents per capita (Trajtenberg, 1999; Ching, 2002).

11. Due to political confrontation between different parties, the annual budget of Taipei City was reduced by 11.2 per cent in 2001. In contrast, that of Kaoshung City increased by 16 per cent at the same time as its mayor belonged to the ruling party. Some key festivals supported by the central government and traditionally held in Taipei City were moved to other places under the rhetoric of 'reducing regional disparity'.

12. These controversies included the location and size of the giant stadium, the cut in sub-vention allocation and the dredging of the Keelung River, which flowed through the city.

13. However, it has been pointed out that less than 500 foreign engineers worked in Taipei until the end of 2000. The low rate of foreign skilled labour possibly was attributed to the returning of the overseas Taiwanese engineers, who provided the channel of technology transfer, and thus reduced the need for other foreign talented people. In fact, the returning workforce rose dramatically in 1990s, and contributed more than two-thirds of the high-technology startups in the corridor (Hsu, 2005).

References

Allen, J., Massey, D. and Cochrane, A. (1998) *Rethinking the Region*. London: Routledge.

Amin, A. (1998) Globalization and regional development: a relational perspective. *Competition and Change*, **3**, pp. 145–165.

Amin, A. and Thrift, N. (2002) *Cities: Reimagining the Urban*. London: Polity Press.

Amsden, A. (1985) The state and Taiwan's economic development, in Evans, P. *et al.* (eds.) *Bringing the State Back In*. Cambridge: Cambridge University Press.

Amsden, A. (1991) Big business and urban congestion in Taiwan: the origins of small enterprise and regionally decentralized industry (respectively). *World Development*, **19**(9), pp. 1121–1135.

Asheim, B. (1997) Learning regions in a globalized world economy: towards a new competitive advantage of industrial districts? in Conti, S. and Taylor, M. (eds.) *Interdependent and Uneven Development: Global-Local Perspectives*. Brookgate: Ashfield.

Byrne, D. (2001) *Understanding the Urban*. London: Palgrave Press.

Castells, M. (1996) *The Rise of the Network Society*. Oxford: Blackwell.

Castells, M. and Hall, P. (1994) *Technopoles of the World – the Making of 21st Century Industrial Complex*. London: Routledge.

Chen, T.J. (1998) *Taiwanese Firms in Southeast Asia*. Cheltenham: Edward Elgar.

Chen, J.X. (1991) *Taiwan de zhongxiao qiye yu guoji fengong* (*Taiwan's Small and Medium Sized Enterprises and International Division of Labour*). Taipei: Lein-JinPress.

Chen, M.C. (2002) Industrial District and Social Capital in Taiwan's Economic Development: An Economic Sociological Study on Taiwan's Bicycle Industry. PhD Dissertation in Sociology, Yale University.

Ching, C.H. (2001) Quanqiouhua yu Taipei de shengchan xingfu wuye fazhan (Globalization and the development of producer services in Taiwan's metropolises). *Dushi yu Jihua* (*City and Planning*), **28**(4), pp. 495–518.

Ching, C.H. (2002) Zhishi jingji shehui yu lingyu fazhan de jihui (Knowledge-based economic society and the opportunities for Territorial development). *City and Planning*, **29**(1), pp. 1–20.

Chung, C. (1997) Division of labor across the Taiwan Strait: macro overview and Analysis of the electronics industry, in Naughton, B. (ed.) *The China Circle*. Washington DC: Brookings Institution.

Daniels, P. (1998) Economic development and producer services growth: the APEC experience. *Asia Pacific Viewpoint*, **39**, pp. 145–159.

Florida, R. (2002) The economic geography of talent. *Annals of the Association of American Geographers*, **92**(4), pp. 743–755.

Frobel, F., Heinrichs, J. and Kreye. O. (1980) *The New International Division of Labour*.Cambridge: Cambridge University Press.

Galenson, W. (1982) How to develop successfully – the Taiwan model, in Proceedings of a conference on *Experiences and Lessons of Economic Development in Taiwan*. Taipei: Institute of Economics, Academic Sinica.

Gilbert, A. and Gugler, J. (1992) *Cities, Poverty and Development: Urbanization in the Third World*, 2nd ed. Oxford: Oxford University.

Gugler, J. (1996) *The Urban Transformation of the Developing World*. Oxford: Oxford University.

Hobday, M. (2001) The electronics industries of the Asia-Pacific: exploiting international production networks for economic development. *Asian-Pacific Economic Literature*, **15**, pp. 13–29.

Hoesel, R. (1999) *New Multinational Enterprises from Korea and Taiwan*. London: Routledge.

Hsia, C.J. (1988) Kongjian xingshi zhuanhua zhong de yilai yu fazhan: Taiwan Zhanghua ge'an (Dependency and development in the evolution of a spatial form: the case of Chang-Hua, Taiwan) *Taiwan shehui yanjiu jikan* (*Taiwan: A Radical Quarterly in Social Studies*), **1**(2-3), pp. 263–337.

Hsing Y. (1998) The work of networks in Taiwan's export fashion shoe industry, in Fruin, M. (ed.) *Networks, Markets and the Pacific Rim*. Oxford: Oxford University Press.

Hsu, J.Y. (2002) From transfer to hybridization: the changing organizations of Taiwanese PC investments in China. Paper presented in the 98th Annual Meeting of the Association of American Geographers, Los Angeles, March 19–24, .

Hsu, J.Y. (2005) New firm formation and technical upgrading in Taiwanese semiconductor industry: is petty commodity production still relevant to high-technology development? in Smart, A. and Smart, J. (eds.) *Petty Capitalists: Flexibility, Place and the Global Economy*. New York: State University of New York Press.

Hsu, J.Y. and. Cheng, L.L. (2002) Revisiting economic development in post-war Taiwan: the dynamic process of geographical industrialization. *Regional Studies*, **36**(8), pp. 897–908.

Hsu, J.Y. and Saxenian, A. (2000) The limits of Guanxi capitalism: transnational collaboration between Taiwan and the US. *Environment and Planning A*, **32**(11), pp. 1991–2005.

Kao, C. (2000) *Taishang dui dalu touzi de zaidihua yu dui Taiwan jingji de yingxiang* (The localization of Taiwanese investment in China and its effects on Taiwan's economy). Zhonghua Jingji Yanjiu Yuan (CIER) Working Paper.

Knox, P. and Agnew, J. (1998) *The Geography of the World Economy*, 3rd ed. London: Arnold.

Kuo, S. (1983) *The Taiwan Economy in Transition*. Boulder, Colorado: Westview Press.

Lai, G.Z. (1986) Gongye quwei (Industrial location), in Ministry of Interior (ed.) *Junheng quyu fazhan decelue* (*The Strategies of Equal Regional Development*). Taipei: Ministry of the Interior.

Lee, T.H. (1971) *Intersectoral Capital Flow in the Economic Development of Taiwan, 1895–1960*. Ithaca: Cornell University Press.

Leng, T.K. (2002) Economic globalization and IT talent flows across the Taiwan Strait: the Taipei/Shanghai/Silicon Valley Triangle. *Asian Survey*, **42**(2), pp. 230–250.

Levy, B. and Kuo, W.J. (1991) The strategic orientation of firms and the performance of Korea and Taiwan in frontier industries: lessons from comparative case studies of keyboard and personal computer assembly. *World Development*, **19**(4), pp. 363–374.

Li, K.T. (1980) Up-grading of science and technology in Taiwan. *Industry of Free China*, August, pp. 2–6.

Li, X.F. (1986) *Taiwan jingji huodong quwei bianqian de jiliang yanjiu* (*The Quantitative Research of the Location Change of Economic Activities in Taiwan*). Taipei: Taiwan Bank Press.

Liaw, Z.H., J.J. Huang & H.H. Hsiao (1986) *Zhanhou nongye zhengce de yanjin* (*The Evolution of Agricultural Policy in the Postwar Era*). Taipei, Taiwan: Institute of Ethnology, Academia Sinica.

Liu, B.L. (2000) Zhanghua Shetou zhiwaye de zaijiegou (The restructuring of the stocking industry in Shetou, Chang-Hua) Master's Thesis in Geography, National Taiwan Normal University.

Liu, J.Q. (1992*a*) *Taiwan zhanhou jingji fengxi* (*An Analysis of Taiwan's Postwar Economy*). Taipei: Ren-Jian Press.

Liu, J.Q. (1992*b*) Siren bumen de fazhan (The development of the private sector), in Liu, J.Q. (ed)*Taiwan de gongyehua: guoji jiagong jidi de xingcheng* (*Taiwan's Industrialization: Formation of the International Processing Base*). Taipei: Ren-Jian Press.

Lo, F. and Marcotullio, P. (2000) Globalization and urban transformations in the Asia-Pacific regions: a review. *Urban Studies*, **37**(1), pp. 77–111.

Malecki, E. (2002) Hard and soft networks for urban competitiveness. *Urban Studies*, **39**(5/6), pp. 929–946.

Maskell, P. and Malmberg, A, (1999) The competitiveness of firms and regions: 'ubiquitification' and the importance of localized learning. *European Urban and Regional Studies*, **6**, pp. 9–25.

Massey, D. (1984) *Spatial Division of Labour*. London: Macmillan.

Mathews, J. (1997) A Silicon Valley of the East: creating Taiwan's semiconductor industry. *California Management Review*, **39**(4), pp. 26–54.

McGee, T. (1998) Globalization and rural-urban relations in the developing world, in Lo, F. and Yeung, Y. (eds.) *Globalization and the World of Large Cities*. New York: United Nations University Press.

Mody, A. (1990) Institutions and dynamic comparative advantage: the electronics industry in South Korea and Taiwan. *Cambridge Journal of Economics*, **14**, pp. 291–314.

Ong, A. and D. Nonini, D. (1997) *Ungrounded Empires: The Cultural Politics of Modern Chinese Transnationalism*. New York: Routledge.

Orru, M. (1991) The institutional logic of small-firm economies in Italy and Taiwan. *Studies in Comparative International Development*, **26**(1), pp. 3–28.

Sassen, S. (2001) *The Global City: New York, London, Tokyo*, 2nd ed. Princeton: Princeton University Press.

Saxenian, A. (1994) *Regional Advantage: Culture and Competition in Silicon Valley and Route 128*. Cambridge: Harvard University Press.

Saxenian, A. and Hsu, Jinn-yuh (2001) The Silicon Valley-Hsinchu connection: technical communities and industrial upgrading. *Industrial and Corporate Change*, **10**(4), pp. 893–920.

Scott, A. (1998) *Regions and the World Economy*. Oxford: Oxford University Press.

Scott, A. (2000) *Global City-Regions: Trends, Theory, Policy*. Oxford: Oxford University Press.

Shieh, G.-S. (1992) *Boss Island-The Subcontracting Network and Micro-entrepreneurship in Taiwan's Development*. New York: Peter Lang Publishing.

Short, J. (1996) *The Urban Order*. Oxford: Blackwell.

Storper, M. (1997) *The Regional World: Territorial Development in a Global Economy*. New York: Guilford.

Sum, N.L. (2002) Globalization, regionalization and cross-border modes of growth, in East Asia: the (re-)constitution of 'time-space governance', in Perkmann, M. and Sum, N.-L. (eds.) *Globalization, Regionalization and Cross-border Regions*. London: Palgrave.

Sun, Y.C. (1988) Taiwan quyu zhengce (Regional policy in Taiwan) *Taiwan shehui yanjiu jikan* (*Taiwan: A Radical Quarterly in Social Studies*), **1**(2/3), pp. 33–96.

Sunley, P. (2000) Urban and regional growth, in Sheppard, E. and Barnes, T. (eds.) *A Companion to Economic Geography*. Oxford: Blackwell.

Tang, F.Z. (1981) Taiwan de dushi fazhan (Urban development in Taiwan). *Taiwan jingji* (*Taiwanese Economy*), **54**, pp 1–35.

Trajtenberg, M. (1999) Innovation in Israel, 1968–97: A Comparative Analysis Using Patent Data. Working Paper No. 7022, National Bureau of Economic Research, Cambridge, Massachusetts, March 1999.

Wade, R. (1990) *Governing the Market: Economic Theory and the Role of Government in East Asian Industrialization*. Princeton: Princeton University Press.

World Bank (1993) *The East Asian Miracle*. New York: Oxford.

Xu, S.G. (1986) Gongyeyong diqu de ziyouhua (The Liberalization of Industrial Land Acquiring) Report to the Committee of Economic and Construction.

Yeung, H. (2002) Towards a relational economic geography: old wine in new bottles? Paper presented at the 98th Annual Meeting of the AAG.

Yeung, H. and Olds, K. (2001) From the global city to globalizing cities: views from a developmental city-state in Pacific Asia. Paper presented at the IRFD World Forum on Habitat.

Zhou, T.C. (1999) *Taiwan zhongxiao qiye de chengzhang* (*The Growth of Taiwan's Small and Medium Sized Enterprises*) Taipei: Lien-Jing Press.

Zhou, Y. and Tseng, Y. (2001) Regrounding the ungrounded empire: localization as the geographical catalyst for transnationalism. *Global Networks*, **1**(2), pp. 131–153.

Chapter Two

The Development of Economic Structure: Producer Services and Growth Restraints

Chia-Ho Ching

How cities restructure their economic activities and what factors influence the restructuring have emerged as an essential research issue in the era of globalization. Shifting to knowledge-intensive services, especially in producer services, is an essential phenomenon in many cities of advanced economies (Clark, 1996; Friedmann, 1986; Harris, 1997; Sassen, 1995). The development of this sector is directly related to the command functions for global accumulation. Some writers (e.g. Douglass, 2000) have observed, as well as suggested implicitly, that the Asian new industrialized economies (NIEs), including Taiwan, have made efforts in restructuring their economic and physical infrastructure, in order to promote their main cities to a higher status within the system of world cities. As Taiwan attempts to promote its role and to adjust its economic development strategy to respond to global economic changes, the functions and the internal economic structure of its capital city, Taipei, change accordingly. A more significant change is likely to be evident from the 1980s, as Taiwan's economy faces more challenges from globalization as a result of joining in the world economic sphere of Asia's other economies, especially, China.

While Taipei has been proposed as a world city (Friedmann, 1986; King, 1990; Reed, 1984; Taylor, 1997; Taylor et al, 2002), its economic development or evolution has been little studied. Further, its economic restructuring is viewed and explained from the experience of those world cities in advanced economies. The elements of industrial organization which rely on the services provided by European and North

American firms may partially explain the development of producer services in the Asia-Pacific economies (Daniels, 1998); however, other elements also influence the development of Taipei producer services. Understanding these elements would reveal the nature of Taipei's economic structural changes and thus lead us to understand the major differences between Taipei and other world cities, especially, Hong Kong, Singapore, and other Asian cities.

This chapter focuses on explaining two essential elements that would constrain the development of Taipei's global commanding functions and thus influence its economic growth and industrial restructuring. First, the subcontractor role in manufacturing industries, played mainly by Taiwan in joining the global economic system, is shaping Taipei – functioning as an industrial production management centre only, rather than a global command centre of diverse flows. The second element is that identity politics confine Taiwan's development policy to anti-China activities which are influencing the economic development and structural change of Taipei.

This chapter is divided into six sections including this introduction. The following section discusses the role of Taipei played in the world economic system. The changes in Taipei's economic structure in general, and the development of its producer service sectors in particular, are, then, examined. The fourth section argues that the structural changes in Taipei are different from those cities in developed countries because Taiwan has chosen the role of main manufacturing subcontractor as the means of entry into the world economic system. The analyses demonstrate that the manufacturing sector in Taipei is transforming rather than retreating due to Taiwan's main function in the global division of labour. It also argues that producer services are not yet well developed in Taipei. This is partly because of the limitation of the subcontractor role of Taiwan's firms in the global market. The following section shows how the 'identity politics' in the current dispute with China leads Taiwan's development policy in a 'de-China' direction. Ignoring the rise of China and treating it as being outside the global economic system politically have resulted in a peculiar development milieu for Taiwan's economy. The impacts of the identity politics on Taipei's economic restructuring are significant and will produce a negative effect in the development of Taipei's trans-border command functions.

The Role of Taipei in Global Economic Systems

Some authors suggest that the globalization of national economies causes the world economy to be organized around and through cities which form interrelated nodes within an urban network that underpins and makes possible capitalist accumulation and reproduction (Timberlake, 1987; King, 1990). This urban system is dominated by a small number of world cities that are the command and control nodes for the world economy (Clark, 1996; Cohen, 1981; Friedmann, 1986; Sassen, 1991; Taylor, 1997). With the intermeshing between these cities, their different positions and functions form a hierarchical world city system (Friedmann, 1986; Smith and Timberlake, 1995; Taylor, 1997; Taylor *et al.*, 2002). In this regard, the niche that a particular city occupies in the system will shape its economic structure and the development of dominant activities (Clark, 1996; King, 1990; Machimura, 1998). This concept is adopted as the framework for analyzing Taipei's economic restructuring.

Since it was established as a capital city in the late nineteenth century (see Chapter 3), Taipei has occupied the dominant position in the Taiwanese economy. Its industrial restructuring is therefore highly connected to Taiwan's overall economic development. A brief review of Taiwan's economic development history over the last five decades illustrates this. Throughout the 1950s, the strategy of Import Substitution Industrialization was adopted by the state to promote Taiwan's economic development. As the largest consumer market for industrial products within Taiwan, Taipei attracted a large proportion of the state's major manufacturing firms to it or its surroundings. The city functioned as the centre in leading Taiwan towards industrialization (see Chapter 1).

However, this inward looking mode soon met a development bottleneck, as Taiwan's internal market was small. In the 1960s, the development of international division of labour, connecting to capitalist restructuring in advanced economies, gave Taiwan an opportunity to change its economic development path. The government shifted the industrial development strategy towards an outward looking approach, an Export Oriented Industrialization (EOI) mode. By this strategy, Taiwan joined the world economic system and became a labour pool for world manufacturing, undertaking low-tech and labour intensive manufacturing and assembly work in the traditional and 'sunset' industrial sectors.

With transport facilities and market access, major cities and their surrounding regions were the most efficient areas for industrial production. Taipei, thus, functioned as the manufacturing core of the Island. A dispersed industrial policy had been promulgated with the first Export Processing Zone (EPZ) established at Kaohsung (city in south Taiwan) in 1966, and two years later, two other EPZs (Taichung and Nanzi) were established in central and southern Taiwan. Simultaneously, the trading services and commercial functions in Taipei grew gradually. This resulted in large-scale labour immigration to fill increasing numbers of manufacturing jobs, which in turn promoted the development of personal service and real estate sectors, causing spatial restructuring. Taipei Metropolis[1] steadily increased its share of Taiwan's population from 15 per cent (1950s) to 21 per cent (1971), 25 per cent (1981), and 28 per cent (1991), while Taipei County's (Taipei's periphery, see figure 2.1) population, in particular, grew more rapidly than

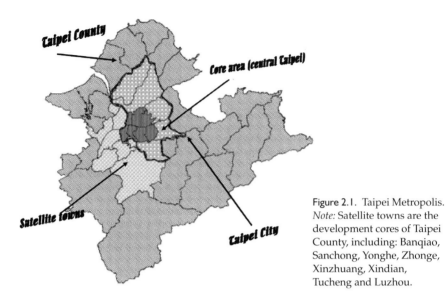

Figure 2.1. Taipei Metropolis.
Note: Satellite towns are the development cores of Taipei County, including: Banqiao, Sanchong, Yonghe, Zhonge, Xinzhuang, Xindian, Tucheng and Luzhou.

other areas in Taiwan. Its population share in the 1950s was only 6 per cent, but in 1981 grew to 13 per cent, and 1991 reached 15 per cent, more than Taipei City's itself. The main cities within the country, surrounding Taipei City, were the areas where manufacturing sectors grew most rapidly from the 1960s to 1980s.

From 1980, following the EOI approach, the Taiwan government promoted the development of a high-tech industry. The creation of Hsinchu (science-based) Industrial Park (located in northern Taiwan, about 70 kilometres (40 miles) from Taipei City and linked to the city by a new highway) provided industrial estate, infrastructure, tax incentives and a high-quality residential environment to attract foreign investment. As a result, Taiwan increased its share of world production of high-tech products. However, the role of Taiwan firms was mainly as subcontractors of multinational corporations of advanced economies, especially from the US and Japan.

Taipei continued to play an important role as Taiwan embarked on its high-tech industrial development. Firms located only production and part of their research and development (R & D) in Hsinchu Industrial Park for tax exemption, while their headquarters for decision-making, management, and marketing functions were in Taipei. Not only the decision-makers and managers of these firms lived in Taipei, but also their engineers and their families, commuting daily or returning for weekends (Castells and Hall, 1994, p. 108). In addition, Taipei provided various services, particularly producer services, to the firms in the Hsinchu Industrial Park, as well as in other areas, thus the city continued to function as the economic centre of Taiwan (Ching, 2001).

From the late 1980s, Taiwan's economic development faced several challenges. The powerful environmental movement and increasing costs of labour and land gradually eroded Taiwanese competitive advantage in manufacturing production. Added to these was competition for foreign direct investment (FDI) from neighbouring countries under pressure of globalization. The result was, for Taipei, not only reduced FDI, but also Taiwan out-sourced production lines to cheaper places, across the border to Southeast Asia and China. In order to avoid or alleviate the crisis of hollowing-out from de-industrialization, from the 1990s, the Taiwan government undertook projects such as the 'Asia Pacific Regional Operational Centre' and 'Knowledge-based Economic Development', and 'Challenge 2008: National Development Plan'. As their titles suggest, the aims of these projects were to promote and transfer the mode of production from a manufacturing to a service economy. Under this influence, Taipei, as a capital city as well as intermediary between Taiwan firms and the world market, underwent major economic restructuring.

Taipei's Economic Structure and Producer Services

Many authors (e.g. Friedmann, 1995; Frost and Spence, 1993; Sassen, 1995) indicate that the driving force of world cities' growth is mainly in producer services. World cities such as London, New York, and Hong Kong have demonstrated large employment losses in manufacturing sectors, together with concurrent gains in producer services (e.g. Daniels, 1991; 1998; Drennan, 1992; Frost and Spence, 1993; Tao and Wong, 2002). The reason for a closer study of the growth of producer services is that it performs a strategic function for transborder economic activities in the era of globalization. Thus, the development of this sector is not only used as an indicator of the economic maturation of advanced economies (e.g. Taylor *et al.*, 2002), but is also associated with the shaping of new roles for a given city (O'Connor and Hutton, 1998). This kind of knowledge-intensive sector has also been observed to cluster in the core areas of the world cities where information flow converges. Also, these cities have become the key locations for export producer services, with a tendency towards specialization (Sassen, 1995; 2002).

With the above development in world cities in mind, to understand the economic changes in Taipei, we need to investigate the growth of producer services alongside the declining manufacturing sector. This section begins with an overall review of the development of producer services and manufacturing industries in Taiwan. Then, by reflecting on other world cities' situations, the changes of Taipei's economic structure, and the spatial distribution of producer services are examined.

To analyze the changes of economic structure, this section is based on Taiwan Industrial and Commercial Census data, undertaken every five years. The census

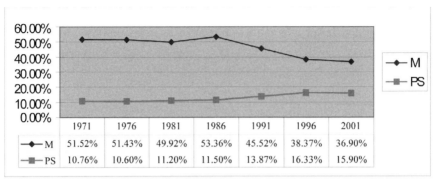

Figure 2.2. Shares of Taiwan's employment by manufacturing (M) and producer services (PS). *Source:* Taiwan Industrial and Commercial Census data.

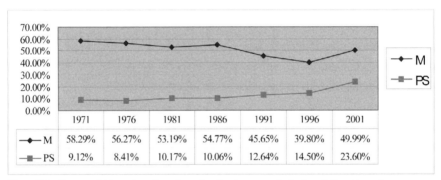

Figure 2.3. Shares of Taiwan's value of production by manufacturing (M) and producer services (PS). *Source:* Taiwan Industrial and Commercial Census data.

data reveal that, since 1986, there has been a trend of stagnation in Taiwan's manufacturing alongside growth in producer services (see figures 2.2 and 2.3). The data also show that the share of producer services is still lower than manufacturing, although it is growing steadily.

As the economic core of Taiwan, Taipei's producer services are growing quite rapidly. The jobs provided by producer services increase to 499,330 from 197,459 in the period 1981–2001. Table 2.1 shows the growth of producer service sectors. Among them, finance, insurance and real estate service sectors as well as business service sectors show substantial growth, with growth rates at 319 per cent and 187 per cent in this period.

Some authors (e.g. Tao and Wong, 2002) posit that the growth of producer services is related to changes in the production system in many industrial sectors. Traditionally, producers provided as many services as possible by themselves. However, this pattern has changed under the pressure of intense competition between firms and high product diversity responding to consumer preference.

Table 2.1. Employment of Taipei City's producer service sectors.

	Transport, storage, communication services	Finance, insurance, real estate services	Business services (professional, scientific and technical)	Producer services total
1981	99,015	58,759	39,685	197,459
1986	112,447	68,008	55,441	235,896
1991	126,608	126,298	93,157	346,063
1996	126,362	176,394	121,317	424,073
2001	138,667	246,574	114,089	499,330
Growth rate, 1981–1996	27.6%	200.2%	205.7%	114.8%
Growth rate, 1981–2001	40.1%	319.6%	187.5%	152.9%

Source: Taiwan Industrial and Commercial Census data.

This means that large-scale and standardized production methods have given way to low-volume but more varied, and more customized production. To respond to this change, firms expanded buying specialized services, as intermediate inputs, from specialized providers. The main reason for outsourcing specialized services is that the production of these services within a single firm can not reach economies of scale. Even if they could, firms might lack the incentive to improve the quality of intermediate services. Therefore, these services are provided by specialized professional firms rather than in-house.

In Taiwan, this changing relationship between manufacturing and producer services can be observed from their input-output coefficients. Table 2.2 shows that selected Taiwan manufacturing sectors increasingly buy professional services as production inputs from 'finance and insurance', and 'trade services'. For example, the amount of trade services needed to produce one unit of textile products was 2.86 per cent in 1991, and increased to 4.02 per cent in 1999. Although these data are limited in scope, they provide a broad perspective that suggests that producer services have been used increasingly as an intermediate input by manufacturing sectors. This reflects a closer business linkage between manufacturing and producer service than before.

Examining the economic structure of Taipei, table 2.3 lists the percentage share of different industrial sectors by employment and value of production. This indicates that Taipei's economic structure has changed significantly since 1981. Although the manufacturing sector still occupies key position, its importance is slipping, while producer services are growing rapidly and probably becoming the most competitive sectors. By 2001, the share of producer services employment accounted for about 22 per cent of the total Taipei Metropolis employment, while in 1981 it had been less than 15 per cent. In contrast, over the same period manufacturing industries' share

Table 2.2. Input/output coefficients of selected manufacturing sectors to trade services and finance and insurance.

	Trade services			Finance and insurance		
	1991	1996	1999	1991	1996	1999
Textile products	0.0286	0.0377	0.0402	0.0234	0.0309	0.0332
Paper and paper products, prints and publishing	0.0440	0.0768	0.0745	0.0380	0.0296	0.0281
Plastic products	0.0441	0.00630	0.0559	0.0239	0.0256	0.0254
Metal industries	0.0586	0.0704	0.0690	0.0315	0.0290	0.0287
Machinery and equipment	0.0652	0.0657	0.0735	0.0244	0.0246	0.0236
Household appliances	0.0550	0.0690	0.0718	0.0235	0.0279	0.0272
Electric machinery and miscellaneous	0.0539	0.0840	0.0806	0.0197	0.0324	0.0289

Source: Directorate-General of Budget, Accounting and Statistics, Bureau of the Census http://www.dgbas.gov.tw/dgbas03/div6all.htm.

of employment declined to 27 per cent from 38 per cent. Manufacturing industries' share of annual total value of production fell dramatically from 50 per cent (1986) to 34 per cent (2001). The producer services sector, in contrast, increased from 19 per cent to 36 per cent in the same period. As expected, it is by far the fastest growing sector in the Taipei metropolitan area. Using employment as a measure, in the period 1981–2001, the producer services sector presents a faster growth rate (153 per cent) than the overall industrial sectors (70 per cent). At present the producer

Table 2.3. Percentage share by industrial sector in Taipei Metropolis.

Years		Manufacturing	Construction	Trade, distribution, catering and drinking	Producer services*	Social & personal services	Others
Employment	1981	38.2	9.9	28.8	14.8	7.3	1.0
	1986	40.0	7.0	29.5	15.3	7.2	1.1
	1991	31.3	7.9	33.4	18.6	8.1	0.8
	1996	28.5	7.2	34.5	20.6	8.6	0.6
	2001	27.4	5.8	35.6	22.1	8.6	0.5
Value of production	1981	37.2	15.7	20.1	19.8	6.4	0.8
	1986	49.9	6.0	13.9	22.5	4.9	3.0
	1991	48.9	6.2	11.4	25.1	4.0	4.6
	1996	37.4	7.9	18.4	29.0	5.5	1.8
	2001	34.4	5.0	17.0	36.4	5.5	1.7

Note: Producer Services include finance, insurance and real estate services; transport, storage and communications services; and business services.
Source: Taiwan Industrial and Commercial Census data

service sector's share of employment is still lower than other world cities, but it has the potential for growth.

Table 2.4 indicates that a significantly high proportion overall of Taiwan economic activities is located in Taipei Metropolis. First, Taipei increases its share of Taiwan's economic activities every year. Second, Taipei Metropolis now accounts for over 40 per cent of Taiwan's economy. Furthermore, the role of Taipei Metropolis in Taiwan's economy excels not only in quantity, but also in quality. In 2001, it had 32 per cent of Taiwan's business establishments, but provided 40 per cent of employment and produced 43 per cent of the value of production. This means that firms with a larger scale and higher value of production congregate in Taipei. This lends support to the notion that Taipei is the economic core of Taiwan. Examining the spatial distributions of Taiwan producer services reveals this very clearly, as seen in table 2.5. In the period of 1981–2001, Taiwan's producer services have obviously clustered in Taipei Metropolis. That is, the share of Taipei Metropolis' producer services increased every year. In 2001, 47 per cent of Taiwan's producer services business establishments and 56 per cent of employments were located in Taipei Metropolis, and contributed 67 per cent of producer services annual value of production.

Table 2.4. Spatial distribution of Taiwan's industries (all sectors).

Year	Taiwan	Taipei Metropolis (1)	Taipei City (1)	Central Taipei (1)	(2)
Total business establishments by all sectors (unit: 000s)					
1981	519.7	153.3 (29%)	97.7 (19%)	78.2 (15%)	51%
1986	624.7	202.7 (32%)	123.0 (20%)	98.0 (16%)	48%
1991	760.6	264.1 (35%)	157.4 (21%)	123.2 (16%)	47%
1996	885.0	300.2 (34%)	164.0 (19%)	124.9 (14%)	42%
2001	968.0	310.2 (32%)	169.6 (18%)	128.3 (13%)	42%
Total employment in all sectors (unit: 000s)					
1981	4,401	1,588 (36%)	989 (22%)	724 (16%)	46%
1986	5,154	1,871 (36%)	1,112 (22%)	836 (16%)	45%
1991	5,856	2,248 (38%)	1,388 (24%)	1,060 (18%)	47%
1996	6,595	2,537 (39%)	1,556 (24%)	1,211 (18%)	48%
2001	6,746	2,702 (40%)	1,708 (25%)	1434 (21%)	53%
Annual total value of production by all sectors (unit: NT billions)					
1981	3,052	1,173 (38%)	395 (13%)	349 (11%)	30%
1986	4,838	1,598 (33%)	891 (18%)	679 (14%)	43%
1991	8,230	2,896 (35%)	1,817 (22%)	1,375 (16%)	48%
1996	13,746	5,478 (40%)	3,665 (27%)	2,910 (21%)	53%
2001	16,439	7,115 (43%)	4915 (30%)	4,287 (26%)	60%

Note: (1) = percentage of Taiwan; (2) = percentage of Taipei Metropolis.
Source: Taiwan Industrial and Commercial Census data.

Table 2.5. Spatial distribution of Taiwan's producer services.

Year	Taiwan	Taipei Metropolis (1)	Taipei City (1)	Central Taipei (1)	Central Taipei (2)
Business establishments in producer services (unit: 000s)					
1981	33.8	12.8 (38%)	9.7 (29%)	8.4 (25%)	65%
1986	59.7	25.9 (43%)	15.1 (25%)	12.3 (21%)	47%
1991	87.5	43.0 (49%)	27.2 (31%)	21.1 (24%)	49%
1996	122.7	57.5 (46%)	33.3 (27%)	25.7 (21%)	45%
2001	129.7	60.4 (47%)	36.1 (28%)	27.8 (21%)	46%
Employment in producer services (unit: 000s)					
1981	489	233 (48%)	197 (40%)	183 (37%)	79%
1986	588	285 (48%)	236 (40%)	218 (37%)	76%
1991	808	416 (51%)	346 (42%)	320 (39%)	77%
1996	1,045	522 (49%)	424 (40%)	389 (37%)	75%
2001	1,075	598 (56%)	499 (46%)	459 (43%)	77%
Annual value of production by producer services (unit: NT billions)					
1981	391	117 (30%)	109 (27%)	105 (26%)	90%
1986	616	358 (58%)	322 (52%)	311 (50%)	87%
1991	1,370	785 (57%)	703 (51%)	674 (49%)	86%
1996	2,787	1,589 (57%)	1,390 (49%)	1,304 (46%)	82%
2001	3,878	2,586 (67%)	2,364 (61%)	2,243 (58%)	87%

Note: (1) = percentage of Taiwan; (2) = percentage of Taipei Metropolis.
Source: Taiwan Industrial and Commercial Census data.

The majority of producer service firms are agglomerating in central Taipei (figure 2.1). As shown in table 2.5, in 2001, 46 per cent of the Metropolis' producer services firms were located in central Taipei, with 77 per cent of job opportunities and 87 per cent of annual value of production. Clearly, the core of Taipei attracts large and high value production firms. Although the degree of concentration is slightly lower than two decades ago, the core still is the commanding centre.

The concentration of the producer service sector is the result of several factors. First, Taipei attracts nearly half of Taiwan's corporate headquarters. The 2001 Census data show that Taipei Metropolis had 2,645 manufacturing headquarters, and 648 producer services headquarters. These headquarters need various kinds of professional services to support the operation of production planning and production control, financial management, market analysis and marketing. As these services need to locate close to their customers, because of essential, face-to-face communication, clustering in the core area is the norm. Second, research and development activities, as well as research institutions, are far more abundant in Taipei than Taiwan's other cities or regions. For example, 33 per cent of Taiwan's manufacturing patents are in Taipei. The dynamic activities of research and invention in Taipei are supported by diversified producer services. Third, Taipei is the largest market of Taiwan, thus the firms located there benefit from easy access to market information, a professional workforce, and expertise from other services. These factors were emphasized by firms which responded to a questionnaire on the main reasons for starting up in or moving to Taipei.[2]

Taipei has indeed experienced a rapid growth in producer services in the past two decades, but its development appears to be less prominent than expected. It only provides 22.1 per cent of jobs and 36.4 per cent of income (see table 2.3). Producer services provide 499,330 jobs for Taipei City (29.2 per cent of the city's total employment) and 98,000 for Taipei County (only 9.9 per cent of the county's total employment). Obviously, Taipei's economy is still dependent on the manufacturing sector, which provides 252,000 jobs in Taipei City (14.8 per cent of the city's total), but 489,000 jobs in Taipei County (49.2 per cent of the county's total).

Since the 1980s, many Asian countries, including China, actively join the global division of labour. Meanwhile, Taiwan's internal production conditions have changed with the rising of environmentalism and the increase in production costs, resulting in pressure on labour-intensive and export-oriented firms to move their production plants to cheaper production sites. Recently, even the high-tech industrial firms have made transborder investments. Otherwise, they would have to expand their production activities towards capital-intensive sectors to replace labour-intensive components. According to statistics from Taiwan's Investment Commission of the Ministry of Economic Affairs, up to the end of 2002 the approved outward investment had reached 9,130 cases and amounted to US$34 billion (http://www.moeaic.gov.tw). This indicates that Taiwan has become a capital exporting territory, and the manufacturing sector, as the traditional mainstay of Taiwan economy, is gradually losing ground.

While the growth of transborder investments increases, the demand for services assisting firms to deal with the complex variety of market analyses, product selling, customer services, and production control and management intensifies. This suggests that a foundation for producer services growth has been laid, and Taipei has the opportunity to shift from manufacturing to service industry. With the clustering of producer services and corporation headquarters, Taipei should have gained the position of command centre for trans-border investment and production. The government has also made policies and plans to promote the growth of the producer service sector, for example such projects as the Asia Pacific Regional Operational Center, Knowledge-based Economic Development , and investment in the Taipei 101 project, for a 101-floor financial centre building in the new CBD of Taipei (see Chapter 5). However, the facts show a reverse tendency. Taipei is still dependent on the manufacturing sector. Few of its producer service firms have expanded their business abroad and exported their services (Ching, 2001), and their contribution to economic growth is lower than other world cities.

It is worth exploring further what leads to this inexplicable situation. The determining factors are various, such as using services outside the Pacific Region and the dissimilarity in industrial organization, asserted by Daniels (1998). In the next two sections, two other factors which influence the economic restructuring of Taipei and constrain the development of producer services are explained. One is the subcontractor role played by Taiwan in joining the global economic system. The other is the identity politics that confines Taiwanese development policy in its interaction with China.

The Role of Manufacturing Subcontractor

Since the 1960s, Taiwan adopted the EOI mode to the world economic system. At first, Taiwan's firms were mainly devoted to the sunset industrial sectors. Since the 1980s, they have promoted many kinds of high-tech products. In reality, they enact the role of subcontractors for multinational corporations (MNCs) of advanced economies, specializing in parts production. They are skilful in such aspects of production as quality control and reducing production costs. However, they are generally weak in the development of new products and in R & D. Few have their own brands or selling channels in the global market. Lacking patents, firms cannot develop the power to dominate production. Lacking named brands and selling channels, making high profits from the production value chains is impossible.

Most of Taiwan's enterprises are small and medium-sized firms. They aim to set up their own brand and sell their products in the global market, but few succeed. The experience of failures further discourages other firms from making this kind of effort. The result is that focus is on the production side, as the subcontractors for other MNCs. The increase of their production share is not sufficient to generate growth of domestic professional services, such as marketing, advertising services, marketing analysis, or customer services. The work of product innovation and marketing is dominated by MNCs in advanced economies. As a rule, these MNCs buy services from firms with which they are familiar, located in advanced economies.

This situation can be delineated by the example of the footwear industry. Several Taiwan firms are the main subcontractors of well-known brands, such as Nike and Adidas. By controlling the brand and selling channels, these MNCs not only make profits for their shareholders, but also generate the growth of producer services in various sectors within their home cities. The production activities are mainly undertaken by the subcontractors, Taiwanese firms and their overseas branches, according to the contracts and instructions of the MNCs. These firms may have 20–30,000 workers, but are unknown in the global market. They specialize in manufacturing activities, but use local professional services far less than Nike and Adidas. Acer and other Taiwan computer firms provide a contrast to the subcontractor firms. Acer has its own brand in the global market. Thus, it buys more professional services from Taiwan producer service firms to assist its operations than other firms who only perform the role of subcontractors. However, these firms are a minority compared to the subcontractors. This provides partial explanation of why the development of producer services in Taipei is less developed than expected, and how its economic restructuring is constrained.

Second, the transborder production network set up by Taiwanese firms has a specific pattern. This relates to their role as subcontractors. To fulfil subcontracting contracts, the main function of an outward expanding production line, mainly in Southeast Asia and now China, is to undertake parts and assembly production. This is only the transborder production mode of Taiwan firms, its purpose being to use cheaper manpower and cheaper land and so reduce production costs. These overseas branch firms are totally or mainly financed by Taiwan firms, and are controlled directly by Taiwanese. They have a stronger connection with firms in Taiwan than the local firms in the overseas country. When transnational production or business connection is established, it is mainly based on the social networks, and not purely on production and economic advantages. The command and logistics functions for transborder production promote some professional services, but the weak production network with local firms produces little demand for professional services, such as agents, credit investigation, investment consultation, legal and accounting services. In addition, the products do not sell in local markets, but are distributed by the MNCs. The need to use producer services, such as market research, marketing, and advertising consumer services, for the operation of the local markets is small. They do not promote local producer service growth either. This explains the differences between Taiwan firms and advanced MNCs. Taiwan firms, unlike MNCs do not practice formal contract supervision and surveillance – the main causes for the demand of professional services.

Third, the state's industrial policies also contribute to the weak demand on producer services. For a long time, the government concentrated mainly on manufacturing production, neglecting the producer service sector and service industries. For example, many incentives (e.g. tax, infrastructure) were provided for manufacturing investment, but not for producer services. A combination of these conditions has meant that the producer service sector firms commonly lack the resources for the development of high-quality labour and the ability to operate internationally and, as a result, many are unable to make a global connection. A survey demonstrates that only 40 per cent of the Taipei producer service firms export their services (Ching, 2001), while examination of Taiwan's outward investment shows that the amount of investment in professional services is significantly lower than in manufacturing services (see figure 2.4). This indicates that Taipei does not play an essential role as a producer services supplier in the global market or even in

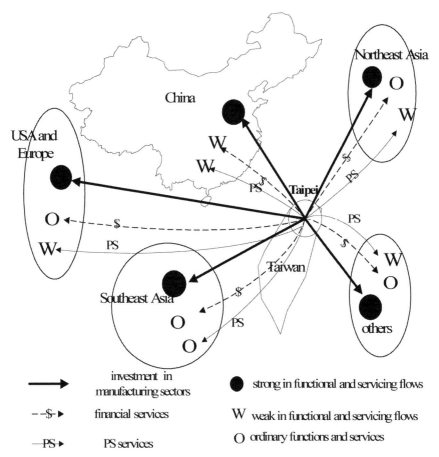

Figure 2.4. The imbalance of flows between manufacturing and producer services (PS).
Source: Ching (2001).

the Asia-Pacific region. Within the producer service sector, those firms that provide services to local production firms to undertake their subcontracting functions are growing faster than other parts of producer services.

In short, although Taipei's producer services have grown steadily over the past two decades, they have not fully developed as major service suppliers in the global market. This is partly constrained by the manufacturing subcontractor role played by Taiwan firms in the global division of labour.

Cross-Strait Relations and Identity Politics

The relations between Taiwan and China also have a major impact on the development of Taipei. Geographically, Taiwan is an island, separate but close to

China. The discontinuity in physical space is one of the causes of the estrangement between the two. Most Taiwanese are the descendants of migrants who came from China in different periods. Thus, Taiwan's culture is traditionally an extension of Chinese culture. However, these relationships and cultural kinship linkages were severed over 50 years ago, in 1949, due to the civil war between two separate governments.

Taiwan has since gained much experience in and a closer relationship with the international trade and production link to global corporations. By developing information and communication technologies, the opportunities in social, economic and cultural aspects, offered to Taiwan are diverse. Meanwhile, Taiwanese social creativity has widened, resulting in a deviation from the Chinese cultural tradition. Thus Chinese influence, both geographically and culturally, has diminished. This has led to a new Taiwanese political agenda – to establish an independent state, and make a clear distinction from China.

The links between the two sides of the Strait have not disappeared entirely. First, many mainlander Taiwanese, who came from China during 1949 and the early 1950s, still identify with their home country (perhaps not with the government) and the Chinese culture. Furthermore, since the late 1970s, due to China's adoption of an Open Door policy, many of Taiwan's manufacturing firms shifted their production plants to China to take advantage of the low production costs available there. According to a survey undertaken by the Ministry of Economic Affairs, 72.9 per cent of Taiwan outward investment manufacturing firms invested in China in the year of 2001 (*Commercial Times*, 30 September 2002). This indicates that a strong industrial connection between the two sides of the Strait has been established. Entrepreneurs acknowledge that China is not only part of the global market, but the currently biggest emerging market in the world. Besides, China provides opportunities to transform small and medium corporations into multinational corporations by expanding their scale of production. Moreover, production in China enables them to set up their own brands and selling channels in this emerging market. China is much more open than the advanced economies where the market has already been carved up by powerful MNCs.

On the political side, China insists on 'one China, and Taiwan is part of China'. With international support, this policy seals Taiwan's international political space. The purpose of the Chinese policy is to prevent Taiwan from becoming an independent country. Therefore, a weak international political position not only reduces the Taiwan government's international diplomacy but also harms the functional flows of international economic, cultural and social linkages, and these linkages are essential elements in global competition (Smith and Timberlake, 1995, p. 86). A substantial proportion of citizens and politicians consider China a threat, and support the policy of de-China.

Disputes about cross-Strait relations are reflected both in the main agenda of political parties and in Taiwan's development policies. These disputes accompanied, by the recent democratization, have led the ruling party in the direction of de-China. The policy of 'No Haste, Be Patient', proposed and undertaken by the former Lee government, is followed by the present Chen government. This policy not only makes the investment from China unwelcome, but also restricts certain kinds of economic activity of Taiwan firms located in China. The key restrictions are in the amount of capital investment and the movement of high-tech manpower. The logic of this policy is that by reducing the economic interactions with China, Taiwan will be less dependent on China's market, thus distancing the domination of Chinese politics. With these restrictions, the Taiwan government hopes to increase its bargaining power with China.

Recognizing that political manoeuvring often conflicts with the demand of firms, and given the trend of Taiwan's economic restructuring, the Lee government attempted to convince firms to go 'South' (to Southeast Asia) instead of 'West' (to China). Also, it endeavoured to link with North America and Japan. The idea was that linking closely with these advanced economies could formulate a strong external network, and position Taiwan in an economic hub away from China, thus reducing the threat of China. However, this strategy failed for two reasons. First, China has many advantages in enhancing Taiwan's economic achievements, by its economic reform and open door policy. These policies attract many Taiwan firms to invest in China. Second, after the 1997 financial crisis, firms lost confidence in the 'going South' policy, and the only alternative for overseas investment is China.

The policy of 'No Haste, Be Patient' to a certain extent means to ignore China as part of the global market. However, while China is rapidly connecting with the global economic system and attracting the largest amount of FDI among Asian countries,[3] economic development of Taiwan is in a difficult predicament. First, the role of the manufacturing subcontractor has been gradually taken over by China, as Taiwan's companies invest a huge amount in China by subcontracting Chinese firms. The shift of manufacturing to China has caused a rising unemployment rate. The 'No Haste, Be Patient' policy also confines the development of producer services in enlarging their businesses in China. The investment of certain producer services in China, such as the finance and real estate industries, is forbidden by the government under this policy, so as to prevent a hollowing-out of Taiwan's capital, and avoid facilitating the opponent's economic development. This strategy, however, can also harm Taiwan's own economic development. First, while firms cannot get appropriate services from Taiwan's producer services, they have to turn to foreign producer service firms, or they encounter investment difficulties and risk. Having to buy services from other countries' firms means that Taiwan's producer services, mainly located in Taipei, lose the opportunity to enlarge their business in

China. Moreover, these restrictions promote the development of other countries' producer services, mainly in Asia Pacific, which now has a competitive advantage over the Taiwanese firms. Thus, Asia Pacific capital cities surge ahead in the race of regional command and finance centres.

Second, many firms bypass government policy and invest in China through a third country. In avoiding being caught, they keep surplus capital abroad or in China, instead of returning it to Taiwan. The de-China policy negatively influences Taiwan economic development and Taipei's ability to develop its global connection and its command functions. It is unusual that the huge outward investment of Taiwan firms has not promoted its own producer services. Part of this irony is bound by the politics of identity.

Another impact of identity politics on Taipei's economic restructuring and its producer service development is regional separation. Voter demographics are different in Taipei and southern Taiwan. The differences come from different identity politics. The Kuomintang Party (KMT) is identified with China, while the DPP (Democratic Progress Party) is against China and promotes a policy of independence as the Republic of Taiwan. The results of recent presidential and mayoral elections (March, 2004; December, 2002) show that the majority of voters in northern Taiwan (Taipei) tend to be KMT supporters, and most voters in southern Taiwan support the DPP. The north-south political split potentially can disrupt Taiwan's economic development and restructuring.

This difference in identity politics causes many problems. As the central government and the capital city have been run by different political parties since 1994, recent policy demonstrates that resources and opportunities for the capital city in promoting its global connecting functions are not at the top of the central government's agenda. Since the DPP swept into power in the presidential election of May 2000, the central government has shifted many important activities to other cities governed by its own party. One example is moving the Lantern Festival from Taipei, run by KMT, to DPP-ruled Kaohsung, a city in southern Taiwan, in the name of balancing development between the north and south. The cultural festival of 2001 'Asia Pacific Cultural Capital' is another example. This festival was organized by Taipei City to promote Taipei's international connections, but was boycotted by cities and counties ruled by the DPP. Even in the case of opening direct links across the Taiwan Strait, dispute over the role of the capital city was raised. The city government announced that the city is almost ready for the opening of direct air links with China, but the national government stated that Taipei will not be selected as a port for handling direct cross-Strait transportation services. All these indicate that the central government is unwilling to support Taipei in developing into a global city, and there is a possible de-linking of Taipei from Taiwan's other areas. Taipei's economic growth will suffer from these domestic identity politics.

Other proponents argued that the small and medium enterprises whose main function is that of subcontractor might not need Taipei as their commanding centre for trans-border investments. If the policy to locate small and medium firms away from the capital city is enacted, Taipei will not be able to develop its service economy according to global commanding functions. Taipei would have to compete with other Taiwan cities for the high-tech manufacturing sector with high production value.[4]

In sum, the contentious relationship between Taiwan and China has raised a host of complex issues of identity politics which in turn will affect the development of Taiwan's economy. The capital city's economic restructuring and the development of the global commanding functions will be restricted, and the development of a strong producer service sector will be uncertain. Taipei's development into a global city will be questionable.

Summary and Conclusion

This chapter analyzes the recent economic structure changes in Taipei, particularly in the shift from a manufacturing to a service economy. The development of producer services, the essential sector for driving world city growth, is examined in some detail. Although Taipei's producer services sector has grown steadily over the past two decades, and the core of Taipei is also attracting Taiwan's large firms with a high value of production, their developments are less robust than expected. This situation can be explained by the development of producer services and economic restructuring related to the production function of Taipei's firms in the global economic system. Many factors influence and constrain the development of Taipei as a global city, thus slowing its economic restructuring. Two important reasons for Taipei's arrested global development are highlighted here. The first is the role of the manufacturing subcontractor that Taiwan has chosen as the entry mode to the global economic system. The huge emerging market in China provides the opportunity for Taiwan firms to establish their own brands and selling channels, allowing them to leap forward into MNCs, breaking away from being just subcontractors. However, this opportunity is undermined by a second factor: that is 'identity politics'. In particular, the domestic dispute over the relationship with China is causing serious conflicts between economic development and politics. This also prompts a conflict between the central and the city government. With the state's current policy of de-China, Taipei is impeded in its attempt to expand its global commanding function, thus damaging its economic restructuring, especially in the development of producer services. The recent proposed development policy for Taipei, considered 'China friendly', could set back the capital's growth potential, and retard its global commanding function.

Notes

1. Taipei Metropolis includes Taipei City and Taipei County, as shown in figure 2.3.
2. This survey was undertaken in 1998 (see Ching, 1999).
3. According to the OECD 2004 report, *Trends and Recent Developments in Foreign Direct Investment*, China has become the world's largest or second largest recipient of FDI among the developing countries.
4. Taipei Mayor's economic policies focus more on the high-tech parks (Nangang Park and Neihu Park) than services sectors.

References

Castells, M. and Hall, P. (1994) *Technopoles of the World: The Making of 21st Century Industrial Complexes*. London: Routledge.
Ching, C.H. (1999) Taipei metropolitan economic structure and spatial distribution changes while becoming a world city. *City and Planning*, **26**(2), pp. 95–112.
Ching, C.H. (2001) Globalization and the development of producer Services in Taiwan's metropolises. *City and Planning*, **28**(4), pp. 495–518.
Clark, D. (1996) *Urban World/Global City*. London: Routledge.
Cohen, R.B. (1981) The new international division of labour; multi-national corporations and urban hierarchy, Dear, M. and A.J. Scott, A.J. (eds.) *Urbanisation and Urban Planning in a Capitalist Society*. London: Methuen, pp. 287–315.
Daniels, P. (1991), *Services and Metropolitan Development*, London: Routledge.
Daniels, P. (1998) Economic development and producer services growth: the APEC experience. *Asia Pacific Viewpoint*, **39**(2), pp. 145–159.
Douglass, M. (2000) Mega-urban regions and world city formation: globalisation, the economic crisis and urban policy issues in Pacific Asia. *Urban Studies*, **37**(12), pp. 2315–2335.
Drennan, M. (1992) Gateway cites: the metropolitan sources of U.S. producer service exports. *Urban Studies*, **29**(2), pp. 217–235.
Friedmann, J. (1986) The world cities hypothesis. *Development and Change*, **17**(1), pp. 69–74.
Friedmann, J. (1995) Where we stand: a decade of world city research, in Knox, P.L. and P. Taylor, P. (eds.) *World Cities in a World-System*. Cambridge: Cambridge University Press, pp.21–47.
Frost, M. and Spence, N. (1993) Global city characteristics and central London's employment. *Urban Studies*, **30**(3), pp. 547–558.
Harris, N. (1997) Cities in a global economy: structural change and policy reactions. *Urban Studies*, **34**(10), pp. 1693–1703.
Hill, R.C. and Kim, J.W. (2000) Global cities and Developmental states: New York, Tokyo and Seoul. *Urban Studies*, **37**(12), pp. 2167–2195.
King, A.D. (1990) *Urbanism, Colonialism and the World-Economy, Cultural and Spatial Foundations of the World Urban System*. London: Routledge.
Machimura, T. (1998) Symbolic use of globalization in urban politics in Tokyo. *Journal of International Urban and Regional Studies*, **22**(2), pp. 183–194.
O'Connor, K. and T. Hutton, T.(1998) Producer services in the Asia Pacific region: an overview of research issues. *Asia Pacific Viewpoint*, **39**(2), pp. 139–143.
Reed, H.C. (1984) Appraising corporate investment policy: a financial center theory of foreign direct investment, in Kindleberger, C.P. and D.B. Audretsch, D.B. (eds.) *The Multinational Corporation in the 1980s*. Cambridge, MA: MIT Press, pp. 219–43.
Sassen, S. (1991)*The Global City London, New York, Tokyo*. Princeton, NJ: Princeton University Press.
Sassen, S. (1995) Urban impacts of economic globalisation, in Brotchie, J. *et al.* (eds.) *Cities in Competition.* Melbourne: Longman Australia, pp. 36–57.
Sassen, S. (2002) *Global Networks: Linked Cities*. London: Routledge.
Smith, D.A. and Timberlake, M. (1995) Conceptualising and mapping the structure of the world city system. *Urban Studies*, **32**(2), pp. 287–302.

Tao, Z. and Wong, R. (2002) Hong Kong: from an industrialised city to a centre of manufacturing-related services. *Urban Studies*, **39**(12), pp. 2345–2358.

Taylor, P.J. (1997) Hierarchical tendencies amongst world cities: a global research proposal. *Cities*, **14**(6), pp. 323–332.

Taylor, P., Walker, D., Catalano, G. and Hoylor, M. (2002) Diversity and power in the world city network. *Cities*, **19**(4), pp. 231–241.

Timberlake, M. (1987) World-system theory and the study of comparative urbanization, in Smitch, M.P. and Feagin, J.R. (eds.) *The Capitalist City*. Oxford: Blackwell, pp. 37–64.

Wang, C.H. (2003) Taipei as a global city: a theoretical and empirical examination. *Urban Studies*, **40**(2), pp. 309–334.

Chapter Three

The Transformation of Spatial Structure: From a Monocentric to a Polycentric City

Tsu-Lung Chou

As continuing globalization has increasingly changed the role of the state in economic development since the 1970s, the profound demise of welfare states in advanced capitalist states has resulted in a surging discourse of 'the end of the state' (Ohmae, 1990; 1995). In parallel, there is also increasing suggestion in mainstream urban literature that the world city has replaced the state as the most important unit in managing world economies (Friedmann *et al.*, 1982; Friedmann, 1986; 1995; Sassen, 1991). The world city hypothesis has recently expanded its influence into debates on urban economic restructuring related to mounting research in advanced producer services (Coffey, 2000), cultural industries (Bryan *et al.*, 2000; Leyshon, 2001; Sadler, 1997; Scott, 1997; 1999*a*; 1999*b*; 2000), urban knowledge-based developments (Knight, 1995; Lever, 2002; Howells, 2002), and city competitiveness (Begg, 1999; Berg and Braun, 1999; Kresel and Singh, 1999; Lever, 1999; Porter 1990; 1995; 1996). Proponents have, thus, created a school of 'new urban economics'. However, literature of the 'new urban economics' school provides only partial insight into the development of the world city. It is primarily for their theoretical root in the institutional economics that they over-emphasize endogenous and exogenous growth mechanism, and downplay the role of the state and vertical governmental conflict beyond the city in the developmental process of the world city (Brenner, 1998; 1999*a*; 1999*b*; Macleod and Goodwin, 1999). This chapter uses the transformation in recent Taipei as a case to explore this omission, and re-emphasize the roles of the state and centre-city governance politics in its spatial and economic restructuring.

As the development mode of Export Oriented Industrialization was adopted in the 1960s, the growth of Taiwan's economic and investment linkages with the world system have brought with them a shift in the development trajectory for Taipei. Recently, Taipei has been in a period of transition in its function and spatial structure in response to globalization and associated to Taiwan's restructuring from an industrial to a post-industrial economy. This chapter aims to examine Taipei's economic and spatial transformation and the state strategies during Taiwan's restructuring in response to globalization. It explores the co-evolution of economic restructuring, spatial reorganization and state intervention in post-industrial Taipei. It also raises political issues in vertical governmental negotiation, and their implications for a globalizing Taipei.

The chapter suggests that the endogenous and exogenous growth discourse inherent in the world city hypothesis has not provided proper policy guidance for Taipei's restructuring because of its over-emphasis on institutional regulation at the city level and downplaying of vertical government negotiation. In Taipei's case, development is strongly conditioned by centre-city governance politics including the complicated identity articulation of cross-Strait politics, the institutional inertia of restructuring strategies at the national level, and the vertical governmental conflicts at Taiwan's regional level.

This chapter is divided into five parts. The first section briefly explores the construction and development of a monocentric Taipei from feudal and colonial periods to post-war industrialization. Subsequently, the polycentric structure and state intervention in post-industrial Taipei are examined. After this, two sections discuss centre-city politics at the centre and city level. The Summary and Conclusion is in the final part.

Monocentric Development in Feudalist and Colonial Taipei

The first two developed areas in feudalist Taipei were located in the western districts of Mengjia and Dadaocheng. They functioned as the primary sites for feudal economic transactions of tea, rice and camphor, which were shipped via the Tamsui River to markets in mainland China. The river port area of Dadaocheng thus became the most prosperous district in Qing Dynasty, while the areas in eastern Taipei were dominated by agricultural production. Dadaocheng constituted the earliest centre of Taipei's urban commercial history, as throughout the feudal period Dadaocheng flourished as a port gateway through which culture, goods and technology were introduced from mainland China and the outside world. In 1875, a walled city was built in Zhongzheng districts near Mengjia as an administrative centre of Taipei. The foundation for spatial development of a monocentric structure was thus laid in western Taipei.

The Japanese entered Taipei in 1895, and remodelled the city through the introduction of urban planning in 1904, dismantling the city wall and amplifying urban areas towards Zhongshan North Road. As the city developed under modern planning, urban infrastructures was laid out, ensuring Taipei as a colonial pioneer of urban development within Taiwan. Modern railways, public schools and parks, central boulevards and other major roads were established with foresight and sound planning. Progressive land readjustment in advance of urban development was also carried out. More importantly, a gridiron spatial structure was introduced to replace remnants of the walled city. In 1914, a new CBD in West Gate area (called Ximending) was built to reinforce the commercial functions of the western areas centred around the railway station. Obviously, commercial core areas had shifted away from the river port to the CBD and railway station areas. Nevertheless, this development re-emphasized the significance of the monocentric spatial structure. After the Second World War, the power and spatial vacancies left by the Japanese were rapidly filled by Kuomintang (KMT) governors, on losing their last bastion in 1949 China. Basically, Taipei, during the 1950s, played a central role in the consumption, administration and management of an agricultural Taiwan. The spatial fabric of Taipei, thus, remained a monocentric structure, centred around the railway station and Ximending.

Formulation and Development of Economic Core in Industrial Taipei, 1960s–1980s

From 1960, a development mode of Export Oriented Industrialization (EOI) was adopted by the Nationalist state and triggered Taipei's functional change from consumer services and administrative management for Taiwan's agricultural development to producer services and decision-making for manufacturing development. Nevertheless, the adoption of an EOI mode and the associated articulation of Taiwan's development with the world system exerted considerable influence on Taipei as well as a change for its economic and spatial structure. From the 1960s onward, the monocentric development expanded to the eastern suburbs of Taipei, and resulted in a spatial shift of the Economic Core with a dramatic decline in the western downtown area. In the industrialization process of post-war Taiwan, a vast majority of export-based manufacturing headquarters, mostly acting as subcontractors of Japanese and Western trans-nationals, flocked to Taipei in order to take advantage of the administrative and policy support from the central government. Most were located in the eastern suburbs between Zhongshan North Road and Keelung Road, because the downtown area in the western city was saturated. Important companies included the Datong Corporation in Zhongshan North Road (the first native consumer electronics giant), Formosa Group in Dunhua

North Road (a native petrochemical giant), Ever Green Group in Minsheng East Road as well as vast state-owned enterprises, such as, Taiwan Power, China Airlines, Taiwan Sugar, Taiwan Fertilizer Company and so on, defining the Economic Core. It was obvious that the spatial shift of Taipei towards the eastern suburbs owed much to the operation of domestic, private and state-owned manufacturing headquarters which increasingly targeted Taipei as an investment locale from the 1960s.

Furthermore, changing relations between urban and rural areas associated with Taiwan's industrialization had also stimulated considerable population growth in Taipei. The eastern suburbs absorbed the vast majority of the population growth. As table 3.1 shows, the resident population of the western downtown traditional districts fell by 17 per cent during the period from 1965 to 1975, while the eastern suburban districts received almost triple growth, gaining approximately 800,000 in population within a 20-year period, from 1955 to 1975. The population in this area accounted for more than 50 per cent of Taipei's total population in 1975. The swelling population turned the areas into a primary location of land speculation and development. In addition, the high growth of manufacturing headquarters in the new Economic Core had increasingly stimulated a centralization of financial and business services towards the most dynamic areas in the city (figure 3.1). A dramatic shift in the economic and commercial centre of Taipei occurred in line with Taiwan's transition from an agricultural to an industrial economy. Newly developing areas in the eastern suburbs emerged as the Economic Core of Taipei and replaced the traditional city centre on the western side of the railway station. Under Taiwan's industrialization, Taipei's major investment in manufacturing sectors came mostly from outside the Economic Core. Nevertheless, above all, the core grew as a centre for foreign trade and management, developing major trade links with advanced capitalist countries, especially the United States, Japan and European countries, while expanding the producer service as its nucleus.

Globalization and Development of Economic Core in Post-Industrial Taipei

Since the mid-1980s globalization has propelled Taiwan's outward-looking

Table 3.1. Urbanization in Taipei, 1950s, 1960s and 1970s.

| | *Population* | | | *Rate of growth* | |
	1955	1965	1975	1955–1965	1965–1975
Western Traditional Districts	239592	271041	223690	13.1%	−17%
Eastern Suburb Districts	464532	864459	1262277	86.1%	46.0%
Other Districts	148546	265035	557291	78.4%	110.3%
Total	852670	1400536	2034318	64.3%	45.9%

Source: Taipei Municipal Government (1978), Planning and Design for Xinyi District.

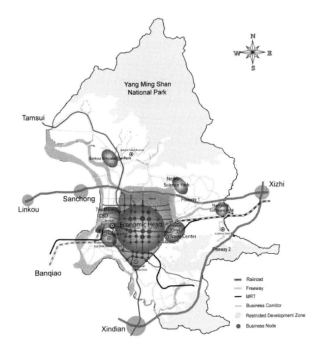

Figure 3.1. The spatial structure of Taipei since the 1990s.

industrial headquarters and transnational companies to centralize further in the eastern suburbs. Taipei hence raised its international image in the world economies through the successful hosting of native export-oriented industrial headquarters and large transnational companies. This development provided a major opportunity for further clustering of producer services and cultural industries, and finally reinforced the international linkages and economic functions of the Core. The Economic Core, thus, not only acts as an engine propelling Taipei's economies, but also serves as a major centre of economic management and decision-making. The growth and intensification of the Core is due to massive centralization of central government agencies, their associated organizations, headquarters of Taiwan's manufacturing, transnational companies and their attendant producer services.

Associated with Taiwan's foreign investment growth in East Asian countries and mainland China since the late 1980s, the headquarters of domestic enterprises were transformed into management centres for cross-border economies. As table 3.2 shows, in 2001, the area was home to sixty-four of Taiwan's top one hundred companies, including domestic and transnational manufacturers, services and state-owned enterprises. Since the late 1980s, this development finally reinforced the functional position of the Economic Core in world economies, serving as a management node in the global manufacturing network.

Obviously, headquarter clustering was the primary driving force for urban development of the Economic Core. The consequence of headquarter agglomeration

Table 3.2. 64 Headquarters of Taiwan's top 100 enterprises in Taipei.

	Domestic enterprises	Government-run organizations	Multinational enterprises
Manufacturing sectors			
Textile	Far Eastern Textile, Ltd.		
Petrochemical manufacturing	Nanya Plastics Corporation; Formosa Chemicals & Fibre Corporation; Taiwan Cement Corporation	Chinese Petroleum Corporation	China American Petrochemical Company, Ltd.
Car industries	Hotai Motor Co., Ltd.; China Motor Corp.; Nissan Taiwan Co., Ltd.; Mitsubishi Motors; Sino Diamond Motors Corp.; San Yang Industry Co., Ltd.; Nan Yang Industries Co., Ltd.		
Electronics	Tatung Co., Ltd.; Teco Electric & Machinery Co., Ltd.		Toshiba Electronic Taiwan Corp.; Samsung Electronic Taiwan Co., Ltd.; Mitsubishi Electric Taiwan Co., Ltd.
Information technology	Inventec Corporation; Asustek Computer Inc.; Compal Electronics Inc.; Wa-Yeu Computer; Synnex Technology International Corp.; First International Computer Inc.; GVC Corp.; Lite-On Technology Corp.		Philips Electronics Industries (Taiwan) Ltd.; Motorola Electronics Taiwan Ltd.; Panasonic Industrial Sales (Taiwan) Co., Ltd.; Hewlett-Packard Taiwan Ltd.
Others	Family Machinery Manufacturing; Yuen Foong Yu Paper Manufacturing Co., Ltd.	Taiwan Tobacco and Liquor Corporation; Taiwan Sugar Corporation; Taiwan Power Company; Directorate General of Posts in Ministry of Communications.	
Producer services			
Finance and insurance	Cathay Life Insurance Co., Ltd.; Shin Kong Life Insurance Co., Ltd.; Kuo Hua Life Insurance Co., Ltd.; Fubon Insurance Co., Ltd.; Central Investment Holding Co., Ltd.; Taiwan	Central Bank Of China; Central Trust Of China; Bureau Of National Health Insurance; Post Remittances and Savings Banks; Bureau of Labor Insurance	Aetna Life Insurance Company of America, Taiwan Branch; Nan Shan Life Insurance Co., Ltd.

Table 3.2 *continued on page 61*

Table 3.2 – *continued from page 60*

	Domestic enterprises	Government-run organizations	Multinational enterprises
	Life Insurance Company; Mingtai Fire & Marine Insurance Co., Ltd.; China Life Insurance Co., Ltd.		
Telecommunication	Walsin Lihwa Corp.	Chunghwa Telecom Co., Ltd.	
Transportation	Evergreen Marine Corp.; Wan Hai Lines Ltd.; Uniglory Line	China Airlines; Taiwan Railway Telecommunications	
Engineering consultation		BES Engineering Corp.	
Consumer services			
Department Stores	Shin KongMitsukoshi Department Store Co., Ltd.; Far Eastern Department Stores Ltd.; Pacific Sogo Department Store Co., Ltd.		Makro Taiwan Ltd.
Trade	President Chain Store Corp.		
Other	Chang Gung Memorial Hospital		Chailease Finance Co., Ltd.
Government		Legislative Yuan; Control Yuan; Executive Yuan	

Source: China Credit Information Service Corporation (1999), Top 500 Companies in Taiwan.

stimulated producer services to cluster in the same areas. The producer services included finance, insurance and real estate, together with business services as well as hotels and department stores. Partly caused by reform and deregulation in Taiwan's financial institutions, the dramatic growth and clustering of banking and equity sectors within the Economic Core, from the late 1980s, has served as an investment funding centre for Taiwan's high-tech and other manufacturing industries. Above all, rapid development of Taiwan's manufacturing investment in China and East Asia (see Chapters 1 and 2), especially in high-tech electronics, has, since the late 1980s, generated considerable demand for investment funding and flow management, reinforcing the clustering development of producer services in the Core. As the investment funding centre of Taiwan's high-tech and other manufacturing enterprises, transactions on its stock market, in 2000, reached US$993.3 billion, which was triple the size of that in Hong Kong, and ten times of that in Singapore (*Taiwan Stock Exchange Statistical Data*, 2000). Thus, the Core, an urban agglomeration of producer services, performed effectively and generated a great economy. As table 3.3 shows, Taipei accounted for the lion's share of producer services – not only in employment and entrepreneurship, but also in GDP production (see Chapter 2). This demonstrated that the industries in Taipei had a much higher productivity than in other cities and counties. Especially in financial services, Taipei had 22.8 per cent of Taiwan's establishments in 1996, but generated 57.5 per cent of Taiwan's GDP production. In advertising services, the percentages were 35.7 per cent and 73.2 per cent respectively.

Table 3.3. Producer services in Taipei, 1996.

County	Taipei (% of total)			Other* 17 cities and counties (% of total)			Total		
	Establishment	Employment	GDP	Establishment	Employment	GDP	Establishment (numbers)	Employment (numbers)	GDP (millions)
Financing and auxiliaries	22.81	43.39	57.51	77.19	56.61	42.49	8,089 100.00	157,761 100.00	688,463 100.00
Securities and futures	47.80	56.77	62.10	52.20	43.23	37.90	887 100.00	29,195 100.00	73,374 100.00
Insurance	25.36	44.77	49.61	74.64	55.23	50.39	3,576 100.00	142,304 100.00	596,130 100.00
Legal and accounting	41.84	53.61	59.90	58.16	46.39	40.10	4,288 100.00	29,447 100.00	24,918 100.00
Architecture and engineering	39.09	53.99	61.70	60.91	46.01	38.30	4,060 100.00	35,725 100.00	47,773 100.00
Merchandise brokers	52.82	61.50	65.82	47.18	38.50	34.18	1,153 100.00	9,082 100.00	17,228 100.00
Consultation services	54.86	56.88	71.46	45.14	43.12	28.54	3,578 100.00	29,270 100.00	36,119 100.00
Advertising services	35.71	52.98	73.23	64.29	47.02	26.77	6,786 100.00	34,858 100.00	69,430 100.00
Specialized design services	39.79	43.04	52.91	60.21	56.96	47.09	3,104 100.00	14,891 100.00	23,692 100.00
Rental and leasing	14.57	19.97	27.26	85.43	80.03	72.74	7,242 100.00	23,375 100.00	30,203 100.00
Other services	25.52	43.91	35.68	74.48	56.09	64.32	6,806 100.00	44,799 100.00	38,294 100.00
Publishing	66.23	67.68	69.16	33.77	32.32	30.84	2,197 100.00	37,029 100.00	62,437 100.00
Transportation	23.43	31.93	44.75	76.57	68.07	55.25	57,482 100.00	322,915 100.00	598,225 100.00

Note: 'Other' includes Keelung city, Hsinchu city, Taipei county, Taoyuan county, Hsinchu county, Ilan county, Taichung city, Miaoli county, Taichung county, Changhua county, Nantou county, Yunlin county, Gaoxiong city, Tainan city, Chiayi county, Chiayi city, Tainan county, Kaohsiung county, Pingtung county, Penghu county, Hualien county, and Taitung county.
Source: The figures are based on data from the 1996 Taiwan Economic Survey.

A significant development of post-industrial Taipei is the emergence and clustering of cultural industries, including advertising, publishing, media, music and others. The driving force for this new industrial development lies in knowledge and creativity. The development used to be suppressed by authoritarian politics and administrative scrutiny. However, Taiwan's democratization after the lifting of Martial Law in 1987 overwhelmingly changed the environment in favour of cultural activities, laying the foundation for media and cultural industrial development. As the literature of innovation economies suggests, industrial creativity is a social product of collective interaction within reciprocal networks (Morgan, 1997; Storper, 1997). Spatial stickiness is their primary characteristic and leads them to agglomerate within the Economic Core.

Taipei has twenty-six colleges and universities, which produced more than 180,000 graduates in 2001 (*Statistical Abstract of Taipei City*, 2002). More than half of them find their first jobs in service sectors of the Economic Core through an alumni personal network which has been developed in school, and is one of the most important networks for career development in Taiwan. The abundant and educated labour supply provides an energetic and disciplined labour force for producer services; Taipei has a good supply of commercial talent. Through the close interaction of personal networks and occupational changes, diffusion and application of know-how and product innovation take place in commercial services. Innovation capacity is high in the consumer services.

Spatial Structure in the Economic Core

The spatial development of the Economic Core is based on the gridiron plan prepared by the colonial Japanese. Main road corridors and nodes in the core are the choice location for the vast majority of economic activities in Taipei, while areas around the corridors and nodes are developed as residential areas to house urban residents. The administrative districts of Zhongzheng, Zhongshan, Da'an and Songshan, circumscribe the Economic Core. As table 3.4 illustrates, the Core's resident population reached 904,913 in 1999. Its GDP, in 1996, reached NT$2,326 billion, 72 per cent of the Taipei total, which was more than double the GDP produced by Hsinchu Science Park in 2000. More than half of Taipei's manufacturing and services employment was located in the Core in 1996, and it was the hub of Taipei's economy.

There are two distinct spatial forms characterizing the Economic Core. The mixed land use of residence and commerce is the first obvious feature. It enlivens the urban life. More importantly, it provides an efficient spatial fabric for work and spatial interaction. The second feature is the internationalized commercial corridors and nodes. The grid-iron infrastructure pattern is efficient for labour mobility and

Table 3.4. Development changes in selected districts of Taipei.

		Western Districts					Eastern Districts					Economic core	Taipei
		Datong (%)	Wanhua (%)	Zhongshan (%)	Zhongzheng (%)	Songshan (%)	Da'an (%)	Neihu (%)	Wenshan (%)	Nankang (%)	Xinyi (%)		
Population	1991	5.51	8.49	8.68	6.76	8.00	12.95	7.90	8.31	4.33	9.03	36.39 (989,077)	(2,717,992)
	1999	5.05	7.87	8.13	6.26	7.86	12.01	9.45	9.41	4.28	9.16	34.26 (904,913)	(2,641,312)
Manufacturing employment	1991	9.89	5.77	16.98	6.47	10.95	10.35	7.92	1.21	11.55	4.32	44.75 (76,903)	(171,851)
	1996	8.00	4.71	17.96	5.97	14.50	14.23	6.59	0.96	8.80	5.89	52.66 (98,514)	(187,075)
Services employment	1991	6.94	4.92	23.76	12.81	14.39	18.48	2.03	1.61	2.06	6.27	69.44 (752,737)	(1,084,011)
	1996	6.38	4.36	21.16	12.51	15.06	18.24	2.47	1.99	2.08	8.13	66.97 (806,394)	(1,204,113)
GDP (NT $ million)	1991	4.38	2.80	22.37	17.91	14.34	20.19	2.14	1.11	3.48	5.24	74.81 (1,359,147)	(1,816,799)
	1996	4.09	2.30	19.66	16.99	15.07	20.40	2.34	1.81	2.94	6.50	72.12 (2,326,383)	(3,225,711)

Note: ( ) = absolute number.
Sources: Taipei Statistics for 1991 and 1999; National Census of Manufacturing and Services for 1991 and 1996.

commuting, as well as goods and services delivery between the Economic Core and surrounding areas. A flurry of skyscraper projects and retail establishments along the main corridors and nodes, give Taipei's new centre a distinctive skyline.

Polycentric Construction in Post-Industrial Taipei: After the Late 1980s

Since the late 1980s, Taipei has experienced a dramatic transformation, responding to Taiwan's post-industrial development. Development in the Economic Core reached saturation point by the late 1980s; there was not sufficient space to accommodate Taipei's new global activities. Two major consequences resulted. First, it fuelled a rampant development in land speculation, and real estate prices soared to a record level. Location in the Core for commercial and residential expansion was limited and available construction sites were extremely expensive. Second, the intensive development imposed an additional traffic burden beyond the capacity of the main corridors, causing severe congestion at peak times in the corridors and nodes. Both traffic accidents and air pollution increased. These negative environmental effects discouraged firms and residents from remaining in the city. Expansion of the Economic Core slowed. By the early 1990s, economic and residential activities began to shift to the neighbouring Taipei County. As a result of out-migration, the population in Taipei dropped by about 10,000 annually. Major companies in Taipei expanded their activities and some even moved their headquarters to neighbouring towns with freeway access and cheaper land. Responding to this situation, new settlements in Taipei County such as Xizhi, Xindian and Linkou were created to house these new developments (figure 3.1).

Since the late 1980s, there has been a growing awareness that Taipei needed to re-construct its infrastructure and expand its economic base in line with that of Taiwan's industrial restructuring – moving away from manufacturing, towards knowledge-intensive industries. In developing the city into an international metropolis, the urban infrastructure and economic base needed to be further strengthened in order to establish global ties within the Asia-Pacific. Since the 1990s, the mounting pressure of post-industrial economic transformation and global competition has impelled the City government to devote much effort to infrastructure and economic restructuring. Infrastructure improvement was the most necessary strategy. The railway was put underground. The most crucial project, the 84.7 kilometre Taipei Rapid Transit System (TRTS), supplementing major traffic corridors and nodes, was planned in 1996 (Taipei Municipal Government, 1996) (see Chapter 9).

Vast tracks of military land were designated for post-industrial activities in order to stimulate Taipei's restructuring. The traditional CBD and administration centre in western Taipei was also redeveloped. The scale of these developments has reshaped the urban fabric of Taipei into a polycentric urban pattern. In other words, spatial development in Taipei has increasingly been manipulated by state intervention, resulting in a shift away from a monocentric to a polycentric mode. As figure 3.1 illustrates, this polycentric mode comprises the Economic Core and several sub-cores, each with specialized functions – the traditional CBD and administration centre in the west, Xinyi international trade centre in the east (see Chapter 6), Nankang Software Industrial Park on the eastern periphery, and Neihu Science Park and Beitou Knowledge Park in the north.

Reconstructions of the Traditional Western CBD

Globalization has produced an uneven development in favour of eastern Taipei, and increasingly divided the city's development between the east and the west. In the 1980s, it strengthened the commercial and management functions in the eastern part, but turned the western district into a recession. The driving force for the divided development lay primarily in the growing competition among the commercial nodes and corridors formulated in the Economic Core. Outdated buildings and infrastructure in the west were unsuitable for the new economic requirements of international business. Further, the western district was difficult to redevelop, because of the extremely complicated and fragmented property ownership, a result of urban land reform in the early 1950s. The western built-up areas were unable to respond to globalization and accommodate the headquarters of transnational and domestic enterprises. A long-standing decline in the traditional west became Taipei's spatial dilemma of global-local nexus in the globalization process. Taipei City's structural shift away from the west towards the east is shown statistically in table 3.4.

Since the early 1990s, the prolonged recession in traditional districts has increasingly translated into a political discourse favouring regeneration of the western district (Jou, 1999). The urban regeneration discourse became a political issue in 1996, finally and overwhelmingly driving the City government to intervene in the western redevelopment. A series of institutional innovations, such as community planner institutions and urban renewal schemes, were introduced. Since the late 1990s, a number of infrastructure reorganizations, including placement of the railway underground and construction of an TRTS-based communication network, were completed. Above all, the Ximending regeneration scheme was initiated as a major redevelopment project to revitalize the traditional centre as the major consumption node for the urban youth, as a potential catalyst for new development in neighbouring districts.

One other important urban regeneration project was launched in 2000 in the Zhongzheng district to renew the area surrounding the Presidential Palace.

Through spatial reorganization in public spaces, historical building preservation, modern urban design and development control, reconstruction of the capital core was implemented by the City government to reshape Taipei's image as a global capital city in East Asia.

Construction of New Industrial Districts

Through the remodelling of traditional industrial zones, appropriation of military land, and reclamation of Keelung River, several satellite centres were created east and north of the Core as new industrial districts to stimulate Taipei's economic transition. Since the late 1990s, these developments have become the most salient strategy of re-territorialization from which post-industrial Taipei attempted to articulate spatially to accommodate globalization. The primary strategies are as follows.

Construction of innovation and learning districts comprises Nankang Software Industrial Park, Neihu Science Park, and Beitou Knowledge Park (see figure 3.1). First, the Nankang Park is a 88 hectare brownfield redevelopment project intended as a software industrial park (see figures 3.2, 3.3, and 3.4). The land came mostly from former railway freight yards and factory sites of the state-owned Taiwan Fertilizer Company. Under the strategic guidance of the Ministry of Economic Affairs, this development was launched in 1996 through a national policy initiative, which encouraged industrial investment for international commercial offices and exhibition facilities, as well as software development and design. Second, on the north-western side of Nankang Park lies the Neihu Science Park (see figures 3.5, 3.6, and 3.7). The land is in an existing light-industry zone and with reclaimed land from Keelung River. This project gained full support from the City government. Flexible land-use control, sufficient public facilities and infrastructure, and a one-stop service system were provided to support private development.

These government-provided advantages, cheap land supply and a suburban location make Neihu a particularly attractive location for the regional offices of high-tech firms. By the late 1990s, Neihu helped to transform Taipei's economic base into knowledge-based production. In the future, this important development will be linked by the TRTS or freeway directly with both Songshan Domestic Airport and Chiang Kai-Shek International Airport, as well as other destinations in the high-tech corridors of northern Taiwan. Through these linkages, high-tech firms in the science park will be closely integrated with regional innovation systems in northern Taiwan. The high-tech regional headquarters are linked internationally with manufacturing sites in both the Pearl River Delta and Yangtze River Delta in mainland China. They also have a close strategic connection with high-tech firms in Silicon Valley.

Figures 3.2, 3.3 and 3.4.
Nankang Software
Industrial Park.

Finally, although a more recent development, the Beitou Knowledge Park is planned for Taiwan's future development. The objective is to assemble bio-related research capabilities and laboratories for bio-industrial development. The designated area has 195 hectares, and encompasses one of the most important hospitals in Taiwan, Veterans General Hospital and its associated research institutes and laboratories. The park is hence expected to create the initial impetus for development of bio-industries and position Taipei as the centre of bio-tech development in East Asia.

The construction of an international financial centre in the Xinyi district (see figure 3.1) is a response to the demand from globalization for office space. The international financial district of Xinyi, 153 hectares, used to be a military factory.

Figures 3.5, 3.6 and 3.7. Neihu Science Park.

The area was designated in 1978 as a satellite-downtown in response to Taipei's eastward expansion, to relieve development pressure on the western CBD (Taipei City Government, 1978). Aimed at stimulating development of Taipei's eastern districts, Xinyi Development Project was launched in 1987. The City Hall was added to this district and an international trade centre was constructed. In 1997, the Xinyi project was further reviewed to meet strategic requirements for Taipei's internationalization, which was the state-led restructuring strategy for Taiwan. Establishing Taipei as the Operation Centre in Asian Pacific region in the mid-1990s was the development goal. The project has since been reformulated as the 'Manhattan' of Taipei's financial services and entrepreneurial headquarters. It has, although faced with threats of rampant land speculation, increasingly constituted as a new downtown in post-industrial Taipei and is the most dynamic area for retail, entertainment and luxurious housing in Taiwan (see Chapter 6).

Limitations of Polycentric Development

Compared with the relatively successful transition of some East Asian cities into world cities, for example Seoul, Hong Kong, and Singapore (see Kim and Cha, 1996; Chang, 2000; Jessop and Sum, 2000), Taipei's evolution towards a global city is not as successful. The city is not yet a priority site for regional headquarters of transnational enterprises, or international conferences and activities (Ho, 2000, p. 2349). Obviously, Taipei's strategies for globalization still face many challenges and conflicts. As illustrated in the following analysis, the polycentric restructuring strategy itself has at least three limitations.

The first limitation lies in the international financial district of Xinyi. As a salient project of globalization in Taipei, the Xinyi project is a state-led mega-property construction project for international trade and modern offices, telecommunication and infrastructure. However, the infrastructure-driven development is only a necessary condition for developing an international financial centre. As Kim and Cha (1996) mention in their critique of Seoul's globalization, support for other socio-economic conditions also plays an indispensable role in a successful trade centre, including a diversity of agglomeration economies, local networks of production collaboration, and sufficient supplies of high-order labour and technology. Lacking such socio-economic support systems, the Xinyi project with its mega-infrastructure investment is inefficient and ineffective in promoting Taipei's globalization. It is for this reason that the Xinyi project is now dominated by developments in luxurious housing, international entertainment and department stores, instead of producer services and international corporate headquarters as planned. The project is facing serious difficulty in performing a global management function (for a detailed analysis of Xinyi, see Chapter 6).

The second is the spatial strategy in restructuring the Economic Core. The construction of a polycentric city in Taipei has spatially de-centralized the new industrial districts and manufacturing activities, but obviously ignored strategic needs for restructuring the Economic Core. It is for this reason that developments in the Xinyi district, the knowledge and software industrial park, as well as the traditional centre redevelopment in the western district, have competed with and threatened the producer services development in the Economic Core. Since the late 1990s, Taipei's commercial nodes and corridors have increasingly shifted away from the Economic Core due to the intra-urban competition. Financial firms and entrepreneurial headquarters in the new development districts of Nankang and Neihu have been relocated primarily from the Zhongshan district of the Economic Core. Thus, economic activities in the Economic Core have been suppressed. Zhongshan district has been driven into a dramatic recession. As illustrated in table 3.4, service employment in the area lost more than 2,600 jobs, during a five-year period, from 1991 to 1996, while the whole city created more than 120,000 jobs in the same period. Its GDP share was reduced from 22.4 per cent in 1991, to 19.6 per cent in 1996. The Zhongshan district has lost about 21,200 in population between 1991 and 1999, responsible for 27.6 per cent of the total population loss in Taipei. Unexpectedly, the sex industry has invaded Zhongshan, and become a prominent informal sector, seriously worsening the urban crime rate. The result is that although Taipei continues to be the wealth creator of Taiwan's economy, Zhongshan district has gone in the opposite direction and is facing growing decay.

The third limitation comes from over-emphasis on the learning and innovation sectors. Since the early 1990s, a development strategy for the learning and innovating sectors has become an indispensable part of economic restructuring in Taipei. With globalization, these sectors now occupy a hegemonic position in the city's redevelopment policy. Nevertheless, this strategy has its industrial and spatial limitations in emphasizing the dispersal of high-tech industries to the Neihu and Nankang districts, while downplaying consumer services for these new sectors in their urban redevelopment. In addition, a labour market strategy is absent in the strategic agenda of Taipei's restructuring.

Centre-City Governance Politics in Cross-Strait Economic Links

The analyses above review the key governance conflicts at the municipal level. However, Taipei is not the only administrative level responsible for the vertical governmental conflicts in its spatial restructuring. Political conflict and centre-city negotiation significantly affect the re-structuring process.

Driven by Taiwan's democratization, politics of identity has emerged as a significant movement since the 1990s (see Chapter 2). Globalization imposes a great impact on the formulation of the economic network across the Taiwan Strait. Especially since the mid-1990s, Taiwan launched a 'two-state discourse', claiming that relationship between Taiwan and China is one of state-to-state, and seriously damaged the cross-Strait economic links. The two-state statement immediately caused a three-day downward plunge in the Taipei stock market, costing US$42.9 billion. The KMT government went on to launch a 'No Haste, Be Patient' policy, prohibiting strategic industries, including semiconductor manufacturers, up-stream petrochemical industries and other large-scale investments over US$50 million, to enter mainland China. The 'patient' policy aims at restraining Taiwan's investment flows into China, it also becomes the primary cross-Strait policy of the Democratic Progressive Party (DPP) regime, which first came to power in 2000 and was re-elected in March 2004. Regardless, cross-Strait investment as well as trade flows continue to expand, further intensifying economic connection and heightening industrial networking. Furthermore, the loss of competitiveness in Taiwan's industries has increased its production dependence on China for cheaper input costs. The continuous cross-Strait economic growth has generated an unexpected political repercussion, and has effectively invalidated the 'patient' policy.

Because of this economic political dichotomy, the policy of 'Active Opening with Effective Management' was enacted to replace the 'patient' policy in order to improve Taiwan's industrial competitiveness and global logistics capability.[1] With the aim of forming a national consensus for Taiwan's restructuring, the Economic Development Advisory Conference, in August 2001, suggested lifting investment bans on high-tech industries in China and facilitating 'three-links' by a direct link of seaports and airports across the Strait.[2] Addressing a group of pro-independence activists on 3 August, 2002, President Chen Shui-Bian argued that each side of the Strait is a country, and urged the Taiwanese to consider a referendum on Taiwan's status, presenting a strong challenge to Beijing's claim of sovereignty over the self-governed island. The next day the stock market plunged 5.8 per cent, costing US$6.4 billion (*Far East Economic Review*, 15 August, 2002). Obviously, the heightening of the cross-Strait economic links has increasingly featured as a common policy discourse for Taiwan's industrial restructuring. However, the political tension has inevitably caused a state and enterprise conflict regarding trade and investment across the Strait. The cross-Strait conflict interrupted the implementation of the national restructuring strategies, including (1) KMT's project of the Asian-Pacific Operation Center in 1997, (2) DPP's project of Three Mini-Links between Kinmen and Xiamen, Global Operation Center and overseas transition centre of Kaohsiung in 2001, as well as (3) Free Port Zone and Corporate Operation Headquarters programmed in the 'Challenge 2008 – National Development Plan'.

At the city level, it impeded the growth of transnational activities and enterprises, and retarded Taipei's establishement as the node of cross-Strait economic networking. The strategic scope for Taipei's integration with the world system and pursuit of globalization was suppressed. In particular, the consequences of the 'patient' policy enormously increased transportation and time costs in trade flows and suspended the creation of an industrial network across the Strait. The direct link across the Strait would have allowed Taiwan industries in China to reduce the shipping time by two days for export to American markets. For instance, American computer giant, Dell, had limited delivery time of Taiwan subcontractors to four-days as a precondition of the manufacturing contract. Dell's purchasing centre in East Asia moved from Taipei to Hong Kong in 2001 because of slow progress in the 'three-link' policy. A report from both the American and European Chambers of Commerce revealed, in 2002, that international banks in Taipei were reduced from forty-six in 1998, to thirty-six. The 875 members of American Business Association in Taipei lost 125 members within one year in 2001. Members of its counterpart, the European Chamber of Commerce Taipei (ECCP), fell from 260 to 230. President of ECCP, Guy Wittich pointed out:

International branch companies in Taipei used to play a regional headquarter role in managing great China economic area. Offices in Shanghai and Hong Kong once had to report to the regional headquarter in Taipei. However, the critical position in transnational companies has deteriorated as their conferences and employee training increasingly move outside Taipei due to the travel constrictions across the strait. (*China Times*, 19 August, 2002)

For these reasons, abolishing the 'patient' policy and promoting the "three-link" policy has become the key to Taipei's restructuring. The 'patient' policy is obviously the major cause of time costs increase hindering the nodal formulation of Taipei. It is a considerable impediment to Taipei's role as a regional hub in the Asia-Pacific region, worsening Taipei's global performance, and seriously damaging the Xinyi Project.

Institutional Inertia in National Restructuring Strategies

Since the 1990s, national strategies of economic restructuring have downplayed the important role of producer services in globalized economies. The institutional inertia in Taiwan's economic system dominated by manufacturing sectors is the key obstacle. Development of financial sectors in Taiwan has consistently been manipulated by the state as an instrument for consolidating its legitimacy, rather than as a critical service sector in Taiwan's economic development. This inertia has imposed structural restrictions on the development of institutionalization, transparency and internationalization in Taiwan's financial sector. The financial industry has been facing constant threats of domestic financial crisis deriving from political intervention, weakening its competitiveness compared to its counterparts in Singapore and Hong Kong. The institutional inertia circumscribes the development of finance, insurance and banking in Taipei, restraining the agglomeration effects of international financial services in the Economic Core and preventing development of an international financial centre in the Xinyi Project.

Centre-City Governance Conflicts and Taipei's Global Project

The political devolution of democratization and associated restructuring in Taiwan's governance are translated into the uneven development between northern and southern Taiwan, and between Taipei City and other counties. Since the late 1990s, this divide has further deteriorated as a result of party political differences between central and city governments. Mayor Ma Ying-Jeou of Taipei city is a second generation mainlander from the opposition KMT party, while the central government is ruled by pro-independence DPP. Taipei's share in the allocation of national resources has been steadily reduced because of these party political differences. In addition, fragmentation of the jurisdiction of Taiwan's local administration system further complicates political identities, causing an inter-agency governance crisis and negatively affecting Taipei's global growth. These can be illustrated in the following three examples.

The first case is the vertical governance conflict in infrastructure construction for global connection. Construction of a rail network linking Taipei with the international airport is an indispensable transport infrastructure and necessary for developing Taipei as a world city (Graham, 2002). The rail link would enable Taipei to become a travel and trade hub in the global economy. The airport-to-city link has proved vital for Asian cities, such as, Seoul, Osaka, Hong Kong, and Singapore. Since the early 1990s, Taipei has advocated an infrastructure project linking Taipei with Chiang Kai-Shek International Airport in Taoyuan to relieve the growing burden on the highway system. However, this project has not yet started due to the cumbersome decision-making process in the Transportation Ministry. In addition, the existing Economic Core, with its developable land already saturated, has the Songshan Domestic Airport nearby. The airport has 182 hectares of unused public land, but it is owned by the central government. The outdated airport needs to be updated or redeveloped, but the City government has no authority as it has no jurisdiction.

The second example of centre-city governance conflict is over the cross-border cultural network. Institutional establishment of a cross-border cultural network has recently become an important part of marketing strategy. Cultural networking is considered a key component in upgrading a city's competitiveness in globalization (see Bianchini and Parkinson, 1993; Chang, 2000; Kong, 2000). In 2000, a Cultural Bureau was established as a key department in Taipei controlled by KMT. It has been actively promoting a marketing strategy of 'Cultural Capital in Asia' in 2001, joined by 15 international cities. However, it is boycotted by counties controlled by the DPP, because of their differences in political identity.

The final case of governance conflict is in the eco-infrastructure of rivers. The Tamsui River system, comprising the Tamsui and Keelung Rivers, forms the waterway for metropolitan Taipei. It is polluted and water contamination is worsening. The polluted length of the river increased from 124 kilometres in 1989, to 151 kilometres in 2000 (*Urban and Regional Development Statistics*, 2001). The river has been a major cause of Taipei's international infamy. River pollution control is a typical example of the governance politics, involving budgets and actions of the central government, Taipei City and County. Effective vertical cooperation has yet to emerge for the pollution control and flood protection. Recreation and communication in both rivers are suffocated by the disagreement between Taipei City and County due to party politics.

The political balance in response to Taiwan's democratization has resulted in various administrative struggles rooted in the identity politics of the two major parties. Accordingly, party politics causes resource squandering as well as administrative ineffectiveness. The political conflicts and discordance between Taipei City, the central government, and its neighbouring counties result in a policy grid-lock. Democratic devolution does not facilitate the creation of social capital (see Putman *et al.*, 1993). Instead, political contention fails to build consensus and formulate policy to restructure Taipei. Policy fragmentation and conflict worsen the decision-making mechanism between central and local government. With democratic devolution and political identity, Taipei City has increasing difficulties in receiving preferential treatment or policy privilege. The capital city has no institutional means to formulate and enforce its global strategies, because it lacks fiscal autonomy or support from the central government. Consequently, this governance crisis hinders Taipei's globalization process.

Summary and Conclusion

In terms of historical development, the spatial structure in Taipei has evolved from a traditional monocentric mode to a modern polycentric mode. The polycentric structure is a deliberate spatial strategy for post-industrial Taipei in response to globalization. In the choice of sector for urban growth, the Taipei government's strategy has focused on industrialization, while downplaying producer services. With several districts designated for specific development, intra-city competition led to the decline of the traditional districts. In policy decision and implementation, Taipei is increasingly affected by centre-city governance politics. This is not surprising; the world city development in the globalization era is inevitably subject to political conflicts. The vertical-governance conflict is further complicated by cross-Strait politics and institutional inertia. In the attempt to develop a global city, Taipei City government has yet to resolve the institutional and governmental obstacles and so formulate a workable global strategy.

Notes

1. The 'opening' policy emphasizes a principle of 'Taiwan first, global deployment, reciprocity and mutual benefit, and risk management' for cross-Strait investment and trade.
2. The 'three-link' policy was raised in 1988 by Chinese government. Its policy goal is through direct trade, mail, and air and sea links to promote reunification.

References

Begg, I. (1999) Cities and competitiveness. *Urban Studies*, **36**(5/6), pp. 795–809.

Berg, L. V. d. and Braun, E. (1999) Urban competitiveness, marketing and the need for organising capacity. *Urban Studies*, **36**(5/6), pp. 987–999.

Bianchini, F. and Parkinson, M. (1993) *Cultural Policy and Urban Regeneration: The West European Experience*. Manchester: Manchester University Press.

Brenner, N. (1998) Global cities, global states: global city formation and state territorial restructuring in contemporary Europe. *Review of International Political Economy*, **5**(1), pp. 1–37.

Brenner, N. (1999*a*) Beyond state-centrism? Space, territoriality, and geographical scale in globalisation studies. *Theory and Society*, **28**, pp. 39–78.

Brenner, N. (1999*b*) Globalisation as reterritorialisation: the re-scaling of urban governance in the European Union. *Urban Studies*, **36**(3), pp. 431–451.

Bryan, J. Hill, S. Munday, M. and Roberts, A. (2000) Assessing the role of the arts and cultural industries in a local economy. *Environment and planning A*, **32**, pp. 1391–1408.

Chang, T.C. (2000) Renaissance revisited: Singapore as a 'global city for the arts'. *International Journal of Urban and Regional Research*, **24**(4), pp. 818–831.

Coffey, W.J. (2000) The geographies of producer services. *Urban Geography*, **21**(2), pp. 170–183.

Douglass, M. (2000) Mega-urban regions and world city formation: globalisation, the economic crisis and urban policy issues in Pacific Asia. *Urban Studies*, **37**(12), pp. 2315–2335.

Friedmann, J. and Wolff, G. (1982) World city formation: an agenda for research and action. *International Journal of Urban and Regional Research*, **6**(3), pp. 309–344.

Friedmann, J. (1986)The world city hypothesis. *Development and Change*, **17**, pp. 68–83.

Friedmann, J. (1995) Where we stand: a decade of world city research, in Knox, P.L. and Taylor, P.J. (eds.) *World Cities in a World-system*. Cambridge: Cambridge University Press.

Graham, S. (2002) Flow city: networked mobilities and the contemporary metropolis. *Journal of Urban Technology*, **9**(1), pp. 1–20.

Ho, K.C. (2000) Competing to be regional centers: a multi-agency, multi locational perspective. *Urban Studies*, **37**(12), pp. 2337–2356.

Howells, J.R.L. (2002) Tacit knowledge, innovation and economic geography. *Urban Studies*, **39**(5/6), pp. 872–884.

Jessop, B. and Sum, N.L. (2000) An entrepreneurial city in action: Hong Kong's emerging strategies in and for inter-urban competition. *Urban Studies*, **37**(12), pp. 2287–2313.

Jou, S.C. (1999) Rebuilding the old Taipei: an analysis of urban renewal policy. *Journal of Geographical Science*, **25**, pp. 15–44.

Kim, Y.W. and Cha, M.S. (1996) Korea's spatial development strategies for an era of globalization. *Habitat International*, **20**(4), pp. 531–551.

Knight, R.V. (1995) Knowledge-based development: policy and planning implications for cities. *Urban Studies*, **32**(2), pp. 225–260.

Kong, L. (2000) Cultural policy in Singapore: negotiating economic and socio-cultural agendas. *Geoforum*, **31**, pp. 409–424.

Kresel, P.K. and Singh, B. (1999) Competitiveness and the urban economy: twenty-four large U.S. metropolitan areas. *Urban Studies*, **36**(5/6), pp. 1017–1027.

Lever, W. F. (1999) Competitive cities in Europe. *Urban Studies*, **36**(5/6), pp. 1029–1044.

Lever, W.F. (2002) Correlating the knowledge-base of cities with economic growth. *Urban Studies*, **39**(5/6), pp. 859-870.

Leyshon, A. (2001) Time-space (and digital) compression: software formats, musical networks, and the reorganization of the music industry. *Environment and Planning A*, **33**, pp. 49–77.

Lovering, J. (2001) The coming regional crisis (and how to avoid it). *Regional Studies*, **35**(4), pp. 349–354.

Lovering, J. (1999) Theory led by policy: the inadequacies of the new regionalism. *International Journal of Urban and Regional Research*, **23**, pp. 375–395.

Macleod, G. (2001) New regionalism reconsidered: globalisation and the remaking of political economic space. International Journal of Urban and Regional Research, 25(4), pp. 804–829.

Macleod, G. and Goodwin, M. (1999) Space, scale and state strategy: rethinking urban and regional governance. *Progress in Human Geography*, **23**(4), pp. 503–527.

Morgan, K. (1997) The learning region: institutions, innovation and regional renewal. *Regional Studies*, **31**(5), pp. 491–503.

Ohmae, K. (1990) *The Borderless World: Power and Strategy in the Interlinked Economy*. Cambridge, MA: Harvard University Press.

Ohmae, K. (1995) *The End of the Nation State: The Rise of Regional Economies*. New York: Free Press.

Porter, M. (1990) The competitive advantage of nations. *Harvard Business Review*, (March/April), pp. 73–93.

Porter, M. (1995) The competitive advantage of the inner city. *Harvard Business Review*, (May/June), pp. 55–71.

Porter, M. (1996) Competitive advantage, agglomeration economies and regional policy. *International Regional Science Review*, **19**, pp. 85–90.

Putman, R., Leonardi, R. and Nanetti, R. (1993) *Making Democracy Work: Civic Traditions in Modern Italy*. Princeton, New Jersey: Princeton University Press.

Sadler, D. (1997) The global music business as an information industry: reinterpreting economies of culture. *Environment and Planning A*, **29**, pp. 1919–1936.

Sassen, S. (1991), *The Global City*. Princeton, New Jersey: Princeton University Press.

Scott, A. (1997) The cultural economy of cities. *International Journal of Urban and Regional Research*, **21**(2), pp. 323–339.

Scott, A. J. (1999*a*) The U.S. recorded music industry: on the relations between organization, location, and creativity in the cultural economy. *Environment and Planning A*, **31**, pp. 1965–1984.

Scott, A. (1999*b*) The cultural economy: geography and the creative field. *Media, Culture & Society*, **21**, pp. 807–817.

Scott, A. (2000) The cultural economy of Paris. *International Journal of Urban and Regional Research*, **24**(3), pp. 567–582.

Storper, M. (1997) *The Regional World: Territorial Development in a Global Economy*. New York: Guilford.

Taipei Municipal Government (1971) *Historical Record of Urban Development in Taipei*. Taipei: Municipal Government.

Taipei Municipal Government (1978) *Planning and Design for Xinyi Satellite Center*. Taipei: Municipal Government.

Taipei Municipal Government (1996) *Urban Development White Paper of Taipei City*. Taipei: Municipal Government.

Chapter Four

Urban Politics and Spatial Development: The Emergence of Participatory Planning

Li-Ling Huang

Modern urban planning in the Euro-American context was born as a tool of the state to balance private and public interests under capitalism. Although planners often claim the tool they use is scientific and neutral, critics remind us that the value-free model of planning is nothing but a myth. Indeed, planning is always a contested arena and full of political conflicts (see Chapter 3), as its history demonstrates (e.g. Hall, 2002).

Since the issue of economic restructuring has been well addressed in previous chapters (see Chapters 1, 2 and 3), this chapter, by taking the practice of urban planning as an example, draws attention to the changing politics and institutions in Taipei. The changing dynamics of urban planning will be explored by referring to the three themes observed from the new politics in the globalization discourse. First, highly interventionist states have weakened, if not hollowed out. Instead, a model of governance of 'partnership' rises among states, capital and society. In this new model, central states, on the one hand, have to deliberate their regulatory power; while on the other hand, play cultural politics to rebuild their legitimacy. Second, in the ever-changing political landscape of globalization, it is the local state, rather than the national state, which better addresses citizens' diversified needs under rapid urban change brought by the global process. Third, urban planning, a political tool of local governments to manipulate the relationship between governments and society by delivering urban services and infrastructure to citizens, brings about urban struggles (Ohmae, 1995; Castells, 1997; Borja and Castells, 1997). Obviously, conventional top-down processes of planning no longer work, while various forms of 'grassroots participation' or 'collaborative' models (see Innes and Booher, 2003; Innes, 1995) are continuously explored to meet the local needs.

In light of these perspectives, urban politics and the shifting planning model of Taipei in the global era are examined. Global forces, orchestrated with domestic dynamics brought on by the democratization process, will be examined to provide an explanation. This chapter first traces past decades to ascertain how the central government has intervened in Taipei's urban planning at different historical stages. Details will show how the distorted approach of planning led to the failure of infrastructure provision, and how the exclusive planning process deprived the society of the possibilities of creating urban identity. After an explanation of the transformation of urban politics in the late 1980s, the new collaborative planning model adapted by the local government, non-governmental organizations (NGOs), and communities will be examined. To illustrate the process, the case of Yongkang Community will demonstrate the citizen values emerging from the cultural and intellectual interaction within the global milieu and from domestic democratization. An assessment of the achievement and limitation of the model of participatory planning concludes this chapter.

International Settings, Development Policy and Urban Planning

Before analyzing urban planning in Taipei, a brief introduction to planning in Taiwan will give background of urban planning in Taipei, which has been highly controlled by the central government. It would be impossible to discuss Taipei's urban development without relating to the intervention of central state. Moreover, planning practice in Taiwan has some traits which make it significantly different from its Western counterparts.

What first characterizes planning in Taiwan is the huge gap between planning ideas and implementation. Although this phenomenon is common everywhere in the world, what happens in Taiwan is definitely very dramatic. Friedmann (1998) argued that while planning ideas diffuse relatively freely, implementation is highly place-bounded, being affected by the particular political culture of each society. For Taiwan, where the planning process has been constantly interrupted by highly conflicted international politics, a rapidly changing economy, and a volatile domestic political culture, this perspective is especially insightful.

In terms of planning ideas, these were introduced by international politics, and Taiwan does not lag far behind the Western countries. A modern planning system was introduced into Taiwan as early as the 1930s by the Japanese colonial government, imposing a modern planning framework of master plan and land-use zoning. In the 1950s, the Western concept of 'garden city' was brought into satellite cities around

Taipei by the planning bureaucrats of the Kuomintang (KMT) government. Later on, in the 1970s, the mechanism of regional and comprehensive planning was incorporated into the planning system. As far as the development of planning ideas and techniques was concerned, Taiwan accepted the intellectual influence of modern planning in the Western world. However, if we delve into the planning results, we will find another story. Most of those planning ideologies disappear.

Modern planning in Taiwan can be dated back to the Japanese period. With a hidden agenda of developing Taiwan as a showcase colony to justify Japan's invasion into South East Asian countries, the colonial government released the first 'Urban Planning Ordinance of Taiwan' in 1936. Incorporating a total of seventy-eight ordinances and 286 sub-ordinances, it stipulated the financial source, enforcement authority and regulating power of an urban planning system, such as zoning regulation, building control and land plotting. Standards for infrastructure provision, such as a system of roads and urban parks, were clearly prescribed in the plans. Following those regulations, the Japanese colonial government completed urban plans for seventy-two cities and towns by World War II.

Unfortunately, the first modern urban plans for cities in Taiwan died early. The outbreak of World War II allowed no chance for implementation. These plans were civil engineering oriented, imbuing imperial power to the Japanese government to carry them out. Most cities only finished parts of the urban construction before Taiwan was returned to mainland China in 1945. Later, the retreat of the KMT government in 1949, announced a new era for planning. It was the time for the heroic role of planning as the Japanese period receded.

In the 1950s, in the aftermath of KMT retreat, a number of factors led to the uncertainty of planning. With over one million political refugees of the KMT government fleeing to Taiwan, the retreat had already exceeded accommodation limits of the main cities. This situation rendered growth control – the kernel of urban planning – a difficult task. Besides, the original planning goals of consolidating urban infrastructure set by the Japanese government were also shifted. Instead, responding to the threat of 'liberation' by the Chinese Communist Party across the Strait, evacuation and military defence served as the primary goals of urban administration. As 85 per cent of the national budget was spent on defence (Gold, 1986) for striking back at the mainland China, little manpower and budget were allocated for long-term plans. In contrast, a government mentality of short-term response prevailed over other concerns of urban development.

The setting of planning altered again in the early 1960s. As the KMT realized that recovering China became increasingly impractical, it started to seek other national goals as its source of legitimacy. Taking advantage of geopolitics in US hegemony, Taiwan joined the new international division of labour, and pursued economic development aggressively. The year 1963 first saw the yield of exported goods outweigh those of imports. In the following three decades, by enforcing a series of Economic Development Plans, the KMT state successfully produced an economic miracle with an average annual GNP growth of around 10 per cent, and economic growth gained status as a socially-accepted measurement of political legitimization.

This miracle came with a price, which is the planning efficacy. From the 1960s on, the government continuously cut taxes to encourage private investment in consecutive economic plans. Although those measures successfully boosted Taiwan's economy, it shrank the government revenue, dwindled public investment, and finally led to under-investment in infrastructure provision. As statistics show, in the 1970s public expenditure comprised 18.3 per cent of the GNP, while in 1988 it sunk to as low as 14.8 per cent. This in turn resulted in a general infrastructure shortage in Taiwan. Moreover, if we take a closer look at the limited provision of infrastructure in Taiwan, we find that roads and schools – more closely connected to the needs of economic production, transportation and labour – were given higher priority, while public housing, parking lots, community centres and parks lagged far behind, in spite of the fact that they were important for improving social life. These phenomena reflected the particular development model of Taiwan.[1] In this context, people's needs for social services and recreation were severely neglected.

In fact, planning failure in Taiwan had its institutional roots. Under the developmental model, planning was deliberately marginalized and neglected by the state. Most clearly, none of the recommendations of national, regional and urban plans were mandatory, with the exception of the zoning regulation in urban plans. Therefore, those three levels of plans have neither independent finance nor *de facto* regulatory power, and whether they would be carried out or not depended greatly on the financial allocation from the central government. This is one of the critical mechanisms for the developmental state in maintaining its centralized power.

As discussed above, in the planning field, the central state enjoyed considerable domination over the local states. Although the Constitution asserted the autonomy of local government, there was no clear definition of the content of 'autonomy'. Actually, by claiming the special administration in wartime, the central government remained in control of the personnel and finance of local states. Besides, the central state was also an authoritarian state, as it forestalled people's participation in public affairs as well as in planning. In the early decades, the KMT government did not have general elections for parliament. This could be attributed to the February 28 Incident in 1947.[2] Martial law was imposed in Taiwan shortly after that event, and restrictions were put in place to suppress political dissidents.[3] Furthermore, the central state organized many surrogate social groups to manipulate public opinion. People's participation in public affairs was a social taboo, and the Western idea of civil society found nowhere to take root in Taiwan. Similarly in planning, by classifying urban planning as confidential administration, the decision-making process of development plans excluded participation by the general public, or even those directly affected residents. This was because the Urban Planning Ordinance did not require public hearings or the gathering of public opinion. The only procedure related to 'citizen participation' was the public posting of the plan for one month. However, this process was more formal than informative.[4] Even if the citizens managed to voice opposition and send their opinions to the planning board, their input would not be seriously reviewed, let alone overturn a planning decision, because the planning board was notoriously manipulated by the administrative officials, councillors and developers (Yu, 1994; Selya, 1995).

The gap between planning ideas and planning practice was rooted in international and domestic politics, economic development and control of knowledge. Most ideas were transplanted without adequate adaptation to fit local conditions. In addition, the ever-changing politics, deeply embedded in geo-politics and the international economy, further undermined the vision of long-term urban planning. Therefore, in this model, the planning skills and ideology transplanted from the West was only a mask for planning reality. In fact, there was very little autonomy for the planning bureaucrats, and what overrode in planning was urban politics determined by the central state which was authoritarian, hierarchical and developmental.

Urban Planning and the Emerging Crisis before the Late 1980s

Since the Japanese colonial period, Taipei has been the most populated city as well as the military, political and economic centre of Taiwan. In 1932, the Japanese colonial government completed an urban Master Plan. It aimed to build Taipei as a model city for its imperialist cities in Asia. To serve this goal, modern concepts and principles of planning, such as the reservation of 10 per cent of land for public facilities, were incorporated into the plan. With it, a grid-iron pattern of roads replaced the original streetscape based on Fengshui principles. Taipei was divided into fifty-two neighbourhoods, separating the colonizers and the colonized. Seventeen urban parks, most of which were located in the Japanese residential area, were planned to enhance public health.

After the KMT retreated to Taiwan and claimed it would strike back China shortly, the central government claimed Taiwan as the 'bastion of freedom and national revival', and appointed Taipei as 'the provisional capital city at wartime'. In planning, it had the following impact. First, the dramatic population growth from the mainland Chinese immigrants made the earlier urban plan ineffective. In order to build Taipei as a fortress city, urban development focused mostly on rapid construction of military infrastructure, such as roads, bridges and cave shelters (Zeng, 1994). The development of other urban infrastructure was suspended or even sacrificed. For example, much of the land reserved for urban parks was allocated to serve as military camps or temporary shelters for immigrants.

During the era of economic take-off, Taipei functioned as a 'magnet for investment and immigrants' for the nation (Drakakis-Smith, 1992). It was not only a key industrial city but also the headquarters for domestic and international corporations. In other words, Taipei was a node city for Taiwan to connect with the world market (see Chapter 1). Thus, the central government aggressively invested in transportation systems and other construction to promote the economic development of the city.

To fulfil Taipei's function, rational growth management was not applied to the city's planning. Instead, a *laissez-faire* approach was the mode for Taipei's growth. Between the 1960s and 1980s, economic development in Taiwan brought a large rural immigration to Taipei City. Though Taipei's comprehensive plan was amended in an attempt to catch up with the rapid migration, population growth could not be controlled. As statistics show, the population of Taipei was 0.97 million in 1962, and increased to 1.9 million in 1972, an average annual growth rate of 6.04 per cent. By 1990, Taipei's population had reached 2.72 million, its historical peak (Taipei City Government, 1998). In only four decades, Taipei's population grew nine times.

Following the rapid growth of population was the shortage of urban infrastructure. As shown above, this was a general condition in Taiwan and it was mainly caused by fiscal policies, which insisted on a low tax rate, thus leading to insufficient public revenue. Given these difficulties, only 53.9 per cent of the land reserved for public facilities had been completely developed in Taipei by 1978 (Tang, 1982). Furthermore, the limited public investment inevitably led to a distorted allocation in infrastructure provision. As table 4.1 shows, a huge gap lies between the heavy investment on roads and the other items. In the municipal budget, road development took between 67 and 86 per cent of infrastructure investment, and in sharp contrast, park development only had a share of 0.7 to 1.5 per cent. Roads were given top priority, because they not only facilitate industrial production but also are necessary for real estate development. Park development was delayed or neglected because both the central government and local government considered it to be a 'waste' of land resources.

Table 4.1 Percentage of budget allocated to public infrastructure, 1968–1977.

Fiscal year	Road	School	Market	Parks	Parking lot	Total
1968	85.89	13.21	N.A.	0.90	N.A.	100.00
1971	67.65	32.22	0.06	0.07	N.A.	100.00
1974	71.86	24.76	0.09	0.09	2.30	100.00
1977	76.21	17.70	1.39	1.53	3.17	100.00

Source: He (1979).

As a result, the planning bureaucrats continuously converted the reserved park lands into other productive land uses, such as road and commercial or industrial development. Documents show that by 1990, a total of 261 tracts for parks and green spaces were rezoned to roads, residential areas and parking lots (Hong, 1992). Consequently in 1984, the area of parks and green spaces per capita in Taipei was only 1.97 square metres. The same standard was set as 8 square metres in the Japanese colonial period and 6 square metres in the amendment of the Master Plan in 1956. Compared with other world cities, the standard was 12.2 square metres for Paris, 13.0 for Seoul, and 23.9 for Vancouver in the same year (Hong, 1992). The shortage of parks in Taipei was an undeniable planning failure.

The poor planning performance was not overlooked by the citizens. As the central government was located in Taipei, the state was especially vigilant in maintaining social order and political stability in the capital city. To facilitate the state's direct command over Taipei City, the central government designated the city the status of special municipality in 1967. Meanwhile, the mayor of Taipei was no longer selected by election, but by designation from the central government. This proved effective in neutralizing political criticism by independent candidates in election.

Political Changes in the Late 1990s

From the discussion above, Taipei was a city short of urban infrastructure, local autonomy, open decision-making processes, and expression of the citizens' diverse values. However, around the late 1980s, urban politics in Taipei underwent a major transformation, and the conventional way of planning was challenged. Two critical movements induced a changing landscape of urban politics. The first is the weakening power of the central state in the face of global economic change and the rise of the middle class. The second is the emergence of Non-Government Organizations (NGOs) and the re-introduction of elections.

Since the mid-1980s, the authoritarian central state, which was steering Taiwan into a developmental state, met with multiple crises. The first formidable crisis came from the dynamic of global economy. In the 1980s, China quickly rose to be the new global factory and replaced the old role of the Asian Four Dragons as manufacturing sites. Many Taiwan firms started to move across the Strait to seek cheaper labour, land and lax environmental regulation. As discussed earlier, the global economy, and not the state, led in the economic transformation.

At the same time, there was a rising demand for democracy from the citizens. Observers argued that the emergence of new politics was attributed to the growth of the middle class, a social transformation generated by over three decades of the KMT's economic development, combined with a Confucian aspiration for high education. In 1962, one year before the milestone of economic take off, Taiwan's per capita GNP was only US$162. Three decades of economic development later this figure was US$10,210, in 1992. The changing economic structure generated a new middle class of skilled workers, professionals and managers in the service sectors, replacing the old middle class in the public sectors, such as military, civil servants, and teachers. Researchers estimated that by the late 1980s, the middle class occupied around 20 to 30 per cent of the total population in Taiwan (Hsiao, 1989*a*).

While the middle class generally tends to possess diversified social values, the new middle class in Taiwan shared the same social political concerns. In the late 1980s, they were sensitive to the social and political inequality, and played a leading role in advocating political transformation. According to the polls of '*Common*' magazine in November 1988, 94 per cent of the middle class reported that they valued democratization more than the improvement of individual life (Xiao, 1989*a*).

The growing political force of the new middle class pushed the KMT government to lift the Martial Law, and abolish the prohibition of organizing opposition parties. The parliament began to practice general election. Therefore, from the late 1980s to the mid-1990s, Taiwan saw a break from the limited electoral democracy of previous decades. In 1994, the mayoral election of Taipei City was restored after nearly 30 years of suspension. That same year, the first election for Provincial Governor took place. In 1996, a general election was called for the presidential election. Political competition was brought on by elections and new political parties – the emerging Democratic Progressive Party (DPP). The KMT no longer held sole control over the government as well as civil society.

These major social and political movements were not entirely instigated by the middle class but an alliance of various social groups. They confronted the central government with a series of social issues. According to Xiao, in the 1980s eighteen different social movements emerged, including a consumer's movement, environmental conservation movement, feminist movement, and so on (Hsiao, 1989*b*). Such social mobilization was unprecedented in scale and variety. These movements finally pushed the national government to lift Martial Law in 1987. This marked a watershed in the process of democratization in Taiwan. The prohibition on organizing political parties and political gatherings, as well as holding public protests was finally abolished.

Political re-structuring was hastened in the late 1980s by two emerging phenomena: the rise of citizen groups and community organizations, and political competition. Brought on by the new opposition parties, they peaked in the restored mayoral election in 1994.

After the lifting of Martial Law in 1987, the right of public participation was re-instated, and self-organizing was the first step. Unlike associations affiliated to the

KMT party, most social organizations formed in the late 1980s and early 1990s had autonomy and were independent of the state. These were the first genuine NGOs in Taiwan, founded by active citizens. By encouraging public participation, they aimed to monitor and influence the policy-making process. In Taipei, the social and political centre of Taiwan, the rise of autonomous NGOs was especially evident. According to statistics, the number of registered social associations in Taipei was 1,010 in 1987, and rapidly increased to 3,333 by 1995, more than tripling in eight years (Taipei City Government, 1998). Aside from registered NGOs, there were also many informal community-based networks flourishing. While some were founded to resist invasion of the unwelcome real estate development into communities, others were dedicated to preserving local culture in the face of rapid urban change.

The members of these formal and informal civil groups came from a wide array of social sectors, such as, intellectuals, professionals, housewives, active students, and so on. A middle-class culture was shared among members, usually expressed as concern for the values of life and living environment, and not merely economic development. They were vocal, and these organized citizens were ready to challenge collectively the government's actions in their cities and communities. Their high alert targeted urban planning, which was no longer free from citizen intervention.[5]

These active citizens were well versed in the strategies of self-organizing and social mobilization. Though they were skilful at negotiating with the government, they were equally adept in pressurizing the local government by public meetings, press conferences, petitions, and lobbying, as well as organizing more militant action, such as, public rallies or boycott campaigns. Their actions not only embarrassed the bureaucrats, but also exposed to the public the inefficacy, unresponsiveness and favouritism of the government. Indeed, urban mobilization shattered the stability of the KMT administration in Taipei, especially later on, when it had to compete with opposition parties in the election.

Responding to the grassroots demand for democracy, the seat of the Taipei mayor was re-instated in 1994. The election campaign was a critical moment for the KMT administration. KMT's local government in Taipei could no longer count on backing from the central state. As voters started to exercise their political power, planning politics shifted again.

Chen Shui-Bian, candidate from the main opposition political party, the DPP, had been a legislator well known for his sharp monitoring of the KMT regime. Different from other candidates,[6] he deliberately avoided splitting issues and prepared a platform which embraced the shared values of the new middle class. He pledged to bring citizens better urban environment and quality of life. Here he proved that he was sensitive to citizens' needs and aware of the role of planning.

To distinguish his approach with that of the KMT regime, he unveiled principles of 'citizen participation', 'no more big constructions, but small improvement of the urban space' and 'preserving historical memory' for urban management and planning. These tactics successfully gained grassroots support, and the mayoral election campaign in 1994 turned out to be a coalition of the grassroots and opposition political forces against the long established KMT.

Chen won the election by a narrow margin. During his tenure, he deliberately built a new governance style. In practice, he did not adhere to all his own principles; instead of 'no big construction, but small improvement', he acted more like a follower of the 'making big things' principle. For example, he tried to ally with developers to speed up the development of the new financial district, a city project named 'Taipei Manhattan', as discussed in Chapter 6. He did, however, aggressively build up new social consensus by revamping the process of urban planning. The most symbolic measure was the so-called 'Space Liberation'. In the city, some buildings and spaces were exclusively reserved for the KMT party, such as those former residential palaces for Chang Kai-Shek and Taipei mayors. He opened them to the public and increased the supply of public facilities. Aside from these individual cases, a series of experiments was initiated to involve the grassroots in neighbourhood planning and historical preservation. By doing so, Chen instigated a major reorientation in urban planning from 1994 to 1998. In the following mayoral election, Ma Ying-Jeou won the seat back for the KMT in 1998. Ma followed the same approach of participatory planning and brought in new measures for the planning system. This process will be elaborated in the following section.

Restructuring Planning Model

From the mid-1990s onward, through the administrations of Chen and Ma, a new system of participatory planning gradually took shape.

As early as in the late 1980s and early 1990s, when the KMT still ruled the city, some planning academics were already involved in community development by taking an advocacy planning approach, speaking out for the grassroots and mediating between the government and communities. After Chen took the mayoralty, the relationship between the government, planners and communities began to be restructured. It was a trial and error experimental process.

In 1995, the government held the first urban design competition and invited community-professional groups to present their ideas for improving the physical environment of neighbourhoods. Twenty-six proposals were selected for awards. This event legitimized the collaborative network between communities, professional groups, and university planning departments as a formal planning process.

In 1996, the Urban Development Bureau of the Taipei City government initiated the Neighbourhood Plan, a programme which served as the first attempt by the government to institutionalize community design through collaborative planning.[7] According to the Plan, Taipei City government would provide budgets for communities, assisted by professionals, to propose plans for improving community spaces through a participatory process. Who were those professionals? Because planning professionals in the private sector were hesitant to adopt this new approach, most of the professionals working with the Neighbourhood Plan were academics in architecture or planning. They learnt the concept and practice of community planning from experiences in Western society and were ready and eager to put them into local practice.

According to the Neighbourhood Plan, after plans were completed and submitted, those considered by the Bureau to be feasible would start construction in the following year. This new method had considerable impact on community planning and revamped the city government's ways of delivering infrastructure and social services at the neighbourhood level. In the past, public construction was decided by the bureaucrats and political negotiation between the government and the councillors – often with no involvement with the public at all. In contrast, the Neighbourhood Plan created an interface for the activists, professionals and community residents to work together, brainstorming, visioning and controlling the future living environment.

Accordingly, from 1996 to 2000, a total of 200 proposals were submitted to the Neighbourhood Plan. Among them, 106 projects passed the competition and received subsidies for conducting participatory design. And by 2001, thirty-five projects were constructed. In terms of planning function, most were for upgrading neighbourhood parks and pedestrian routes. Some communities aimed to remodel vacant public buildings to accommodate community activities.[8] These projects reflect and serve the neighbourhood's needs for public facilities and urban amenities.

In the early years of the Neighbourhood Plan, there was a shortage of expertise for community design. By 1999, the Bureau introduced a mechanism called 'Community Planner System' into the process of collaborative planning. This policy aimed at recruiting professionals for neighbourhood design, and thus expanded the programme considerably.

According to the Community Planner System, the tasks of community planners include: establishing community studio for contact with local residents; providing consultant service to communities to facilitate the Neighbourhood Plan; and distributing planning information to residents. Supposedly, each local office would provide these services to every 10,000 to 12,000 citizens throughout the city. In the Community Planner System, Taipei City government provided the incentives, including both entitlement and consultant fee, to professionals who were committed to serve as community planners. Thereby, a number of planners and architects from the private sector were incorporated into the new planning system. In order to coordinate the Community Planner System at a district level,[9] the municipal government started a new scheme called 'Community Planning Centre' in 2001. In this scheme, Community Planning Centre was either run by NGOs interested in community affairs or planning related departments in universities.

Figure 4.1 indicates the mechanism of integrating community, professionals and organizations in community design, through which Taipei City government has created a collaborative framework to transform the antagonistic relationship between the sate and society. Although from time to time, sporadic and minor conflicts still occur, this new approach, which is highly symbolic, has functioned well in the face of vocal citizens.

After years of practice, the limitations of this system gradually showed up. First, the 'participatory process' does not give equal access to various social groups. In fact, although the poor communities have more urgent needs for resources for the Neighbourhood Plan, most Neighbourhood Plan grants went to prestigious communities with residents of high education and income, who possess higher social capital and better knowledge of the participatory discourse and process (OURs, 1999). As a result, the new participatory approach tends to reproduce the social inequality in the city.

Second, communities, even the middle-class ones, find that they do not have equal footing with the government to form a partnership. Although the Neighbourhood Plan system invites citizen participation, the institutional support from government is insufficient. The administrative bureaucracy often overrides and frustrates the

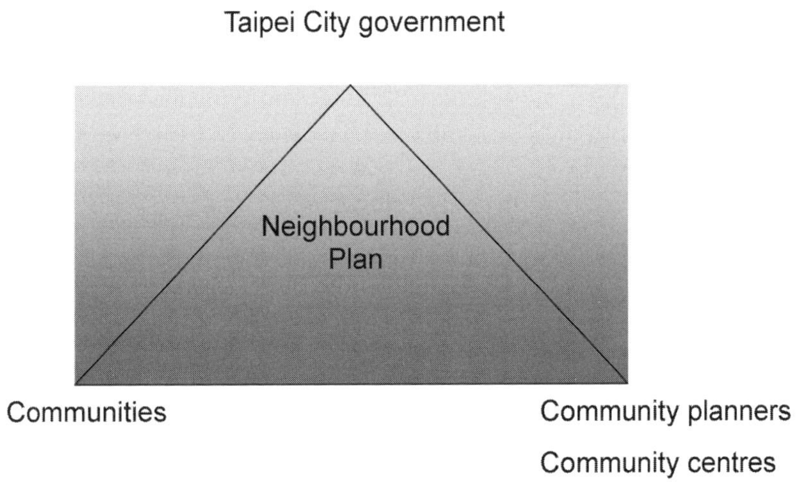

Figure 4.1. The structure of collaborative planning in Taipei.

participatory design. For example, the schedule of Neighbourhood Plan projects must closely follow the timeline of the governmental fiscal year rather than the tempo of community consensus-building. Furthermore, the lack of coordination among government agencies in vertical and horizontal negotiations often leads to the delay or rejection of construction, and undermines the effects of participatory design (OUR, 2000).

Third, it becomes clear that community participation is no panacea for all urban problems. While the community planners and resident networks focus on neighbourhood planning, the planning issues at the city level are left out. Activists have to redirect social attention and create a new vision for planning at a higher level.

By the following case study of Yongkang community, we shall provide a clearer picture on how the participatory process works in the context of the new urban politics.

Participatory Planning in Yongkang Neighbourhood

Located at the south-eastern part of Taipei City, Yongkang neighbourhood is a community of mixed residential and commercial land-uses. For decades, this neighbourhood has had a rich sense of urbanity, due to its particular geographic and historic background. In the Japanese colonial era, Yongkang neighbourhood was designated for the exclusive residence of Japanese officials. Therefore, it is no accident that in the 1930s, the largest urban park in Taipei, the 'No. 7 Park', later named Da'an Urban Park after its completion, was planned to be developed here to provide environmental quality (see figures 4.2, 4.3, and 4.4). After the KMT retreated to Taiwan, the former Japanese residences were turned over to the KMT officials. Later on, churches, schools, and universities were set up one after the other, giving the area the milieu of a pleasant neighbourhood. In the 1980s, when the middle class was well established, numerous gourmet restaurants and craft-shops opened. These new consumption activities turned the area into a cultural consumption hub for all urban citizens and visitors from abroad, far removed from the original sense of residential neighbourhood.

In the early 1990s, urban growth had a strong impact on the Yongkang neighbourhood. Geographically, the Yongkang community is close to the city centre and only about 200 metres away from Da'an Park. Across from the Park are the Weekend Flower and Jade Markets, which form a popular attraction node for citizens and visitors. This visitor attraction renders Yongkang neighbourhood open to urban growth. Especially during the weekend, traffic jams often occur around and within the community. To alleviate the traffic problem, in July 1995, the city government decided to develop a road through this neighbourhood.

This government plan under the new DPP city government proved to be an

Figure 4.2. Da'an Urban Park. In Taipei, urban parks serve as natural parks, and provide large spaces for trees and lawn as was first employed at Da'an Urban Park. (Photo by Li-Ling Huang)

Figure 4.3. Da'an Urban Park. Open spaces and playground facilities give a functional balance at the park. (Photo by Li-Ling Huang)

Figure 4.4. Da'an Urban Park. People, and even birds, are provided with kiosks at the park. (Photo by Li-Ling Huang)

ill-considered decision. First, the development project needed to cut through Yongkang Park, a small, 0.4 acre, park east of Da'an Park, which had served as an open community space for its surrounding neighbourhood since the 1960s. According to the plan, about two-thirds of Yongkang Park (see figure 4.5) would be demolished and transformed into road surface. At the same time, about 50 trees would have to be removed. Second, city government did not properly inform or consult with residents in the Yongkang community. This news was announced abruptly, but semi-openly.

A university student member living in the neighbourhood discovered the news from posters on the trees just weeks before the bulldozer was to arrive. After talking to neighbours, she was convinced that the road development was a poor idea. She then decided to launch a community action. Within one week, she successfully mobilized a network by founding a group called 'Friends of Yongkang Park', which comprised mainly of young people and housewives in the community. Several strategies were adopted by this group. First, they held a public meeting in the community, explaining the government's road plan, and collected signatures from more than 300 community residents for issuing an emergency appeal to the government. They kept close contacts with the press and called for public support. At the same time, in order to build up wide local support, Friends of Yongkang Park also held community fairs in the park for children, parents and shopkeepers in the community. Third, they sought support from other activists and NGOs, such as the Organization of Urban Reformers (founded by advocate planners), Awakening (an NGO set up by feminists), and the Alliance of Home Makers (an NGO organized by female environmentalists, most of whose members were housewives). These organizations were invited to lead a community discussion on what kind of community environment would be desirable. Once the project became a public issue, the media were interested to report the community actions. The project and community dissent were widely circulated and the issue of Yongkang Park received widespread citizen attention. To be responsive, officials from both the Planning and Construction Bureaus arrived at the community to re-evaluate the project, and, the government promised to halt construction. The whole process of halting the project was swift, as it took less than one month after the university faculty member decided to take action.

The solution quickly dissipated the tension between the government and community. For the rest of the dissenting urban communities, the community action and the government's response were taken as the new norm for interaction between government and community under the DPP urban regime. To dispel the negative effects of this episode and to appease the community, the city government actively encouraged Yongkang community to join the Neighbourhood Plan and conduct a participatory design for the park.

Figure 4.5. Yongkang Park.

Two teams, one included academics from the Architecture Department of Chung-Yuan University, and the other from National Taiwan University came to assist the Yongkang residents on park design. The team from Chung-Yuan University, pioneers of promoting urban design, adopted an approach of the United States in the 1970s, which aimed to preserve the community equilibrium in the process of urban development. The team from National Taiwan University had long focused on the issue of community mobilization, and the academic department had a strong commitment to the advocacy planning approach introduced in the 1960s and 1970s in the United States. The intellectual forces and working methods introduced by these planning approaches empowered Yongkang community and gave substance to this new planning method. A new social experiment was initiated.

The participatory design was dynamic and it involved issues of physical space and social identity. Because there was no community centre in Yongkang neighbourhood, the first issue of the park design was how to provide a space for community events. This turned out to be the first controversial issue because a statue of Chiang Kai-Shek had occupied the centre of the park for the past decades, and residents had divided opinions over how to deal with the statue in order to make room for the centre. Some thought the statue was already a part of the collective memory and did not offend their political ideals, while others considered the statue an offending icon. After negotiation, mediated by the professionals, a compromise was reached. The statue was moved to the fringe of the park, and a performance stage was placed in the centre of the park to support community activities.

Additional features were included in the participatory design process, as participants often made suggestions for improvement. For example, the wall of the park was razed to be replaced by a bush-fence to serve as a visual and sound barrier. Yet a section of the wall, decorated by mosaic, was built. It was to link the residents' memory to the past, because the original wall was built in the 1960s with mosaic. Later it was torn down and replaced with standardized design. Other improvements included a side-gate built to enhance accessibility and the replacement of steel benches with wooden ones to be more user friendly. A corner in the park was reserved for ecological experiment. In this corner, fallen leaves would be collected into compost as fertilizer for the park. In addition to these ecological features, the park design incorporated the community's action to save trees.

The park improvement project was by no means an entirely rosy story. Even middle-class residents found collaboration with the government difficult. Community members complained mostly about the inefficiency of the government. Endless red-tape often blunted their enthusiasm. For example, in order to change the design of the drainage lids, they had to get the approval from almost a dozen sections from various bureaus. Each step was so tedious that some participants considered participation a punishment.

Within the community, there were other groups with complaints. Obviously, the participatory process was inclined to incorporate the opinions of the most vocal residents. Some of the disadvantaged groups, such as, vendors around the park and homeless people who used the park as a shelter, were excluded from the process. Although some members of the Friends of Yongkang Park tried to involve those disadvantaged people, most participants did not consider them entitled to share the decision-making.

Community politics turned out to be more complicated than initiators of the park design envisaged. As Yongkang neighbourhood enjoyed being a recognized 'successful community' and received a budget for a number of improvements from the government, the community leadership started splitting. The most radical members dropped out as they refused to compromise, leaving the battle to the more conciliatory. Apart from the regular community activities, commercial community fairs were often held in this park (see figures 4.6 and 4.7). Suspiciously, the current community leader is using the park to increase her social and political capital, and possibly, material gains. Community activities tend to follow the existing formula, rather than serve as an instrument for social improvement.

The action of upgrading Yongkang Park inevitably led to gentrification. After the community action to save trees and the park design became an urban legend,

Figures 4.6. and 4.7.
Community activity at
Yongkang Park.

a number of fashionable restaurants opened around the parks to take advantage of its popularity. This brought the second restaurant boom to this area seen in recent decades. Consequently, the properties of this community keep soaring in price. Such rises are welcomed by landowners, but costly to the tenants. Traffic has increased, even to the extent of endangering children en route to school. Continuous community actions cannot be, and have not been, initiated.

Summary and Conclusion

Within the context of political forces functioning at both global and local levels, this chapter attempts to develop an argument for the shift in Taipei's urban planning at different stages of economic development. The era from the late-1980s to mid-1990s is identified as the watershed for a radical change. Prior to it, urban planning had a long tradition of transplanting planning ideology from the Western world, and being dominated by the centralized, authoritarian and developmental state. This planning approach planning did not respond to urban reality and citizens' needs, but served the national goals of economic development and political stability.

The accelerated global process in the late 1980s brought on a new political landscape for change in planning practice. The global economy expanded the middle class who weakened the controlling power of the central state, thus releasing a tide of democratization, which shook the central authority. At this juncture, the political party competition over the 1994 mayoral election prompted a new local agenda, community participatory planning, which democratized planning practice. The meaning of this policy initiative can be interpreted in its political significance. It was the first governmental attempt to institutionalize participatory planning by conceding power. It was also the first time that community activists and planners became protagonists to combine civil society and technology, apply Western practice in the production of community actions and social service, and reduce the state to a supportive role.

While it may still be too early to generalize on the achievements of participatory planning at the community level, some interim conclusions can be drawn from the pioneering case of the Yongkang Park project. Participatory planning in Taipei is predominately a middle-class project. It was dedicated to mobilizing community power, creating a better public environment and building new citizen identities but over time it has gradually turned into a formalized and routine practice, and lost its innovation and capacity as the critical force for transforming and improving society. On the other hand, the community planning training course for the general public seems to continue to enjoy popularity. And it does offer evidence of the change in planning model practiced in Taipei.

Notes

1. In contrast to Hong Kong and Singapore, where the states intervened in social reproduction by providing large-scale public housing, the state of Taiwan boosted the capitalist development mainly through establishing transportation systems and advancing education of nationals. Public housing only comprises about 3 per cent of total housing stock, and if housing for exclusive groups, such as, teachers and military personnel, is included the total is 8 per cent. Public housing provision is extremely low, compared with that in Hong Kong and Singapore, where over 50 per cent of the respective populations live in public housing.
2. On 28 February 1947, a cigarette vendor was interrogated, beaten and shot by KMT policemen on the street in Taipei. This event, which reflected the high tension between the government and local society, finally went out of control and triggered island wide civil-uprising. KMT quashed this event with military force. More than 20,000 people, most of whom were social elites, were killed in the massacre.
3. Under the Martial Law, hundreds of dissidents were incarcerated or executed, and ordinary

people were deprived of major civil rights, including rights of initiating autonomous social groups, political parties or gatherings to express political opinions.

4. The government usually played tricks with it. For example, it published the details of a plan in an unpopular newspaper and therefore did not violate the regulation of the ordinance about 'publicizing' the plan, but did not release it too widely and so incur opposition (See Yu, 1994).

5. Many actions targeted the local government's plans for undesirable facilities, such as, electric transmission stations, garbage processing fields, and gas stations. Some communities close to hillsides mobilized against the government's plan to change the conservation land into development land. These planning decisions were previously made within the planning departments, without informing or consulting residents.

6. Besides Chen, there were two other candidates. One was Huang from the KMT, the other Zhao from the New Party. But neither addressed the urban planning issues as Chen.

7. According to the Neighbourhood Plan, neighbourhood design would be open to civic groups and community organizations. Once the proposal passed the review by scholars and professionals, the Bureau would provide each case a subsidy of around $10,000 to $20,000 US dollars.

8. In Taipei, around 64 per cent of the urban land is owned by the government. Because of the dispersed ownerships by different institutes and different levels of government, much public land and many buildings are poorly managed, and even remain vacant. Community residents started to list and check out the public premises in the community, and pushed the local government to negotiate with the public institutes to release the right of land use and management to the community.

9. In total, there are twelve districts in Taipei. The population of a district on average is 215,000.

References

Borja, J. and Castells, M. (1997) *Local and Global: The Management of Cities in the Information Age*. London: Earthscan Publications.

Castells, M. (1997) *The Information Age: Economy, Society and Culture, Volume II, The Power of Identity*. Oxford: Blackwell.

Drakakis-Smith, D. (1992) *Pacific Asia*. London: Routledge.

Friedmann, J. (1998) Planning theory revisited. *European Planning Studies*, **6**(3), pp. 245–253.

Gold, T. (1986) *State and Society in the Taiwan Miracle*. Armonk, New York: M.E. Sharpe.

Hall, P. (2002) *Cities of Tomorrow*, 3rd ed. Oxford: Blackwell.

He, D.P. (1979) Taipei Shi gonggong sheshi yu caizheng guanxi zhi yanjiu (Research on the relationship between the public infrastructures and finance). Master's Thesis, Graduate Institute of Urban Planning, National Chung Shin Law and Business School, Taipei.

Hong, I.R. (1992) Dushi gongyuan siren touzi yu fangdichan liyi zhi jian de guanxi (The relationship between the private investment on urban parks and the interest of real estate). Master Thesis, Building and Planning, National Taiwan University, Taipei.

Hsiao, H.H.M. (1989*a*) Taiwan xinxing shehui yundong de fenxi jiagou (The analytical framework of the new rise social movements), in Xu, Z.G. and Song, W.L. (eds.)*Taiwan xin xing shehui yundong* (*The New Rise Social Movement in Taiwan*). Taipei: Ju Liu Publisher.

Hsiao, H.H.M. (ed.) (1989*b*) *Bianqian zhong* Taiwan shehui de zhongchan jieji (The Middle Class in the Transforming Society of Taiwan). Taipei: Ju Liu Publisher.

Inness, J. (1995) Planning Theory's Emerging Paradigm: Communicative Action and Interactive Practice. Working Paper of the Department of City and Regional Planning, University of California, Berkeley.

Innes, J. and D. Booher, D. (2003) The Impact of Collaborative Planning on Governance Capacity. Working Paper of the Department of City and Regional Planning, University of California, Berkeley.

Ohmae, K. (1995) *The End of the Nation State: The Rise of Regional Economies*. New York: Free Press.

OURs (Organization of Urban Reformers, Dushi gaige zhuzhi) (1999) *Diqu haunjing gaizao jihua zhi xinchenguo pinggu yu qi zhi qianghua celue guihua yanjiu* (*The Strategy Development and Evaluation of Neighborhood Environment Improvement Plan*). Taipei: Weituo danwei, Taipei Shi dushi fazhanju (Bureau of Urban Development, Taipei Municipal Government).

OURs (Organization of Urban Reformers, Dushi gaige zhuzhi) (2000) *Diqu haunjing gaizao jihua anli chenguo pinggu* (*The Evaluation of Neighbourhood Environment Improvement Plan: Projects from 1996 to 2000*). Taipei: Bureau of Urban Development, Taipei Municipal Government.

Selya, R.M. (1995) *Taipei*. New York: Wiley.

Taipei Shi Zhengfu (Taipei City Government) (1998) Taipei Shi tongji yaolan (Statistics Summary of Taipei City). Taipei: Shizhengfu Zhujichu. Taipei: Bureau of Budget, Accounting and Statistics).

Tang, F.Z. (1982) Dushi wenti yu dushi zhengce yanjiu (Research of Urban Problems and Urban Policy). Taipei: Xingzhengyuan Yangkaohui (Taipei: Research, Development and Evaluation Commission, Executive Yuan).

Yu, D.L. (1994) She qu shi jian ju min kang zheng dong yuan zhi yan jiu: sange Taipei ge an (A study on the mobilization process in community controversies: three cases in Taipei). Guoli Taiwan daxue jianzhu yu chenxiang yangjiusuo shuoshi lunwen (Master's Thesis, Civil Engineering, National Taiwan University, Taipei).

Zeng, X.Z. (1994) Zhanhou Taipei de dushi guochen yu dushi yishi xinggou zhi yanjiu (The urban process and the formation of urban ideology in postwar Taipei). Guoli Taiwan daxue tumu gongchenxue yanjiusuo boshi lunwen (Ph.D. Dissertation, Civil Engineering, National Taiwan University, Taipei).

Chapter Five

Provision for Collective Consumption: Housing Production under Neoliberalism

Yi-Ling Chen

Many of the world's cities have experienced economic restructuring as a result of capitalist expansion on a global scale. The change in employment structure in the city hastens social polarization. Social inequality not only affects people's everyday life but also transforms the spatial structure of the city. Segregation, exclusion, and the shortage of low-income housing become common phenomena in the city. In particular, the rising ideology of neoliberalism in economic and social policies has exacerbated housing problems. Cutbacks in welfare expenditure greatly reduce the role of the state as the major provider of low-income housing. Mitigating social inequality and housing problems has been a major concern of research on global cities.

Beginning in the mid-1980s, privatization and liberalization became goals of public policy in Taiwan. The rise of neoliberalism in the 1980s has affected the role of the state on housing production. The central government in Taiwan provides a strong leadership in economic development but only plays a minor role in housing provision. Without public assistance, low-income people in Taipei have relied on the informal sector and rental housing to solve their housing problems. The neoliberalist policies further reduce the responsibility of the government in providing low-income housing – hence the source of affordable housing in Taipei city becomes limited. Moreover, the clearance of squatters and illegal housing in the city greatly reduce the provision of low-income housing.

This chapter aims to explain why low-income housing remains a marginal urban issue in Taipei in the process of economic liberalization and political democratization of Taiwan. Analysis of Taipei housing must posit the central government's policy as the context because local housing development responds to the policy of the central state. Central government enacts housing policy and local government implements it. Taipei's housing department is the local agency of that of the central state. The chapter first discusses the rise of neoliberalist ideology in the 1980s in Taiwan and its impact on housing policy. It examines the housing boom in Taipei at the end of the 1980s against the background of global economic development, and concludes with a review of the three key features of housing policy in the neoliberalist era.

Neoliberalist Reform in Taiwan in the 1980s

The crisis of the Keynesian welfare state in the late 1970s led to the rise of neoliberalism that aimed at market-led development. Thatcherism and Reaganism, during the 1980s, began reforms toward neoliberalist restructuring. The reforms were intended to 'extend market discipline, competition, and commodification throughout all sectors of society' (Brenner and Theodore, 2002, p. 3). The reform projects included:

the deregulation of state control over major industries, assaults on organized labor, the reduction of corporate taxes, the shrinking and/or privatization of public services, the dismantling of welfare programs, the enhancement of international capital mobility, the intensification of interlocality competition, and the criminalization of the urban poor. (*Ibid.*, p. 3)

Through the policies of such agents of transnational neoliberalism as GATT, WTO, the World Bank, and the IMF, Third World countries are exhorted to enhance 'market forces and commodification' (*Ibid.*, p. 3). However, restructuring processes, under the doctrine of liberalism, take place in very varied contexts, both geographically and in terms of institutional frameworks (*Ibid.*, p. 4).

In Taiwan, neoliberalist reforms in the 1980s were accompanied by the process of democratization in the mid-1980s. The policies of privatization and deregulation were perceived as a mechanism to weaken the dictatorial Kuomintang (KMT) party which had governed Taiwan since 1945. These policies, thus, gained society's support at the beginning. However, after almost two decades of these political and economic experiments, instead of social stability and equality, the social trends have gone in the opposite direction.

The most significant reform under the neoliberalist principle in Taiwan was the privatization of the state-owned enterprises from the late 1980s. State-owned enterprises had provided the means for the KMT government to maintain its dominance in Taiwan. These enterprises monopolized not only industries that supplied basic facilities, such as, water, electricity, gas, oil, but also up-stream industries that provided key raw materials. Therefore, the KMT state was able to lead economic development and restrict private capital (Chang, C.F., 2003).

Due to the strong economic foundation that supported the KMT regime, privatization of the state-owned enterprises was one of the goals of the opposition movements. Meanwhile, economic scholars in Taiwan advocated the neoliberalist ideology. Increasing deficits and inefficiency also brought the state-owned enterprises under attack. In the late 1980s, the KMT state began liberalist reforms, including allowing private capital to buy state-owned enterprises or to enter the monopoly. There are three major reasons why the KMT government was willing to implement the reforms (Chang, C.F., 2003):

1. To reduce the central government deficits from the 1980s. Due to the 'Six-Year National Development Plan', which initiated several large public construction projects, the increase of welfare programmes, and the acquisition of land for public infrastructure, the deficits have increased since 1989. Selling the property, the public-owned enterprises or the public share of stocks would add to the central government's revenue.

2. To increase support from the capitalists and reduce resistance from the opposition movements. After the demise of Chiang Ching-Kuo, the succeeding President, Lee Tung-Hui, faced a power struggle within the KMT party and political protest from opposition movements. Through tactical manipulation to ensure profits for private capital, the privatization process ensured the partnership of the capitalists and the KMT government.

3. To reduce the inefficiency of the state-owned enterprises and avoid increasing labour movements organized by the employees in state-owned enterprises.

The strong pressure for democratization from society and the search for a new political coalition for the KMT state explain why neoliberalist reforms gained wide initial support from Taiwan's society. The dual process of political democratization and economic liberalization is not a unique case in the world. However, what is special in Taiwan's transformation is that the old regime had 'led the political and economic transformations' and 'was able to maintain its hold on political power until the presidential election in 2000' (Chang, C.F., 2003, p. 1).

In 1989, the Banking Law was revised to lift interest rate controls. The principle of privatization and deregulation applied to reduce the role of the state not only in the economy, but also in public policy. Urban planning aimed at encouraging the mechanism of market economy and reducing state intervention (see Chapter 4). The new practice included the deregulation of land-use control, market-led land development, and the charge of user fees. Private developers, rather than the state, increasingly played an active role to direct urban planning (Chou, 2001). Due to the lack of funding for urban renewal, Taipei City government in the 1990s used bonus floor space, i.e. permitting building at higher densities, as the major incentive for private developers to rebuild rundown buildings or neighbourhoods (Jou, 1999). In the 1990s, welfare privatization also became a goal of social policies (Chen, 1997). Local governments subcontracted the private sector, including both profit and non-profit organizations, to disperse such welfare services as care of the handicapped, the elderly, the homeless, children and battered women.

Neoliberalist reforms are important to an understanding of the nature of housing problems in Taipei city. There are three consequences of the neoliberialist reforms and democratization. First, both privatization and democratization have increased political influence of the capitalists (Wang, 1996). Privatization opens opportunities for capitalists who had been controlled by the KMT; at the same time, it builds a new coalition between capitalists and the state. Further, democratization gives capitalists opportunities to become directly involved in the policy-making process through the election system. Hence, their political influence continued even after the KMT stepped down in 2000. The development of global neoliberalism in many countries transforms a state-led economy to a new form of market-led economy (Crotty, 2002). In Taiwan, this process involved democratization, and thus, had little resistance from society at the beginning. After economic liberation in 1986, business groups began to play an increasingly vital part in Taiwan's economy and they have increasingly consolidated their position. The market gradually came under the control of a small number of large business groups (Chu and Hung, 2002).

Secondly, democratization also increased the participation of citizens and welfare programmes. While most welfare states are cutting down their welfare expenditure in the neoliberalist era, Taiwan society is increasingly demanding a move towards a welfare state (Wang, 2001). Political liberalization provides opportunities for welfare movement by popular protest or by lobbying representatives for welfare policies (Hsiao and Liu, 2002). Therefore, welfare expenditure rose during the 1990s (see figure 5.1). However, the Taiwan state carefully manipulates welfare programmes and maintains them at a minimum level so as not to hinder economic development (Wang, 2001).

Finally, the provision of welfare is based on the strength of collective bargaining and is unevenly distributed among different groups. Military personnel and government employees have received the largest benefit. Their welfare expenditure includes social insurance, social relief, and welfare services. Among the welfare service, the elderly and disabled people share a large proportion. Children, juveniles and women have a smaller amount. The passage of different welfare programmes or legislation is due to several successful social movements. The only exception is the pension for the elderly, which is a political platform for all parties during the election (Hsiao and Liu, 2002).

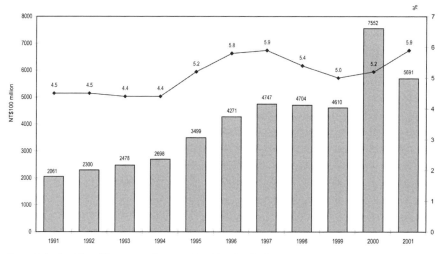

Figure 5.1. Social welfare expenditure, 1991–2001 (including retirement pension). *Source:* GIO (2002).

The provision of welfare programmes increases the government's deficit. The outstanding debt to GNP ratio for the central government increased from 14.6 per cent in fiscal year (FY) 1999 to 25.3 per cent in FY 2000 (GIO, 2002). This financial deficit worsens not only because of the increase in government expenditure on welfare and public construction, but also because economic growth has slowed down due to global economic recession and a large investment outflow overseas, especially to China. The policies continue to encourage cooperation with the private sector in the provision of social welfare and infrastructure. The privatization of publicly-owned enterprises also continues. The logic of deregulation and privatization reduces the protection of labour. An increasing unemployment rate further demands more welfare expenditure. In the neoliberalist era, market-led restructuring leads to greater economic, political and social instability in Taiwan. Nevertheless, capitalists have gained an upper hand.

Neoliberalism in Housing Policy in the 1990s

Democratization enhanced the coalition between the state and the capitalists. Their relationship transformed from a top-down leadership to a more equal partnership (Wang, 1996). The neoliberalist reform of housing policies was to further enhance the state's role in facilitating the housing market. The state reduced government-supplied housing (see figure 5.2) and alleviated its already minor responsibility in providing low-income housing. With the state retreating from housing production, market mechanisms became a major solution for housing demands.

The early neoliberalist reform of housing started at the end of the 1980s in

Figure 5.2. Early public housing in Da'an Park, Taipei. *Note:* Da'an Public Built Housing is located at the city center. It was targeted for the middle-to-lower income people, but now the residents are mostly middle-to-upper income people.

response to the largest housing movement. The provision of low-interest mortgages for general homebuyers without houses began in 1989. The housing authority claimed that this policy initiated the switch from a supply-oriented policy to a demand-oriented policy. The mortgage helped the middle-class homebuyers and actually expanded the housing market.

The most controversial housing policy was the NT$150 billion mortgage plan at the beginning of 1999, which showed the political influence of developers. The Asian Financial Crisis in 1997 intensified the problem of excessive unsold housing that was mostly built after the announcement of the land-use or plot ratio. The land-use ratio would set stricter limits of floor space for the new building. The state accepted the suggestions from developers to provide NT$150 billion in low-interest mortgages (5.95 per cent). The national treasury made up the difference between market interest rates and the rate of low-interest mortgages. The policy also increased the mortgage interest allowance on income taxes. With fiscal policy supporting the buyers in the housing market, public housing projects were suspended for two years (Li, 1999).

The NT$150 billion mortgage programme initially did not set any limit for applicants. The only restriction was that it applied only to new houses. In order to placate the realtors of older houses and those who could not afford the price of new houses, NT$30 billion was provided for first time homebuyers to buy used houses. This adjustment could not change the real intention of the policy which was to help developers solve the overproduction problem rather than to cool down speculation and high housing prices. The policy actually violated the rule of free market because the state intervention artificially raised housing demand, increased housing prices and impeded the selective process of the market. Lower-quality housing and developers were eliminated in the process. The reason for the policy was to prevent the collapse of the housing financing system by providing a large number of loans to homebuyers and developers. Upholding the housing market and the financial system was the major purpose. The overall effects were a high housing demand while those on low incomes were left out of the housing market.

The very open conditions and tax subsidies had serious impact on social justice. The largest tenant organization, Tsui-ma-ma, and many scholars were strongly against this policy. With this new subsidy, new housing buyers rushed in to take advantage of the financial benefit. Within six months, the mortgage fund was drained. Due to the popularity of the mortgage programme, the new government under President Chen Shui-Bian's administration continued to subsidize the mortgage interest. From 2000 to August 2003, this programme subsidized about NT$800 billion. The selection criteria were too unspecific – any citizen over twenty years old who has never applied to a government mortgage programme is eligible to apply for the mortgage.

The housing policy essentially safeguards the housing market, but does not maintain social equity. In the 1990s the public housing construction by the government was greatly reduced and, since 2000, has stopped. The policy orientation initially changed from supply to demand. Then, it stopped supply altogether. The switch to a mortgage programme aimed at promoting the buying power of the middle class, hence facilitating the housing market, served the interests of developers. The housing needs of low-income people were overlooked during the economic downturn.

Housing Market and Global Economy

As the largest city and the political economic centre of Taiwan, Taipei has attracted the wealth of the state. Among the top one per cent of wealthiest households in Taiwan, 74.25 per cent of them live in Taipei City (DGBAS, 1992, p. 13).[1] The average household income in Taipei is 1.44 times the average income of Taiwan (CEPD, 2002). The standard housing price in Taipei is also much higher than that in other major Taiwan cities (Taiwan Real Estate Research Center, 1999). Therefore, the problem of housing affordability for the below average income families is most severe in Taipei City as indicated in housing price to family income ratios in table 5.1. In 2001 homeownership rates were 78.4 per cent in Taipei city (Taipei City Government, 2001), and 85.6 per cent in Taiwan (DGBAS, 2001). For poorer households, the homeownership rate is much lower: only 16.77 per cent in Taipei City and 32.46 per cent in Taiwan (Ministry of Interior, 2002) (see table 5.2).[2]

Table 5.1. Standard housing prices and average family incomes in selected areas in Taiwan, 1996.

	Taipei City	Taipei County	Kaohsiung City	Taichung City
Standard housing price (NT$1,000)	6,988	4,409	3,777	3,702
Average family income (NT$1,000)	1,422	1,128	1,077	1,041
(Standard housing price)/(Average family income)	4.91	3.91	3.51	3.56

Source: TRERC (1999), p. 49; DGBAS (1996).

Table 5.2. Housing in Taiwan and Taipei.

	Average current income, 2001 (NT$)	Standard housing price, 1997 (NT$ 10,000)	Homeownership rate, 2001	Homeownership rate for poor households, 2001
Taiwan	1,108,461	Taipei County 440.86 Kaohsung City 377.73 Taichung City 370.22	85.6%	32.46%
Taipei	1,596,257	698.81	78.4%	16.77%

Source: DGBAS (1992), p. 13; CEPD (2002); Taipei City Government (2001); DGBAS (2001); Ministry of the Interior (2002).

The housing market in Taiwan is closely related to fluctuations in the global economy, as housing affordability in Taipei is related to housing speculation triggered by global forces. The two oil price shocks in the 1970s caused the first and second waves of speculation as housing price increases kept up with inflation caused by these shocks. Consequently, investment in housing became the mechanism to hedge against against inflation and a way to safeguard the value of money (Chang,

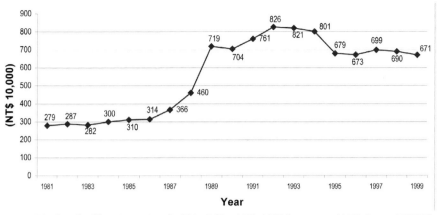

Figure 5.3. Standard housing prices for Taipei City, 1981–1999 (base year: 1996). *Source:* TRERC (1999), p. 49.

1995, pp. 160–161). Housing prices, therefore, rose twice in the 1970s, but at about the same rate as inflation so there was no real price increase. There was no real price insurgency in the 1970s. Instead, the most dramatic rise occurred in the mid-1980s, when prices rose to more than double in Taipei in the six years from 1986 to 1992 (see figure 5.3). The standard housing price[3] for Taipei City rose from NT$3,130,000, in 1986, to NT$8,260,000, in 1992, but in 1997 this figure reduced to NT$ 6,988,000.

Land speculation in the mid-1980s was generated by economic liberalization. As a result of rapid economic growth and financial policy, a huge amount of capital was accumulated in the domestic market and provided a major source for housing investment and consumption. Taiwan's trade surplus increased rapidly after 1981, and reached 19.3 per cent of GNP in 1986 (Hsueh, 1994, p. 199). A large amount of trade surplus from the United States pressured the central government to relax economic protection and deregulate the domestic financial system. Several measures of financial deregulation triggered housing investment and consumption. The first was the vast appreciation of Taiwan currency. The rate of increase value of the NT dollar was more than 50 per cent between 1986 and 1989 (*Ibid.*, p. 203). This was due to the relaxation of foreign exchange restrictions in 1987. Foreign capital surged into Taiwan's financial market to invest in Taiwan dollars (Hsiao and Liu, 1993, p. 5). Taiwan's savings remained at 30 per cent of GNP in the 1980s (Wu, 1993, p. 30). As the central government decontrolled the interest rate, it began to decrease (Li, 1998, p. 136), which encouraged both consumption and investment. More investors could get a low-interest loan and depositors sought better returns than from bank savings. Both consumers and investors converged in the housing market, resulting in a surge in housing speculation (see figure 5.4).

Figure 5.4. Newly built private housing in a Taipei suburb.

In order to cool down the skyrocketing housing prices, the central government instructed financial institutions to set limits on the amount and length of loans on land in 1989. The housing price finally dropped a little in 1990. The momentum of housing speculation, however, continued, and housing price rises were maintained between 1990 and 1992 (see figure 5.3). Since 1992, overproduction and disastrous mudslides finally induced a housing price decline in Taipei. The economy during the 1990s could no longer maintain high and lasting growth. From 1992 to 2002, the net GDP growth rate decreased from 7.5 per cent to 3.1 per cent (Taiwan Year Book 2002). In 2001, the growth rate became negative (–2.2 per cent). The Asian financial crisis induced an economic recession, and gradually reduced the housing value, but only marginally. However, during the economic downturn, housing prices in the city continued to remain high.

The housing boom since the mid-1980s caused a serious problem of housing affordability. The average price of a 30 ping apartment grew to 11 times the average annual disposable family income, in 1989, in Taipei City (Shih, 2001, p. 6). Thirty ping (1067 ft²) is the average size of apartments in Taipei City; they usually contain three bedrooms, one bathroom, one kitchen, and one living room. Although the housing price to disposable family income ratio fell to 6.2 in 2000 (*Ibid.*), the housing price was still expensive for many people in the city. As mentioned above, the standard housing price to average family income in Taipei City was 4.91 in 1996 (see table 5.1). In comparison, in the United States, the median housing price was US$115,800 and the median family income US$42,300 (HUDUS, 1999), and the ratio of the median housing price to median family income was 2.74 in 1996. With the high housing price to family income ratio, many lower income families are left out of the housing market. Urban slums and suburban squatter settlements are the housing supply for the poor.

High Homeownership Rate and Social Inequality in Taipei

Even though the housing price in Taiwan has remained high, the homeownership rate has been rising. It was 65.2 per cent in 1985 before the housing boom, and rose to 80.2 per cent in 2000 (see figure 5.5). One explanation is that as housing prices remain high, housing becomes a safe investment which is good for the consumers (see figure 5.6). As there are abundant buyers in the market, housing prices remain

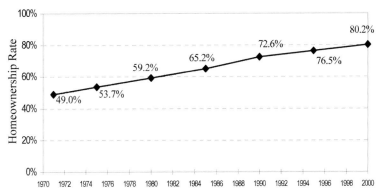

Figure 5.5. Homeownership rate, Taipei City, 1971–1999. *Source:* Taipei City Government (2001), p.15.

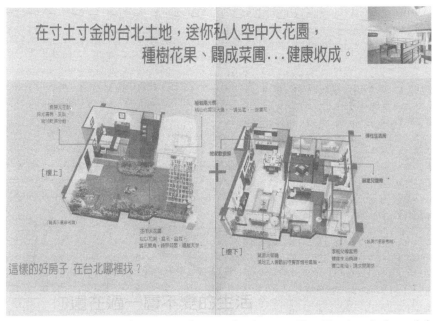

Figure 5.6. Advertisement for a private housing development. *Note:* The three-bedroom loft apartment advertised here has a garden on the roof. The caption says 'We send you the gift of a private garden on the roof in Taipei City, where every inch of the land is worth an inch of gold'.

high. The society embraces Confucian social values, such as perseverance and stability, and owning a home reflects the value of maintaining a harmonious household (Hua, 1999).[4] Therefore, even if the mortgage is a heavy financial burden, many people still want to be a homeowner for economic and psychological reasons.[5]

The concept that housing is an investment good, a good way of saving money, is deeply rooted in the minds of Taiwan people (Chang and Peng, 1998; Hua, 1999). In Tseng's (1994) study of the urban consciousness of migrants from their experiences of buying houses in Taipei City, the urban migrants included political refugees from China in 1949 and rural-to-urban migrants. Two characteristics were significant in their consciousness: 'self-reliance is the only way to own a house' and 'housing prices always rise and never fall'. The former showed the role of the state as it extolled the value of self-reliance. The latter motivated the newcomers to participate in housing speculation. The exchange value of housing had a much more important status than its use value. As a result, Taipei is a city with real estate speculation but a low quality of living (Tseng, 1994, pp. 187–193).

Taiwan's housing authority has been encouraging housing ownership, and is very proud of the high level of ownership (DGBAS, 1993, p. 31). High homeownership, however, hides many problems. First, the measurement of homeownership cannot adequately reflect real housing tenure (Hua, 1996, p. 73). Many people live in units owned by their parents or relatives.[6] Although the homeownership rate in Taiwan is much higher than that in Europe, the United States, or Japan (their proportions are around 60 to 70 per cent) (DGBAS, 1993, p. 31), the number of persons per household in Taiwan is also higher. It was 3.77 in Taiwan in 1995, while in the United States it was 2.67 in 1994.[7] It is also important to note that Taipei had a high doubling-up rate: 14.5 per cent of households in Taipei City in 1990 shared their housing unit with another household. Living in 'owner-occupied' housing does not necessarily mean that all the residents own the housing.

Second, many housing problems are not shown in the government reports. The issue of inequality is one example. There are no statistics for the actual amount of subsidies that have been used for different groups of people, such as military personnel, government employees, etc. There is, however, no concern about the housing need of the under-advantaged. As for housing amenities, the official reports do not set criteria for substandard housing. If there are such standards as crowding ratio, doubling-up, light, noise, or maintenance, a large proportion of housing would be considered low quality (Hua, 1999, pp. 73–74).

Third, Taiwan society places much emphasis on housing ownership, as it is, relative to the stock market, a safer investment. This causes a serious waste of family and social resources. Most people, even many middle-class families have problems financing their homes (Yang, 2000). Monthly payment for mortgage is a heavy financial burden so becoming homeowners is actually equivalent to being housing slaves . The problem of affordable housing affects a large proportion of households in Taipei. Chang et al. (2001) divided households in Taipei into five income groups. The middle-income group (third in Table 5.3) paid 28.2 per cent of their disposable income in 1983; 38.4 per cent in 1988; 46.2 per cent in 1993, and 34.1 per cent in 1998 to purchase an apartment in Taipei.[8] After the housing boom the middle-income group had to pay more than one-third of their disposable income for housing mortgage. In other words, more than 80 per cent of the households in Taipei had to pay more than one-third of their disposable income on mortgage if they bought a housing unit between 1988 and 1993. In 1998, the situation improved due to a slow down of the housing market, however, more than 60 per cent of the households had to pay more than 30 per cent of their disposable income on housing mortgage. The housing boom from the late 1980s to the early 1990s continues to impose a housing affordability problem.

Table 5.3. The percentage of housing mortgage payment to disposable income, 1983–1998.

Income Group	Lowest fifth			Second		Third		Fourth		Highest fifth	
Year	Standard housing prices (NT $ 10,000)	Annual disposable income (NT $ 10,000)	% of income on mortgage	Annual income (NT $ 10,000)	% of income on mortgage	Annual income (NT $ 10,000)	% of income on mortgage	Annual income (NT $ 10,000)	% of income on mortgage	Annual income (NT $ 10,000)	% of income on mortgage
1983	174.81	19.42	51.0	27.77	35.7	35.13	28.2	44.48	22.3	69.98	14.2
1988	323.80	26.64	68.9	38.01	48.3	47.83	38.4	61.05	30.1	93.32	19.7
1993	699.96	46.06	86.1	68.29	58.1	85.93	46.2	109.53	36.2	165.78	23.9
1998	651.31	51.57	71.6	83.74	44.1	108.06	34.1	137.93	26.8	216.77	17.0

Note: Chang *et al.* (2001) assume that reasonable payment for housing mortgage is between 20 per cent and 40 percent of income, the interest rate of a twenty-year mortgage is 7 percent, and down payment is 40 per cent of the housing price. *Source:* Chang *et al.* (2001), tables 3 and 4.

The problem of housing affordability is more severe for the lower income groups. After 1983, the lowest and the second lowest fifth income groups were not able to buy an apartment in Taipei, as housing purchase required more than 44 per cent of their income for mortgage (table 5.3). The lowest income group has smaller households, and these householders are youngest, mostly single with lower education attainment (Chang et al., 2001). Therefore, lower income households rely heavily on the rental housing market in Taipei.

In sum, high housing prices and the high homeownership rate show that housing has become an expensive commodity as homeownership has been perceived as an important way for household saving and investment. The social functions of housing are greatly undermined and neglected.

Housing Movement in Taipei

While democratization has increased opportunities for citizen participation in politics, the social attributes of different classes determine their bargaining power with the government. Indeed, the class composition of a community affects its resources, networks, and ability to attract attention from the media and the authority for collective action (Hsiao and Liu, 2002). This explains the inability of the urban poor to take collective action and why their housing movement has only marginal political importance (Shih, 2003).[9]

The weakness of social movement is also due to conflicting interests that exist between the poor and society as a whole (Hsiao and Liu, 2002). High homeownership rates imply that a large proportion of the citizens participate in the housing market which, so far, maintains high housing value. It is difficult for the housing movement to switch from the pro market-led platform when homeowners want to preserve the value of their private property.

Conflicting interests also exist between the middle class and the urban poor. Following democratization the urban regime in Taipei is increasingly based on the interests of the middle class as it has the strongest political voice. Taipei is gradually becoming a 'middle-class city' (Huang, 2002) (see Chapter 7).[10] The middle class as well as the elite in Taipei consider 'social order, city aesthetics and efficiency' their main urban goals (Shih, 2003). They have formed a new culture of citizen participation and contribute to the improvement of collective consumption in the city (see Chapter 4). However, the middle class is less concerned about the issue of social justice or the problem of the urban poor (Hsiao and Liu, 2002; Huang, 2002; Marsh, 2003).

One instance is that, in the 1990s, the City government implemented projects to build city parks, removing the slum dwellers that had lived on the land for decades. These projects created green and open space in favour of the urban middle-class voters, but they greatly reduced an important source of cheap housing. The government did not construct any low-cost housing to compensate for the slum clearance. The construction of city parks becomes a means of expelling the urban poor from the city. It raises a serious problem of social justice in the city (Hsiao and Liu, 2002), the urban poor often having to resort to informal housing on the city periphery (see figure 5.7).

A further example is that of the largest urban housing movement which protested on affordability, in Taipei City in 1989. The movement successfully pressured the central government to intervene in housing speculation. A new mortgage programme was targeted at increasing homeownership for those who could not otherwise afford the high housing prices rather than fundamentally changing the housing market. The housing movement is organized by the middle class, with the supply of low-income housing as a low priority, because its primary goal was the problem of housing affordability for the middle-class people (Shih, 2001, p. 26). Housing for the poor is still not fully recognized as an urgent social problem.

Figure 5.7. Treasure Hill, squatter housing in Taipei.

Housing Policy: The Roles of Central and City Government

What are the reactions of the government at different levels to the housing problems? Housing provision for the urban poor is more difficult now due to the rise of neoliberalist ideology, which dominates in Taipei's city politics. As Taipei shifts towards an entrepreneurial city, the neoliberalist project began with the first elected mayor, Chen Shui-Bian, in 1994. His urban policy was to build 'an efficient, entrepreneurial, globally-competitive, and citizen-based city'. In order to build a city with order and beauty, he removed 1,000 residents to construct a park in 1997. The park project was to improve the city image, and was small scale. The project was continued under the present mayor, Ma Ying-Jeou. With the recent economic downturn, the city is now more determined to restore economic growth as the important goal, rather than the social issue of housing.

In terms of housing policy, the policy implementation is a top-down and state-centred process. The central government enacts polices and regulations, and the local government implements them. The central government refers to the reports from local governments in formulating housing plans, but it is the power to decide the quantity and priority of public housing development and mortgage. Therefore, the central government has the dominant position to enact housing policies.

The central government provides strong leadership in the economy but plays only a minor role in housing. Fu-Kuo Mi (1988) explains the marginal status of housing policy in Taiwan, by applying the work of Castells, Goh, Kwok and Kee (1988) on Hong Kong and Singapore's public housing. He argues that although the political need, maintaining political stability and legitimization, were the same as these governments' concerns, Taiwan's government never treated public housing as an important element in reducing the cost of reproducing the labour force. Instead, a substantial proportion of public housing is to reward the supporters of the KMT state – military dependents and government employees. Thus, the housing programme was excluded from public investment for economic development. As a result, the private sector has become the major housing provider; 95 per cent of all housing stocks are privately constructed (Lin, 1996, p. 84).

Increasing homeownership has been the dominant goal of Taipei's housing policy. Among the housing that was either constructed or subsidized by the state between 1950 and 1999, less than 3 per cent of the units in Taipei was rental housing; 97 per cent was for sale (Shih, 2001, p. 26). The qualification for housing subsidies is lax so that the middle and upper-middle income class are eligible to apply. Due to the high housing prices in the city, the citizens who benefit from housing subsidies are predominantly the middle class. Among them, military families and government employees who are supporters of the state receive the largest subsidies. Housing subsidies for low-income people are limited. Very few policies are related to renters, especially low-income renters. A small proportion of public rental housing, little subsidy for low-income renters, and a housing law that does not protect tenants all contributed to the lack of affordable housing for the poor. The housing policy favours buyers over renters. As a result, housing policy worsens social inequality.

The private sector plays the major role to supply housing. The KMT state enacted market-led development to ensure support from the local elite. By authorizing the power of land-use planning to local governments (see Chapter 4) that were mostly under private developers' control, the state allows land speculation, which benefits land developers and the economic elite (Chang, 1992; Chen, 1995). The housing market functions in the absence of strict regulations from the state (Hsu, 1988; Li, 1998; Tseng, 1994). Without an effective and fair policy to redistribute profit, there is little to impede land speculation and the concentration of wealth to real estate developers.

The lack of adequate regulations in housing has contributed to the pervasive existence of an informal housing sector. Hsu's 1988 research into the housing market in peripheral Taipei concluded that the informal sector in housing production, exchange, and consumption played an important role in mitigating housing shortage as a stop gap measure. The extensive development of the informal sector was the result of the state's negligence because the profit from real estate has been the major revenue source for local politicians and business groups. Currently, informal housing in Taipei appears to be in check. The proportion of the city's population in squatter settlements greatly reduced from more than 30 per cent in the 1960s to about 5 per cent in the 1990s (Shih, 2003).

The design of housing policy implicitly encourages speculation due to the tolerance of the state. The land sales tax system does not redistribute real estate profits appropriately to the rest of society. The system also allows the resale of real estate within a short period of time. Because of the low property tax, homeowners who own more than one housing unit can afford to keep their houses vacant rather than to rent them out, since the cost of housing maintenance is relatively low. One other reason is that housing ownership is a long-term household investment; owners are looking for long-term value gain rather than short-term returns. Any downturn in housing prices is viewed as a short-term fluctuation, while long-term housing value increase is assumed to be assured. Another reason for the high vacancy rate is due to the lack of effective legal protection for renters. Landlords often avoid potential trouble that tenants may cause. Therefore, the proportion of vacant houses was about 17 per cent in Taiwan and 12 per cent in Taipei in 1998 (TRERC, 1999). These high vacancy rates were partly due to the excessive housing construction after 1992. The speculation in the late 1980s greatly increased housing demand based on the investment incentive (Peng *et al.*, 1995, p. 410). After the rise in housing prices slowed down in the 1990s, many investors held on to their housing and waited for a better time to sell. Therefore, the vacancy rate remained at a high level in Taipei City.

Consequently, housing speculation has increased the concentration of ownership. In 1979, 15 per cent of homeowners had two or more housing units, and multiple-ownership consisted of 32 per cent of the total housing units in Taipei. In 1994, the distribution of housing was more unequal; 17 per cent of homeowners had two or more housing units and they owned 35 per cent of housing units in Taipei City (CPA, 1996, p. 264; Li, 1998, pp. 97–98). In the same period of time, the Gini coefficient increased from 0.285 to 0.316 and the ratio of the highest fifth's income to the lowest fifth's rose from 4.34 to 5.42 (CEPD, 1996). As economic restructuring contributes to the increasing social inequality, the social gap manifests itself most prominently in homeownership.

Summary and Conclusion

The housing boom in the late 1980s worsened the problem of housing affordability in Taipei City. More than 60 per cent of the City's households have to spend more than 34 per cent of their disposable income on mortgage in pursuit of homeownership. The high housing prices encourage land speculation as housing demand for ownership remains high. The homeownership rate in Taipei has been rising. Other signs of speculation are the high portion of multiple housing unit ownership and high vacancy rate.

Low-income housing was given a marginal status in Taiwan's housing policy and urban policy of Taipei in the 1990s, when political democratization and economic liberation became the two major forces restructuring the society. Economic liberation increases the coalition between the capitalists and the state at the levels of central government and local government. Political democratization opens the opportunity for participation of the capitalists as well as the middle class through the election system and collective action. Without strong political organization speaking out for low-income classes, their influence on policy formation is negligible, and their housing problems are ignored.

There are three key features of housing policy in the neoliberalist era. First, the power of the private developers has increased, so has their influence over housing policy and the housing market. Second, the lower classes in Taipei suffer the problem of affordability due to the housing speculation. The market-led housing policy predominantly aims at stimulating housing demand and maintaining housing prices. Third, the market-led development of housing policy does not provide housing for the low-income class in the city.

The economic recession spurred on by the Asian financial crisis in the late 1990s brought about a rising unemployment rate – it increased from 1.5 per cent to 4.57 per cent from 1992 to 2001. Economic and social inequality also increased. The ratio of the highest fifth's income to the lowest fifth's rose from 5.24 to 6.39 between 1992 and 2001. Social equality has never been an objective in urban policy or housing policy in Taiwan. Urban development in Taipei aims at increasing the amenity of the city for the middle-class, and it also intends to build a favourable business environment to attract international corporations. While social inequality is growing, urban and housing policies do not address the housing need. The living space of low-income groups is diminishing. Therefore, the housing condition in Taipei raises the question of 'whose global city', raising a serious social justice issue. Taiwan's housing policy of relying almost entirely on the market clearly fails to address this issue. The state will have to consider active intervention for the underclass in order to close the social inequality gap.

Notes

1. The calculation of wealth includes the value of real estate, stock, income, and other family property.
2. The poverty line is very strict in Taiwan. Only 0.82 per cent of all households or 0.55 per cent of all population receive low-income welfare in Taiwan (DGBAS, 1998) (In the United States, this percentage is about 5 per cent).
3. Standard housing prices use 1996 as the base year to adjust housing prices by consumer price indexes. Therefore, the standardized prices take inflation into account.
4. There are several popular sayings relating to homeownership. 'You hengchan si you hengxing' means 'owning immovable property will lead to perseverance'. 'Anjia liye' means 'establishing a stable home and career', which are the social expectations of young men.
5. Housing prices have begun to fall recently in many places in Taiwan except Taipei City. The factors are related to the military threats from China since 1996, the typhoon in 1996, the Asian financial crisis in the late 1990s, and the earthquake of 21 September 1999, all of which have reduced the incentives to buy houses.

6. A few articles mentioned the possibility that more young people stayed with their parents when housing became very expensive. However, there has been no research on this topic.
7. The size of the average household in the EU countries, for example, was from 1.7 persons in Denmark to 3.4 persons in Spain in 1990. It was 3.0 in Japan in 1990.
8. Chang *et al.* (2001) assumed that reasonable payment for housing mortgage is between 20 per cent and 40 per cent of disposable income, the interest rate for twenty years' mortgage is 7 per cent, and down payment is 40 per cent of the housing price.
9. Shih (2003) also questioned whether social movement is an effective way for the poor.
10. Hsueh *et al.* (2003) also found that the out-migration from Taipei City to its surrounding areas was strong during the period of peak housing prices in Taipei City. The income of the residents in Taipei City also rose more quickly than the income of those in the outskirts of the city. This is a possible reason for the concentration of the relatively wealthy people in the centre of the city.

References

Brenner, N. and Theodore, N. (2002) Cities and the geographies of 'actually existing neoliberalism', in Brenner, Neil and Theodore, Nik (eds.) *Spaces of Neoliberalism: Urban Restructuring in North America and Western Europe*. Oxford: Blackwell Publishers, pp. 2–32.

Castells, M., Goh, L., Kwok, R. and Kee, T.L. (1988) *Economic Development and Housing Policy in the Asia Pacific Rim: A Comparative Study of Hong Kong, Singapore, and Shenzhen Special Economic Zone*. Monograph 37. Berkeley, CA: Institute of Urban and Regional Development, University of California at Berkeley.

CEPD (Council for Economic Planning and Development) (1996) *Taiwan Statistical Data Book*. Taiwan: Executive Yuan.

CEPD (2002) *Urban and Regional Development Statistics*. Taiwan: Executive Yuan.

Chang, C.F. (2003) *Taiwan gongying shiye minyinghua: Jingji misi de pipan* (*The Privatization of State-Owned Enterprises in Taiwan: A Critique of the Economic Myth*). Taiwan: Institute of Sociology, Academia Sinica.

Chang, C.O. (1995) *Taiwan diqu zhuzhai jiage zhishu zhi yanjiu* (*Research on Housing Price Indexes in Taiwan Area*). Taipei: Taiwan Council for Economic Planning and Development.

Chang, C.O. and Peng, C.W. (1998) Qiye weiji yu fangdichan jingqi (Business crisis and real estate boom). *China Times*, 1 December.

Chang, C.O., Kao, K.F. and Lin, V.C.C. (2001) Taipei Shi heli fangjia – xuqiu fenxi (Reasonable housing prices in Taipei – demand side analysis). *Zhuzhai Xuebao* (*Journal of Housing Studies*), **10**(1), pp. 51–66.

Chang, J.S. (1992) Xugou de geming (A fictitious revolution: the formation and transformation of KMT's land reform policies: 1905–1989). *Taiwan: A Radical Quarterly in Social Studies*, **13**, pp. 161–194.

Chang, T.C. (2003) Economic Liberalization, Party-state, and Political Coalition in Taiwan's Democratic Transition. Paper presented at the Ninth Annual Conference of the North America Taiwan Studies Association, Rutgers University, New Brunswick, NJ.

Chen, T.S. (1995) *Jinquan chengshi* (*Cities of Money Power: Sociological Analysis of Local Factions, Business Groups and Taipei Urban Development*). Taipei: Chuliu Publisher.

Chen, W.H. (1997) Woguo tuidong shehui fuli minyinghua de juti zoufa yu zhengce fazhan (The practice and policy development of social welfare privatization in Taiwan). *Shehui fazhan jikan* (*Journal of Social Development*). No. 18, pp. 4–9.

Chou, T.L. (2001) Taiwan guotu jingying guanli zhidu jiegou bianqian (The evolution of the management structure for state-owned land). *Renwen ji shehui jikan* (*Journal of Humanity and Society*). **13**(1), pp. 89–132.

Chu, W.W. and Hung, C.Y. (2002) Ziyouhua yu qiye jituanhua de qushi (Business groups in Taiwan's post-liberalization economy). *Taiwan: A Radical Quarterly in Social Studies*, No. 47, pp. 33–83.

CPA (Construction and Planning Administration) (1996) *Zhuzhai zixun tongji huibao* (*Statistical Report on Housing Information*). Taiwan: Ministry of the Interior.

Crotty, J. (2002) Trading state-led prosperity for market-led stagnation: from the golden age to global neoliberalism, in Dymski, Gary A. and Isenberg, Dorene (eds.) *Seeking Shelter on the Pacific Rim: Financial Globalization, Social Change, and the Housing Market.* Armonk, NY: M.E. Sharpe, pp. 21–41.

DGBAS (Directorate-General Budget, Accounting and Statistics) (1992) *Guofu diaocha* (*National Wealth Report*). Taipei: Executive Yuan.

DGBAS (1993) *Report on the Housing Status Survey in Taiwan Area, 1993.* Taipei: Executive Yuan.

DGBAS (1996) *Report on the Survey of Family Income and Expenditure in Taiwan Area of Republic of China.* Taipei: Executive Yuan.

DGBAS (1998) Relaxed Standard Caused the Increase of Low-Income Households. Taipei Executive Yuan, http://www.dgbasey.gov.tw/dgbas03/bs3/report/n871130.htm.

DGBAS (2001) *Report on the Survey of Family Income and Expenditure in Taiwan Area of Republic of China.* Taipei: Executive Yuan.

GIO (Government Information Office) (2002) *The Republic of China Yearbook – Taiwan 2002.* http://www.gio.gov.tw/taiwan-website/5-gp/yearbook/.

HDTCG (Housing Department of Taipei City Government) (1987) *Gouzhai shinian: Taibei shi.* (*Housing in Taipei: 1976–1985*). Taipei: Taipei City Government.

HDTCG (1996) *Taibei Shi gouzhai tongji nianbao* (Annual Report on Public Housing in Taipei City). Taipei: Taipei City Government.

Hsiao, M.H.H. and Liu, H.J. (1993) Taiwan de tudi zhuzhai wenti yu wu zhuwuzhe yundong de xianzhi (Land-housing problems and the limits of the non-homeowners movement in Taiwan). *Hong Kong Journal of Social Science*, No. 2, pp. 1–38.

Hsiao, M.H.H. and Liu, H.J. (2002) Collective action toward a sustainable city: citizens' movements and environmental politics in Taipei, in Evans, Peter (ed.) *Livable Cities? Urban Straggles for Livelihood and Sustainability.* Berkeley, CA: California University Press, pp. 67–94.

Hsu, K. J. (1988) Taibei bianyuan diqu zhuzhai shichang zhi shehuixue fenxi (A sociological analysis of the housing market in peripheral Taipei). *Taiwan: A Radical Quarterly in Social Studies*, **1**(2/3), pp. 149–210.

Hsueh, C. (1994) Zongti shiheng yu geti tiaozheng (The inbalance of macro economy and the adjustment of micro economy), in *Chanye jiegou yu gongping jiaoyi fa* (*Industrial Structure and Equal Trade Law*). Taiwan: Institute of Humanity and Social Science, Academia Sinica.

Hsueh, L.M. (1992) Pingjun diquan tiaoli xiuzheng fang'an pinyi (Revising the law of equalization of land rights). *Jingji qianzhan* (*Economy prospects*), **28**, pp. 127–131.

Hsueh, L.M. (1996) *Taiwan diqu heli fangjia zhi tantao* (*The Exploration of Reasonable Housing Prices in Taiwan*). Taiwan: Council for Economic Planning and Development, Executive Yuan.

Hsueh, L.M., Chen, Y.C. and Tseng, S.P. (2003) Quyu renkou qianru Taibei duhuiqu didian xuanze zhi shizheng yanjiu (Locational choice in cross-regional migration: an empirical study of the Taipei Metropolitan area). *2003 Annual Conference of Chinese Society of Housing Study.* Taipei: Chinese Society of Housing Study.

Hua, C.I. (1996) Qingyi fei-zhengzhixing shuju yanni quanguo zhuzhai zhengce (A plea for non-political, quantitative approach to housing policy). *Zhuzhai xuebao* (*Journal of Housing Studies*), **4**, pp. 73–75.

Hua, C.I. (1999) Da po zhuzhe you qiwu misi (Breaking the myth of home ownership). *China Times*, 31 January.

Huang, L.L. (2002) Dushi gengxin yu dushi tongli: Taibei he Xiangang de bijiao yanjiu (Urban redevelopment and urban governance: a comparative study of Taipei and Hong Kong). PhD Thesis, Taipei: Graduate Institute of Building and Planning, National Taiwan University.

HUDUS (Department of Housing and Urban Development, United States) (1999) http://www.huduser.org/periodicals/ushmc/winter99/histdat3.html.

Jou, S.C. (1999) Zaizao lao Taibei (Rebuilding the Old Taipei: an analysis of urban renewal policy). *Journal of Geographical Science* (Taipei Department of Geography, National Taiwan University), No. 25, pp. 15–44.

Li, K.C. (1999) Burst Bubble? Taiwan's troubled property market. *Quanghua zazhi (Sinorama).* February.

Li, W. (1998) *Housing in Taiwan: Agency and Structure?* Aldershot: Ashgate.

Lin, T.C. (1996) *Woguo xianyou zhuzhai butie ziyuan zhenghe yu yunyong zhi yanjiu (The Integration and Application of Resources on Housing Subsidies)*. Taiwan: Council for Economic Planning and Development, Executive Yuan.

Marsh, R.M. (2003) Contestations in Taiwan society: social class and government welfare. Paper presented at the Ninth Annual Conference of the North America Taiwan Studies Association, Rutgers University, Brunswick, NJ.

Mi, F.K. (1988) Tawian de gonggong zhuzhai zhengce (Public housing policy in Taiwan). *Taiwan: A Radical Quarterly in Social Studie*s, **1**(2/3), pp. 97–147.

Ministry of the Interior, Statistics Department (2002) *Survey on the Living Conditions of Low-Income Households.* Taipei: Ministry of the Interior.

Peng, C.W., Chen, Y.S., Chang, C.O. and Lin, C.C. (1995) Taiwan diqu kongwu diaocha yu ge'an Yanjiu (Survey and case studies on Taiwan's vacant houses), in *Fourth Annual Conference of Chinese Society of Housing Study*. Taipei: Chinese Society of Housing Study.

Shih, C.H. (2001) The emerging rental housing market in Taiwan. Master's Thesis, Graduate Institute of Building and Planning, National Taiwan University, Taipei.

Shih, M. (2003) Rethinking progressive planning for squatter settlement: the case of Pao Shen Yan in downtown Taipei, Taiwan. Paper presented at t*he Ninth Annual Conference of the North America Taiwan Studies Association,* Rutgers University, New Brunswick, NJ.

Taipei City Government (2001) *Report on the Family Income and Expenditure Survey, Taipei City*. Taipei: Department of Budget, Accounting and Statistics, Taipei City Government.

TRERC (Taiwan Real Estate Research Center at Cheng-Chih University) (1999) *Season Report on Housing Information.* Taipei: Construction and Planning Administration, Ministry of the Interior, http://www.housing.nccu.edu.tw/center/.

Taiwan Yearbook (2002) Taipei: Government Information Office, http://www.gio.gov.tw/Taiwan-website/5-gp/yearbook/contents.htm.

Tseng, S.C. (1994) Zhanhou Taibei de dushi guocheng yu dushi yishi xinggou zhi yanjou (The study of urban process and urban consciousness in post-war Taipei). PhD Dissertation, Graduate Institute of Building and Planning, National Taiwan University, Taipei.

Wang, J.H. (1989) Taiwan de zhengzhi zhuanxing yu fandui yundong (Political transition and opposition movement in Taiwan). *Taiwan: A Radical Quarterly in Social Studies*, **2**(1), pp. 71–116.

Wang, J.H. (1996) *Shei tongzhi Taiwan (Who Governs Taiwan).* Taiwan: Chuliu Publishers.

Wang, J.H. (2001) Contesting flexibility: the restructuring of Taiwan's labor relations and spatial organization. *International Journal of Urban and Regional Research*, **25**(2), pp. 346–363.

Wu, C.Y. (1993) Jinrong ziyouhua de misi (Financial liberalization reconsidered: a critique from economic sociology). *Taiwan: A Radical Quarterly in Social Studies*, No. 15, pp. 1–37.

Yang, M.L. (2000) Zhongchan jieji, ni weishemo bu shengqi? (Middle class people, why aren't you angry?). *Common Wealth*, January.

Chapter Six

Domestic Politics in Urban Image Creation: Xinyi as the 'Manhattan of Taipei'

Sue-Ching Jou

During the 1990s, a new downtown, named by Taipei City Government the 'Xinyi Planning District', appeared in the eastern part of Taipei City. At present, this district is perceived by the general public and international tourists as synonymous with the most prestigious and international-oriented area in Taipei City. Business headquarters, the international financial centre, convention centres, the Civic Centre, five-star hotels, shopping malls, entertainment centres, luxury residential complexes are agglomerated in Xinyi Planning District, a CBD cityscape typical of all major global cities (figure 6.1).

Similar to the 'urban mega-projects' implemented in other global cities, this newly created urban centre has been purposefully promoted and imaged by Taipei City government as a miniature of New York's Manhattan, a response to global-city competition and network building. It also expresses the convergence of landscape and developmental process in global cities around the world. These phenomena have already been well documented (Ford, 1998; Olds, 1997, 2001; Zukin, 1992). However, development of global cities generalized by a comprehensive global-city model (Smith, 1998; Taylor, 1999; Yeoh, 1999; Hill and Kim, 2000; Marcuse and Kempen, 2000; Wang, 2003) is, in fact, much embedded in local political and spatial contexts. Therefore, the purpose of this chapter is to examine the features of Taipei's new downtown, which is highly imbued with global images, by exploring its local context and processes.

The formation of this new city centre can be examined in its two stages

Figure 6.1. Cityscape of the Xinyi Planning District *Source:* Flytiger Co., Ltd.

of development. The first is related to the area's role and function of urban development in general and, specifically, its effects on land speculation. The new city centre development will be analyzed via the area's planning processes and its land-holding transition. The second is related to the district's initial development, which was defined by the landscapes and activities as well as the image of the city the state intended to project. In short, the developmental process of this new downtown shows that it has created a playground for Taipei's land speculation as well as a fantasy city for international capitals. In addition, this chapter attempts to analyze how the most globally-imaged new downtown has been shaped through the intertwining forces of globalization, state transformation, the real estate market and the evolution of a new consumption society.

The Planning of Xinyi Centre

Based on the orthodox CBD functions of business and consumption activities, Taipei has developed into an urban structure with two nuclei (figure 6.2). These two urban centres are described as the 'Western District' and the 'Eastern District' of Taipei City. They are characterized by a nucleus of retail and entertainment activities. The business function of the two urban cores is concentrated in surrounding areas. In the old city centre ('Western District'), the early business district was located south of the Taipei Train Station, along Chongqing South Road. In the new city centre ('Eastern District'), business activities are concentrated mainly along commercial corridors radiating from the crossroads of Renai Road and Dunhua South and North Roads, the Eastern Core. Therefore, these two urban centres are the basic central commercial districts. The government's newly-planned centre, the Xinyi Planning District city centre extended east of the Eastern Core, and has changed Taipei's traditional spatial structure (Jou, 1997; Tseng, 1994). Taipei does not have a single central business district (see Chapter 3) as most downtowns do in Western cities.

The Xinyi Planning District is located in the eastern part of central Taipei, occupying 153 hectares with housing for 38,576 people (Taipei City Government, 2001). The purpose of this special planned district is to function as 'the window of Taiwan's internationalization'. It is now the fastest growing business and entertainment area in Taipei City. Its landmark skyscraper, Taipei 101 (shown in figure 6.2), is now the tallest building in the world since it was opened at the end of 2003. The new CBD is replacing the traditional 'Eastern Core' and is becoming Taipei's dominant urban centre. In brief, Taipei's bi-nuclei spatial structure is now marked symbolically by two skyscrapers, Hsin Kong in the Western District and Taipei 101 in the Eastern District, located on either side of the central (west-east) axis of Taipei City (figure 6.2).

The origin of the Xinyi plan dates back to 1975 when under the direction of the late President Chiang Kai-Shek its purpose was the relocation of military sites[1] away from the city centre. The removal of the military base was to provide land to accommodate the rapid population growth of Taipei City. This order was carried out by the Taipei City Public Works Department,[2] under the instruction of the Executive Yuan,[3] in response to the housing crisis caused by rapid urban growth. The city government planning staff made three proposals. The first proposal was to build low-income housing communities in response to Executive Yuan's request. The second was to build new residential communities plus an administrative district

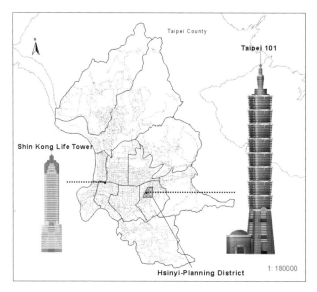

Figure 6.2. Bi-nuclei urban structure of Taipei and the location of Xinyi Planning District.

to compensate for space shortage in the old City Hall. The third was to build new residential communities with a commercial district to relieve the over-congestion in the central commercial district – the 'Western District'. Finally, the decision was made by the Secretary General of Executive Yuan, as the first plan, which was called Xinyi New Community. In this proposal a high-income residential community was incorporated.

Taipei City Government started to implement the plan for Xinyi New Community under the guidance of Executive Yuan, until a new Taipei Mayor, Lin Young-Kan, was appointed. In January 1977, under the new mayor's instruction, the plan was revised to include a new centre, because, in the second half of 1976, when the new mayor held three expert meetings for the Xinyi plan, several local planners and scholars recommended that the plan should include a new centre with multi-functions rather than just a new residential community. Although the idea of a new centre was incorporated into the planning, the Xinyi Plan was still mainly for a residential and local commercial centre.

What brought the Xinyi plan to its current state occurred under the following mayor, Lee Teng-Hui.[4] Mayor Lee adopted the design of a well-known Chinese architect in Japan, Kaku Morin,[5] who proposed to re-orient the planned centre with a new vision. His design upgraded the district into an administrative, cultural and economic centre, which would catapult Taipei into a modern, international city with a western CBD (figure 6.3). The specific tactic was to exchange the sites of the New City Hall and the National Central Library, that is to move the New City Hall to the site originally designated for the National Central Library. In addition,

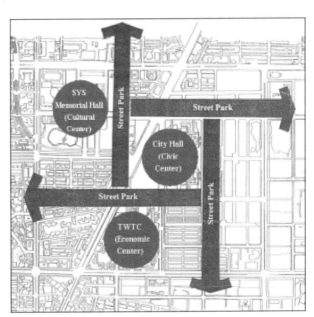

Figure 6.3. Functional layout of the Xinyi Planning District. *Source*: Chen (1998), figure 1.

it was proposed to enlarge the boundary of the Xinyi plan to include the Sun Yat-Sen Memorial Hall and to develop a Taipei World Trade Centre within the planned district. The new plan was officially announced on 30 August 1979, by the Taipei City Public Works Department, and the master plan was published on 1 May 1980, followed by detailed plan on 17 August 1981.

In order to avoid piecemeal development prevalent in Taipei's land development and to achieve successful implementation, the Xinyi Planning District adopted the strategy of land consolidation and staged development. This was to ensure that later development would follow the objectives of the whole development. In doing so, only the large developers could participate. Moreover, in order to produce a modern and international cityscape, an urban design guideline, the first in Taipei's planning history, was initiated and enforced in order to control the district's landscape (Lin, 1995).

To safeguard the successful implementation of land consolidation, a temporary construction ban was imposed for the district. Land consolidation was estimated to be completed by the end of 1986. This caused a long lag in development and, later, according to the Land Consolidation Corporation's report in 1983, disinvestments for the district.[6] As a result, the construction ban was terminated, and development was promoted by the next mayor in 1984 – the end of the first phase of land consolidation.

Development of the Xinyi Planning District

The new blueprint for the Xinyi Planning District to raise Taipei City to an international city was inaugurated, but initial development was sluggish. As described above, following the announcement of the master plan in 1980, there was a long wait until development commenced in 1987. In 1991, completed floor space accounted for only 20 per cent of overall planned floor space, increasing to 30 per cent by 1997. Before 1997, most of the development activities in the district were either public projects or luxurious residential condominiums (figure 6.4). In the early 1990s, development for commercial business was stagnant and most of the land designated for those activities was fenced off with no sign of development. Apart from the Taipei World Trade Centre and Civic Centre, and the gateway to the district, for many years the whole Xinyi Planning District was disjointed with scattered construction sites, dotted with piecemeal high-rise commercial buildings in the centre, surrounded by the new luxurious residential condominium complex at the edge (figure 6.5). It was not until the late 1990s that development began to speed up and the emergence of Taipei's Eastern District became visible (figure 6.1).

Xinyi is a benchmark urban project that aims to remake Taipei City into an international city. Why did it have such a sluggish start in the first decade? Partly, it

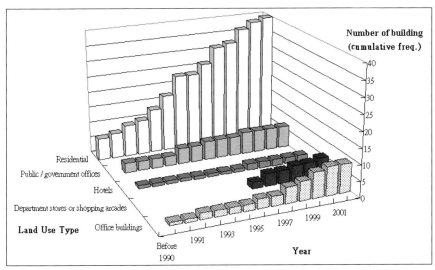

Figure 6.4. Total number of buildings completed by land-use type and by year. *Source*: Adapted from databanks of *China Times* (http://news.chinatimes.com) and *United Daily News* (http://udnpaper.com) and field survey.

Figure 6.5. Xinyi Planning District before 1997 *Source:* Chen, M.M. et al. (1999) *Above Taipei*. Taipei: Yuan-Liou Publishing Co., Ltd., pp. 128-9.

was due to inefficiency in land preparation by the public agency, but mostly it was due to the area's pivotal role as the arena for real estate intrigue. The development lag combined with the weakening state power and the escalation in land prices in the late 1980s provided the district with an unrestricted opportunity for large-scale land speculation, monopolized and manipulated by large business groups.

As Xinyi Planning District was developed by using former military land, government owned land accounted for almost two-thirds of the total area (figure 6.6). Land ownership enabled the government to play a significant role in the

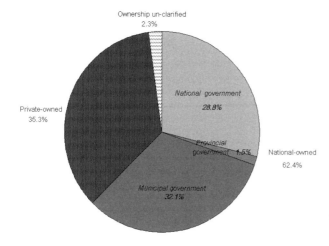

Figure 6.6. Distribution of land ownership in Xinyi Planning District, 1980. *Source:* Quin Huan Consulting Company (1997).

district's development at the planning phase. By the end of the 1980s when the area started developing, the state was no longer a coherent unit[7] since the authoritarian regime was replaced by democratized politics. At the developmental stage, the district was under a totally different polity from the one under which the Xinyi Plan was initiated. Government agencies were no longer under unilateral central control, but were subordinated to different branches of the government (as illustrated in figure 6.6). These branches now had certain autonomy, power and legal rights. Holding land parcels in Xinyi Planning District, which had extraordinarily high value, became economic and political assets for bartering and bargaining. The newly gained assets and power significantly affected their actions in Xinyi's development, which will be discussed later.

Although one-third of the district's land was owned by the private sector, the large-scale development and the potential profits generated by the land market had limited the players in the private sector. Only large business groups with property development or financial subsidiaries and affiliates competed in purchasing private land or bidding for government land. In total, large business groups currently own around 57 per cent of the private land. Land deals during 1987 and 1988 started the district's land speculation, which generated the escalation of land prices in Taipei (Jou, 1997; see also Chapter 5). Figure 6.7 illustrates the escalation of land prices in Xinyi Centre and the large business groups' land purchasing activities and transaction prices.

Development Stages of Taipei's Eastern District

In addition to land speculation, the distribution of land ownerships in Xinyi Centre displayed the power which governed the district's development. Although the

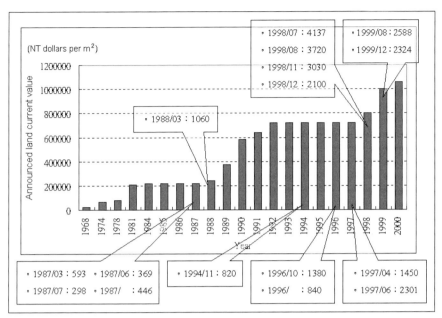

Figure 6.7. Growth of land prices and land transaction events in Xinyi Planning District. *Note:* Transaction events are documented in boxes by date (year and month) and by price (thousand NT dollars per ping). Ping is the local unit to measure the area of land, which is equivalent to 35.6 square feet.
Source: Derived from *Taipei Statistical Book* (various years) and adapted from databanks of *China Times* and *United Daily News.*

city government took the lead in the final planning of Xinyi Centre and controlled around one-third of the land, this still has not guaranteed the local government's power in controlling development. The role of city government has been strictly limited to land-use-related planning, since the project was initiated. To implement the planning of Xinyi Centre, the city government still had to rely on other resources allocated by the central government. The central government, in fact, directly or indirectly controlled the planning and implementation of the Xinyi development.

Before 1990, the district plan was first carried out by the Ministry of Economic Affairs. As the Taiwan government was in a developmental state, the Ministry is the most powerful central government agency for development and construction. In January 1986, Taipei World Trade Centre was officially introduced by the China External Trade Development Council,[8] an unofficial affiliate to the Ministry, in the Xinyi Centre to promote Taiwan's international trade. The World Trade Centre[9] includes the International Trade Building, Exhibition Hall and Grand Hyatt Hotel, which were built to form an integrated business complex. With the World Trade Centre, the icon representing the international and economic centre of Taipei, the Xinyi Centre became the most important site for global reach in Taipei, functionally or symbolically. The Ministry played a critical role in navigating the Centre to become an 'international and economic centre' in Taiwan.

At the same time as the World Trade Centre was initiated, a large shopping centre in this new district was proposed by the Department of Commerce, a department within the Ministry. The proposal was based on the rationale that a modern shopping centre was an important commercial and leisure node for a large metropolis. The consumption activities would stimulate the consumption level of the city. It was to bring in new management technology to generate new and advanced service industries for the whole of Taiwan as well. The shopping centre was a policy instrument to promote the modernization of domestic commercial industries. For a successful shopping mall project, the central government decided that extensive land had to be provided, urban infrastructure (especially the subway connection) had to be improved, and urban land zoning probably had to be changed. All these preconditions had to rely on the local government's coordination and management. The Ministry was willing to assist in financing by soliciting private investment, but expected Taipei City Government to take the lead in organizing and implementing the project.

The proposal was finally withdrawn. Two critical factors hindered the shopping mall project and forced the city government to give up the project by 1988. The first was related to the lack of cooperation from the Ministry of National Defence and the municipal government. As the land in this district was largely to be converted from military sites, the most accessible land for commercial uses was controlled by the Ministry of National Defence. As the land value began to escalate in the district, the Ministry of National Defence preferred to sell the land to the private sector than to transfer it to the Taipei City Government. The second was related to the unwillingness of the Ministry to relax the regulations of land purchase financing for the shopping mall. At the same time, the Executive Yuan also sent a directive forbidding Taipei City Government's participation in a private commercial project. With regards to promoting the shopping mall project in the Xinyi Centre, the central government played a passive, and at times, obstructive role compared to the World Trade Centre project.

In the late 1980s, the political transformation in Taiwan had just begun. Essentially, the authoritarian state remained in operation. The inactiveness of the central state in promoting the shopping mall in the Xinyi Centre was one of the many signs of its negligence over the role of service industries for Taiwan's economic development, because the central government still considered Taiwan an industrial developmental state, continuously promoting manufacturing policies at the post-industrial age.

Between 1990 and 1995, Xinyi Centre could barely fulfil its original plan. It was not working as the economic centre, civic centre or cultural centre of Taipei (see figure 6.3), even after most of the public investment projects had been completed.[10] The Xinyi plan was tarnished as a promised successful and glorious urban project because only two private office buildings were completed. The private commercial developers were hesitant, and there were public accusations of government's inefficacy in promoting private development. The criticism was due to the government's inability to control the land speculation, and to attract sufficient investment from the private sector or the public sector.[11] Instead, several luxurious residential condominiums were built and reached the highest selling prices in Taipei's housing market. The success of the residential development began to direct the new Eastern Urban Centre into a high-income housing area in Taipei City. At the same time, most of Taipei's citizens were suffering from a serious shortage of affordable housing (see Chapter 5), and the district's development was synonymous with social and spatial injustice within the city. The entire project was severely criticized in a public forum.

In order to put the project back on the original tract, Taipei City Government began hesitantly to release its land for sale or lease, in order to diffuse the intense land price escalation. It bought out all its own land tracts reserved for land consolidation. This action had a considerable negative effect on the city government's treasury, as the city-owned land was inefficiently used. The incompetence, incapability and inefficacy of the central state was explained by shifting the blame to the city government's mismanagement in infrastructure development, especially in transportation planning and routing. When the new City Hall was put into operation in 1994, the influx of thousands of new city government employees and clients caused congestion in local traffic. As the traffic conditions deteriorated, Xinyi Centre became inaccessible, and traffic over-flowed into Taipei's southern and eastern traffic routes.

By the second half of the 1990s, Xinyi Centre began to establish itself as the new downtown, as it is now recognized by Taipei's citizens. The first Taipei mayor's election was a crucial time for the district's development. Active promotion of Xinyi Centre development became the most visible item of the newly elected mayor's urban policies. Immediately after Mayor Chen Shui-Bian took office, he requested the Bureau of Finance and the Department of Urban Development to formulate an effective strategy to revitalize the district's development. In attracting development to the idle land, the Bureau of Finance proposed that the city government should lease developmental rights of the city-owned land to the private sector, and actively encourage public-private partnership. The Department of Urban Development initiated the release of public land as a strategy to promote the district's development. The Department made a specific proposal for Taipei Financial Centre along similar lines as the central government's plan for the Asian Financial Centre. In addition, after an overall review of the Xinyi Planning District Master Plan and

Detailed Plan, the Department used floor space subsidies and fines as instruments to activate commercial developments for both private land and public land.

With these new stimuli, the district's development speeded up. The new mayor's actions on Xinyi Centre sent out symbolic but important messages to Taipei City. The first elected mayor of the capital city, Chen Shui-Bian recognized the potential and strategic role of the Xinyi Centre for Taipei, and even for Taiwan, in the globalization era. He began actively promoting the project of Taipei Financial Centre, which had been proposed by the previous mayor in 1991. He declared the critical role of Taipei Financial Centre in enhancing Taipei in the competition for a regional financial centre in the Asia Pacific.

Xinyi Centre was significant politically and economically in two aspects for the new urban regime. First, as a mayor from the opposition party to the central government, this 'urban mega project' was a perfect medium to alleviate the confrontation between the central state and the local state. He adopted a pragmatic strategy to regulate the two-tier governments' relationship. The realization of the Taipei Financial Centre needed the financial endorsement of the central government, and it relied heavily on central government's promotion and deregulation of financial control. The leasing of the developmental rights by tender was a new method[12] for public-private partnership. Chen enabled the Taipei City Government to change its role in major urban projects by providing the land and setting up the regulations to facilitate the government agencies, private developers and users. Under a flexible, fair and reasonable investment environment, all parties gained mutual benefits. This new regime significantly changed the anti-capitalist image of the Democratic Progress Party, the party of the new mayor.

This project served as a catalyst for a new growth coalition, between different levels of the government and the private sector, for urban development of Taipei and economic development for Taiwan. With the demand of very large capital investment for a high-rise in the Taipei Financial Centre, no single domestic enterprise could undertake the project alone. Seven business consortiums were formed to bid for the developmental rights of the Financial Centre. The combinations and compositions of these corporate coalitions, in some ways, reflected the corporate networks of Taiwan's large business groups. In addition, to supporting the development of the Taipei Financial Centre, the central government, especially the Ministry of Finance, showed a great deal of flexibility and deregulated many security firms and banks who invested in real estate. Specifically, the Ministry provided around NT$20 billion of low-interest loan to the Taipei Financial Centre Corp. In short, the Taipei Financial Centre was a demonstration project on how to organize a mega-urban project, and to sell Taipei as a global city, similar to the Petronas Tower in Kuala Lumpur, Malaysia. A coalition of the central government, local government and domestic large business groups had to be formed.

Although the Taipei Financial Centre project was symbolic for the district's development, the Xinyi Centre's vitality in the second half decade of the 1990s owed much to a series of large-scale outdoor activities organized by the city government and the successful investment of Warner Village. The spate of popular activities and building projects mutually enhanced each other, and together they were powerful for image making in promoting Xinyi Centre as the place for investment.

Imaging the Xinyi Planning District

Similar to recent development in other world cities, the Xinyi Centre development has focused on place promotion and image making to attract investment and consumption in recent years (Bradley, *et al.*, 2002; Goss, 1997; Hubbard, 1996; King, 1995; Short and Kim, 1999; Wu, 2000*a*, 2000*b*). What made the experience of place promotion and image making of this new urban centre different from those of other cities was more in the political realm than in the economic one. Promoting the development of the Xinyi Centre had a great symbolic meaning for the first elected mayor in gaining political legitimacy and promoting a new political ideology.

At the beginning of 1996, the second year of Chen's term as mayor, he focused on finding mechanisms to accelerate the development of Xinyi Centre. Promoting the Xinyi Centre development was closely related to image-making activities, especially to the image of the district's future. 'Creating the Manhattan of Taipei' became the slogan and mission for the city government led by the elected mayor. Taipei Financial Centre was the most symbolic and representative landscape for the city's mission and image making.

The major objective for the Xinyi Planning District in the Second Review had to do with developing the District into the 'window of Taiwan's Internationalization'. This objective was in accordance with the economic policy of the Asia Pacific Operation Centre (APOC), a project by the central government. The district was to function as the international financial, business and entertainment centre, the key ingredients for a global-city function. In order to make the Xinyi Centre a hub of high-rise offices to match the image of a Manhattan, the city government purposefully reduced the 10 per cent building coverage ratio without changing the building bulk control, thus drastically increasing building height. In the overall review of the master plan and detailed plan, land-use management was also changed from a rigid control for a modernist cityscape, which was stipulated in the original land-use plan and urban design,[13] to a mosaic of postmodern urban landscape (Tsai, 1998). Taipei City Government used urban planning instruments effectively through the Second Overall Review of the Xinyi Planning District to achieve its urban image objective. Taipei's Manhattan was synonymous with Xinyi Planning District.

As Xinyi Centre became a multi-functional centre, the Civic Centre was incorporated as one of the major components. The City Hall had a special meaning to the newly elected mayor. The geographical location of the City Hall was at the eastern end of the Renai Road. In contrast to the Presidential Hall of Taiwan, which is located at the western end of the Renai Road, Chen demonstrated spatially the difference between his regime and the central regime. Xinyi Centre became an effective instrument for expressing symbolically contending politics.

During his term of office, Mayor Chen worked hard on 'City Diplomacy', resolving the difficult obstacles imposed by the central government. The visibility of Taipei City Hall was important in promoting the city and city diplomacy.[14] As the Xinyi Centre functioned as the 'window of internationalization for Taiwan', Chen actively sought to twin Taipei with overseas cities, the intention being to raise the status of the city. The Taipei City Government eagerly participated in the International Union of Local Authorities (IULA).[15]

The new urban regime embraced the political ideology of democracy. Citizens were the master of the country and the clients of the city government. The lobby of the City Hall was remodelled as a gallery to hold city-related exhibitions. A bookstore and a cafeteria were opened in the hallways inside the City Hall. The double-ten architectural design (a national symbol) was colourfully attached to the City Hall to demonstrate that Taipei had charm and life, not just a city with drab political iconographies.

Chen's regime purposefully created a citizen friendly environment in the City Hall. The public space in front of the City Hall was redesigned and renamed Citizen Plaza. Client oriented and citizen friendly spaces were consciously provided not only in the Civic Centre, but also in the whole Xinyi Centre. Taipei City Government organized public activities in the Xinyi Centre with festivals, hosting or encouraging large-scale events in public spaces to enliven the whole district. These programmes paved the way for the Xinyi Centre to become a higher-class consumption space. To this end, investment in the Warner Village, discussed later, was critical.

Practically all Asian-Pacific major cities race for the sky in office construction. Ownership of the tallest building in the world is equivalent to a legitimate membership of the global-city club. Skyscraper towers are promoted for global recognition and national identity to the citizens (Bunnell, 1999; Ford, 1998; Olds, 2001; Wu, 2000a, 2000b). Taipei Financial Centre, Taipei 101, the tallest skyscraper in the world when finished raised an issue. The local government took a dramatically different position from those of other world cities in the Asia-Pacific. Why was not Taipei Financial Centre initially an important project to Taipei's citizens?

There were many reasons for the omission. The most prominent was the disagreement and doubt over constructing the skyscraper, mainly related to the earthquake safety, as Taiwan is in the earthquake zone. Another reason was related to the capability of geological loading in Xinyi Planning District. Others included concern that the proposed skyscraper exceeded the allowed navigation height limit for the nearby Taipei Songshan Airport.[16] The most important reason of all, however, was related to the land speculation scandal in Xinyi Centre. The Taipei Financial Centre would be a positive symbol for Taipei City in city promotion and global city competition, but the timing was wrong for the city government during Chen's mayoralty.

Mayor Chen carefully promoted Xinyi Centre's development to illustrate the capability of the new regime in cooperating with the large business groups, which had become rich under the KMT regime. The city government proposed that spatial and social injustices that were caused by the Xinyi Centre would be balanced by transferring the financial benefits from the centre to redevelop the old city core. This proposal was widely broadcasted in the succeeding mayoral election in 1998 by Chen's camp. The purpose of the Taipei Financial Centre was to rectify the negligence and physical decay of the old city core. Despite the mayoral and city government's promotional efforts, this had little effect on most of the citizens in the old city core, as shown in the following election.

The urban regime changed during the second mayoral election at the end of 1998. The new mayor Ma Ying-Jeou used 'the axial overturn for urban development' as the main slogan in his election campaign, and Xinyi Centre lost its importance in urban policy. In order to avoid the association with large corporations and real estate speculation, Mayor Ma focused on urban redevelopment. Xinyi Centre became one of the urban planning projects but without preferential treatment; with a different slant, the role of the Centre in city promotion was now to be the cyber-city for Taipei City Government. The rhetoric of global-city competition was changed. This strategy of geographical location and the political position of City Hall, however, remained unchanged under Mayor Ma, as Chen was elected as the president of Taiwan. With the reversal of opposition party politics, city diplomacy was still relevant, and continued to play a critical role in city promotion for Mayor Ma. The Civic Centre was still promoted as a place for the citizen, and outdoor activities were still organized for the weekends. These functions fitted in with the new mayor's agenda of the healthy and citizen friendly Taipei.

The Private Sector in Place-making

After 1998, Xinyi Planning District, as a globally oriented financial centre, became the fastest growing entertainment and consumption centre in Taipei. This growth was attributed to the opening of the Warner Village multiplex. Warner Village was a joint venture between Warner Brothers International Theaters and Village Roadshow Internationals, which brought a multiplex revolution in cinema business to Taiwan. The opening of the Warner Village not only brought lucrative profits and market potential for both companies, but also determined the functional change in Xinyi Centre development.

Taiwan, one of the top ten world markets for Hollywood films, had long been an investment target for international cinema developers (Groves, 2001; Wu, 2002). Were rigid control of foreign investment removed, penetration of international capital to Taipei's entertainment would have been earlier than Warner Village's opening. Along with the apparent attempt to vitalize Xinyi Centre by Taipei City Government and the district's comparative advantages for multiplex cinemas, Warner Village brought around three million customers per year to the district by promoting American-style leisure and entertainment.

The operation of Warner Village was aided by frequent promotion and image-making activities in the surrounding public space. Those activities not only invigorated the district, but also differentiated customers to create place identity (Hsu, 2002). Differentiation of entertainment space could be clearly seen by comparing promotion activities held in Warner Village and those in Ximending, the Western District. Relatively speaking, Warner Village was more international and Western, Hollywood actually, while Ximending was more local and Asian. Many activities, especially movie premiers with famous Hollywood stars, shaped the district as an image of a globally synchronized entertainment centre. Warner Village in Xinyi Centre reflected Taiwan's market position in a Hollywood-dominated world movie industry.

In addition to large and multi-screen venues, the multiplex cinema centre was accompanied by other leisure and consumption activities. Otherwise, similar to a suburban shopping centre in Western cities, the Xinyi Centre is an urban centre. In Asia-Pacific cities, this kind of fantasy downtown has expanded quickly since the 1990s (Hannigan, 1998). Taipei is one of the typical examples. The success of Warner Village in Xinyi Centre also benefited the surrounding department stores, such as, New York New York, Hsin Kong Mitsukoshi and Neo 19. This newly emerged consumption and entertainment centre distinguished itself from centres in other districts, because consumers were willing to travel and pay higher prices. The district's image was greatly enhanced as the department store, in Taipei 101, opened at the end of 2003 with brand-name collections targeting the high-end of the consumption market and culture. In short, the whole district has now established itself as the multi-purpose new downtown of Taipei.

The status and prestige of the Xinyi Centre was greatly strengthened by the concentration of high-income condominiums. Although residential development in this district was associated with land speculation, the high land price naturally led to top market residential development. Since the early 1990s, before Xinyi Centre was recognized by the general public as a high-class entertainment and consumption centre, residential development had already been known as distinct with a high concentration of second- and third-generation (1986 onwards) luxury condominiums (table 6.1).

Table 6.1. Evolution of Taipei's high-income residential development.

Generation	Time	Type	Location	Residents
First	Before 1986	Mansion	Suburban, surrounding the Taipei Basin	Top government officials & Wealthy businessmen
Second	1986-1991 Early Stage	High-rise buildings	Renai Rd. & Dunhua S. Rd.	Top government officials & celebrities
	Later Stage		Renai Rd., Dunhua S. Rd. & Xinyi Planning District	Top government officials & Wealthy businessmen
Third	1998	High-rise complexes	Xinyi Planning District	Wealthy businessmen (esp. in information industry) & celebrities

Source: Adapted from various news reports in http://magazines.sina.com.tw/businesstimes/.

As land prices escalated in the second half of the 1980s, the high-income residential development concentrated in the most expensive locations within the city. Expensive high-rise residential condominiums were developed along Renai and Dunhua Southern Roads. These buildings housed top governmental and party officials and celebrities. In the later years, luxury condominiums in the City Centre were designed with floor space of 3,500 square feet[17] and equipped with advanced safety devices for the security and privacy of the residents. Residential development in Xinyi Centre was famous for its large housing units constructed in the early 1990s. Luxury condominium complexes have been extensively developed in recent years, which greatly enhanced Xinyi Centre's status as a high-end housing area.

The image of luxury condominiums was demonstrated by the buildings' names. Amongst the luxury condominiums constructed in the second half of the 1980s, two buildings were named as King and Queen and Xinyi National Treasure. For those constructed in the late 1990s, luxury condominiums were named Xinyi Fubang (Rich Country), Diamond 5000, National Gallery of Art, and so on. Developers used building names to reinforce the luxury image. Only a few architects would be hired to design these condominiums, and internationally known architects monopolized these projects. Following the globalization process, two international architects, Kenzo Tange and Remo Riva (P & T Group) were brought in, enhancing the global image and prestige of the district. The upper-class and globally-connected ambience of the Xinyi Centre was affirmed.

The recently opened iconic project, a symbolic landscape in the Xinyi Centre, is Taipei 101 (Taipei Financial Centre), which joined the race for tallest skyscraper in the world. In doing so, it promotes Taipei as one of the global cities in city promotion and competition (Ford, 1998). Taipei 101 is now a major player in that the international skyscraper is attracting international coverage (for example, *The New York Times International*, 11 January 2004). It is a monumental structure which produces a symbolic image for Taipei as well as Taiwan. Its status allows Xinyi Centre to compete for the regional financial hub in the Asia-Pacific, even though Taipei does not have a sufficiently strong economic base, as the state's economy has recently been facing a serious downturn and has a severe problem of capital outflow (see Chapter 2).

The symbolism of the skyscraper for a modern city can be dated back to the late nineteenth century and continues to the present (Bunnell, 1999; Cartier, 1999; Davey, 2002; Domosh, 1988; Ford, 1998; Wu, 2000*a*, 2000*b*). The skyscraper race produced a myriad of buildings more than 500 metres tall around the world (figure 6.8) and the Manhattan syndrome created a new global cityscape. Joining the global trend, Taipei 101 is the symbolic landscape and becomes the key element of the 'Manhattan of Taipei' project. This iconic building represents the power of the local corporate consortium, and brings international capital to finance current construction as well as future operation.

A city with monumental skyscrapers, as the mark of modernity, signifies the city's ability in world-class infrastructure development, which is a key ingredient for identity construction (Ford, 1998; King, 1996; Olds, 1995). A series of critical issues – the interference of airplane navigation at the planning stage, a construction accident caused by an earthquake in 2002, and a fire accident in March 2003 – initially damaged Taipei 101's role as the place-maker for local identity and

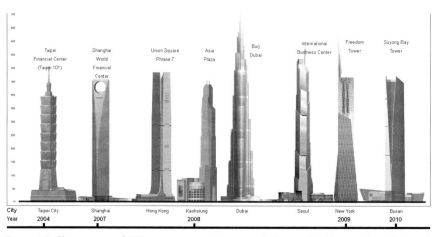

Figure 6.8. Skyscrapers of 500-metre generation around the world. *Source:* Compiled and redrawn skyscraper buildings from http://skyscrapers.com.

international reputation. As Taipei 101 is the tallest building in the world, it is now effectively winning reputation on the global-city stage.

Summary and Conclusion

Development of a downtown area is an urban process signifying that a city is pursuing globalization. In most Asian global cities, developing a new downtown is the prevalent trend (Ford, 1998; Olds, 2001; Short and Kim, 1999). Taipei is a third-tier global city in the world-city system, and its function is to link Taiwan's economy to the world market, but its downtown development process, in the face of global-city competition, has not been documented. This chapter aims to fill this gap by examining the developmental process of creating a new urban centre, the Xinyi Planning District.

Xinyi Planning District as the new city centre in Taipei now projects a global image, but its development is enmeshed in local politics. The spatial process has generated two political economic issues. The first relates to the new city centre's role and function in the urban political economy and its effects in generating the real estate market, illustrated through the district's planning processes and the history of land transfer. Although the central state initially played a leading role in planning this new city centre, a weakening of the state's role followed. The erosion of the authoritarian state has given rise to a new political interaction and caused a continuous confrontation between the city and central government. The weakened state is increasingly incapable of counter-balancing the corporate power in the real estate market, because land shortage and high rent permeates the Xinyi Planning District. The second relates to the politics of spatial form. How the spatial activities and the cityscapes are determined and how the city image is produced are the two key issues. The success of the district's development is built on the new leisure and high-income consumer classes rather than on producing a built environment for producer services. The former responds to the new rising affluence. The latter facilitates global city growth which is sluggish in Taipei (see Chapter 2). 'The Manhattan of Taipei' is a globally synchronized fantasy city rather than an international finance commanding post. Xinyi Planning District is projecting a global image, but its spatial activities are only domestic. Instead of building global activities, creating 'The Manhattan of Taipei' creates a playground for land speculation and fantasy space awaiting international capital.

Notes

1. The sites were mainly occupied by the Joint Services Forces (currently the Joint Logistic Command) under the Ministry of National Defense. The sites included the 404 arsenal factory, vehicle base service division and military vehicle division.

2. There was no planning agency in the Taipei City Government then. City planning was implemented under the authority of public works.
3. At that time, Taipei as the Capital City of the Republic of China was governed by the central government.
4. Lee is the former president of the Republic of China (Taiwan).
5. Kaku Marin is well-known for his design of several skyscrapers in Japan.
6. The construction ban applies to private development but allows public buildings to be constructed before the completion of land consolidation.
7. Jou (1997) used the concept of loosely-coupled structure to discuss the relationships of different state agencies.
8. It is the top non-profit trade promotion organization in Taiwan, founded in 1970 to help promote foreign trade. The Development Council is in fact an important outreach organization for the Ministry in promoting foreign trade, since Taiwan is not a member of the United Nations and does not have a formal relationship with many countries.
9. The Taipei World Trade Centre was opened in 1990 and Taipei World Trade Centre Exhibition Hall 2 was completed later on 26 November 1999.
10. As discussed above, the World Trade Centre was inaugurated on 9 January 1990, which was the major component of the economic centre. As for the Civic Centre, the Taipei Municipal Council was opened on 8 October in the same year. Taipei City Hall opened on 14 March 1994, and in the same year, the Xinyi District Administration Centre was also opened. The Taipei Fire Department was then moved into the Xinyi Planning District on 10 July 1996. With regards to the cultural centre, the Sun Yat-Sen Memorial Hall was already there.
11. This refers to the Ministry of National Defence and some National-owned enterprises.
12. Taipei City Government adopts the Build-Operate-Transfer mechanism to the development of the Taipei Financial Centre.
13. Xinyi Planning District is the first district that has implemented urban design control in Taipei and in Taiwan.
14. A showroom in the City Hall was open to show the achievement of city diplomacy by the Taipei City Government.
15. Taipei gained the role to host the IULA World Capitals Forum in 1998. There were 179 mayors or representatives from sixty-seven cities in fifty-eight countries attending the forum on 29 May 1998.
16. This was raised between the Taipei City Government and the Ministry of Transportation and Communications and caused the Taipei Financial Centre to change its design. This disagreement was resolved later and the Taipei Financial Centre was brought back to its original design.
17. Usually a local unit, ping, is used to measure. In most cases, floor space for a luxury condominium contains around 100 pings, equivalent to 3,500 square feet.

References

Bradley, A., Hall, T. and Harrison, M. (2002) Selling cities: promoting new images for meeting tourism. *Cities*, **19**(1), pp. 61–70.
Bunnell, T. (1999) Views from above and below: the Petronas Twin Towers and/in contesting visions of development in contemporary Malaysia. *Singapore Journal of Tropical Geography*, **20**(1), pp. 1–23.
Cartier, C. (1999) The state, property development and symbolic landscapes in high-rise Hong Kong. *Landscape Research*, **24**(2), pp. 185–208.
Chen, L.C. (1998) Anatomy of the original Xinyi plan. *Architect*, No. 8709, pp. 73–76.
Chen, M.M. *et. al.* (1999) *Above Taipei*. Taipei: Yuan-Liou Publishing Company.
Davey, P. (2002) Eastern highrise. *Cranes Today*, July, pp. 16–18.
Department of Urban Development (1997) *1996 White Paper for Taipei City's Urban Development*. Taipei: Department of Urban Development, Taipei Municipal Government.

Domosh, M. (1988) The symbolism of the skyscraper: case studies of New York's first tall buildings. *Journal of Urban History*, **14**(3), pp. 321–345.

Dovey, K. (1992) Corporate towers and symbolic capital. *Environment and Planning B*, **19**, pp. 173–188.

Fainstein, S. (1994) *The City Builder: Property, Politics and Planning in London and New York*. Oxford: Blackwell.

Ford, L. (1998) Midtown, megastructrure, and world cities. *The Geographical Review*, **88**(4), pp. 528–547.

Goss, J. (1997) Representing and re-presenting the contemporary city. *Urban Geography*, **18**(2), pp. 180–188.

Groves, D. (2001) Biz blues may run deeper than perplexing answer. *Variety*, 24–30 September, p. 13.

Hannigan, J. (1998) *Fantasy City: Pleasure and Profit in the Postmodern Metropolis*. London: Routledge.

Hill, R.C. and Kim, J.W. (2000) Global cities and developmental states: New York, Tokyo and Seoul. *Urban Studies*, **37**(12), pp. 2167–2195.

Hubbard, P. (1996) Urban design and city regeneration: social representations of entrepreneur landscapes. *Urban Studies*, **33**(8), pp. 1441–1461.

Hsu, Y.K. (2002) The production of Warner Village: a political economy approach. Master's Thesis, Department of Journalism, National Chengchi University.

Jou, S.C. (1997) *Urban Politics and Policies of Urban Development: The Cases of Xinyi-Planing Districts and Nakang Economic and Trade Park*. Final report of research project funded by the National Science Council, Republic of China. Taipei: Department of Geography, National Taiwan University.

King, A.D. (1995) Re-presenting world cities: culture theory/social practice, in Knox, P.L. and Taylor, P.J. (eds.) *World Cities in a World-System*. Cambridge: Cambridge University Press, pp. 215–231.

King, A.D. (1996) World in the city: Manhattan transfer and the ascendance of spectacular space. *Planning Perspectives*, **11**, pp. 97–114.

Lin, C.J. (1995) *Urban Design in Cities of Taiwan*. Taipei: Chuang Hsing Publisher.

Marcuse, P. and Kempen, R. (2000) Introduction, in Marcuse, P. and Kempen, R. (eds.) *Globalizing Cities: A New Spatial Order?* Oxford: Blackwell, pp. 1–21.

The New York Times International (2004) 11 January, p. 10.

Olds, K. (1995) Globalization and the production of new urban spaces: Pacific Rim megaprojects in the late 20th century. *Environment and Planning A*, **27**, pp. 1713–1743.

Olds, K. (1997) Globalizing Shanghai: the 'Global Intelligence Corps' and the building of Pudong, *Cities*, **14**(2), pp. 109–123.

Olds, K. (2001) *Globalization and Urban Change: Capital, Culture and Pacific Rim Mega-Projects*, Oxford: Oxford University Press.

Quin Huan Consulting Company (1997) *Technical Report for Overall Review of the Xinyi Planning District Detailed Plan*. Taipei: Department of Urban Development, Taipei Municipal Government.

Short, J.R. and Kim, Y.H. (1999) *Globalization and the City*. New York: Longman.

Smith, C.S. (1999) Race for the sky. *Wall Street Journal* (Eastern Edition), 2 June, **233**(106), p. B1.

Smith, M.P. (1998) The global city – whose city is it anyway? *Urban Affairs Review*, **33**, pp. 482–488.

Taipei City Government (2001) *Second Overall Review of the Xinyi-Planning District*. Taipei: Taipei City Government.

Taylor, P. (1999) The so-called world cities: the evidential structure within a literature. *Environment and Planning A*, **31**, pp. 1901–1904.

Tseng, H.C. (1994) Urban processes and formation of urban consciousness for Taipei City after World War II. PhD Dissertation, Department of Civil Engineering, National Taiwan University.

Tsai, C.K. (1998) Power structure under urban development processes: the case of Xinyi-Planning District. Master's Thesis, Department of Geography, National Taiwan University.

Wang, C.H. (2003) Taipei as a global city: a theoretical and empirical examination. *Urban Studies*, **40**(2), pp. 309–334.

Wu, F.L. (2000*a*) Place promotion in Shanghai, PRC. *Cities*, **17**(5), pp. 349–361.

Wu, F.L. (2000*b*) The global and local dimensions of place-making: remaking Shanghai as a world city. *Urban Studies*, **37**(8), pp. 1395–1377.

Wu, M.C. (1991) Comparative studies of land uses in Taipei City's Central Business Districts. Master's Thesis, Department of Geography, National Taiwan University.

Wu, N.H. (2002) Multiplexes eat up B.O. *Variety*, 24–30 June, p. 10.

Yeoh, B.S.A. (1999) Global/globalizing cities. *Progress in Human Geography*, **23**(4), pp. 607–616.

Zukin, S. (1992) The city as landscape of power: London and New York as global financial capitals, in Budd, L. and Whimster, S. (eds.) *Global Finance and Urban Living*. London: Routledge, pp. 195–223.

Chapter Seven

Social Polarization and Income Inequality: Migration and Urban Labour Markets

Po-Fen Tai

Globalization leads to a new pattern of international labour migration. Labour migration affects the urban labour market and employment structure, and is often accompanied by social transformation. Liberalizing and deregulating a state's cross-border economic activities results in international movement of capital and people. Following capital flows, a new migrant system in Asia – the workers from the low-wage countries flowing across national boundaries to the newly industrialized areas – has been noted (Stahl and Appleyard, 1992; Athukorala, 1993; Lim and Abella, 1994; Findlay *et al.*, 1998).

Friedmann and Wolff (1982) first developed a hierarchy of types of city, culminating in the 'world city'. Looking exclusively at occupational structure, they reveal the dramatic changes in the distribution of employment, the polarization of class divisions, physical expansion and decaying older areas, and political conflict. The world city economy results chiefly from the growth in high-level business, professions, and international tourism, which is taking place at the expense of manufacturing employment. Simultaneously, government services, which are concerned with the maintenance and reproduction of the world city, 'informal economy' and the undefined category of those without a steady income, also grow. Sassen (1991) illustrated an ideal type of 'the global city' by comparing London, New York, and Tokyo. In Sassen's empirical study, social polarization meant that the gap between the top and bottom occupational groups increased and grew, whereas the middle occupational group decreased. She argued that capital circulation, especially foreign investment, influenced the formation and the direction of international labour migration. First, the internationalization of production resulted in the shift of manufacturing and routine office work to less developed areas and constituted a push factor for new immigration. Second, the geographic dispersion of manufacturing contributed to more headquarters and producer services being centred in major cities. Finally, decentralized production reduced the supply of middle-income jobs while centralized managements and services generated the expansion of both high-income and low-wage jobs. The occupational shifts in these global cities tended towards the extremes – an increase in technical and professional workers and in casual, highly flexible, and low-cost workers.

Though an attractive hypothesis, this social polarization has evoked some debates about its theoretical and empirical validity. The crux is whether social polarization is a general tendency for cities in the globalization process or a specific phenomenon arising from the changing social structure of major cities in Western capitalist countries. Using occupational change and income distribution statistics to test this dual tendency in labour markets has received wide support in the studies of major global cities (Sassen, 1991; O'Loughlin and Friedrichs, 1996). However, the development of some European and Asian cities seems to contradict Sassen's conclusion (Baum, 1999; Hill and Kim, 2000; Wang, 2003). The empirical inconsistency of Asian cities with the global city paradigm generated a debate on global cities and developmental states (Hill and Kim, 2000, 2001; Friedmann, 2001; Sassen, 2001).

There were two general lines of critique questioning the applicability of Friedmann's and Sassen's models to cities other than the ones they specifically deal with. The first came from the developmental state theory, which emphasized that 'states have played a strategic role in taming domestic and international market forces and harnessing them to national economic interest' (White, 1988, p. 1). The second critique problematized the generalized application of the experience of specific global cities to all cities in the globalization process. First, global city theory was criticized for underestimating the role of the state, at both the national and the local level, and overemphasizing the market as the primary determinant of spatial form and social structure. The state's power is manifested in the tight control of a clearly defined territory and of the population trapped within its boundaries. Political controls are imposed in the attempt to break a movement impelled by the operation of a global labour market. Based on the developmental state theory, Hill and Kim (2000) constructed two world city types to demonstrate how state-centred, political-bureaucratic cities, such as Tokyo and Seoul, were different from Western market-centred bourgeois world cities. They proposed that Tokyo and Seoul's divergence from the world city model indicated that the legitimacy of global markets depended upon the legitimacy of a national political regime. The occupational structure in market-centred cities showed a polarized structure with a missing middle class, high inequality and segregation. The state-centred city presented a compressed structure with missing extremes, low inequality and segregation. Other Asian world cities under the control of developmental states have provided similar evidence to challenge the validity of the global city thesis (Baum, 1999; Wang, 2003).

Second, global city theory neglected cities' historical trajectories, and generalized the development of Western capitalist cities to all cities worldwide. One of the significant differences was based on the different immigration experiences in various world cities. Theory about social polarization based on the experience of high-immigration cities like Los Angles and New York (Sassen, 1988) may not be applicable to cities that lack an immigration tradition and consider themselves against immigration (Hamnett, 1994). After the Second World War, the Newly Industrialized Economies (NIEs), of Taiwan, South Korea, Singapore and Hong Kong, all implemented tight immigration restrictions for the sake of political and regional security. With rapid economic growth in the 1980s, the NIEs began to absorb a growing number of workers from the surplus-labour pool in neighbouring countries, because local workers were simply unavailable for many low-skilled jobs. A comparative study of manpower policies in Asian countries showed that states were forced to renew border controls as a short-term solution to address labour shortages but also set immigration restrictions for those contracted labourers (Abella, 1994). Compared with the experience of immigration in the global city, the foreign workers recruited for economic expansion in the NIEs have formed a flexible labour market and generated a new, flowing, and temporary underclass.

At the end of the global cities and developmental states debate, Sassen (2001, p. 2538) responded to Hill and Kim (2000) and reemphasized that her global city model was only an analytical construct seeking to capture a partial reality. In an empirical sense, the development of the global city function was 'filtered partly through thick local institutional environments and legal and administrative frameworks'. This claim returned to Fainstein *et al.*'s argument (1992), which treated the concepts of social polarization as a hypothesis rather than a conclusion. Although Wang (2003) has provided a theoretical and empirical examination of Taipei City from a global city paradigm, few studies on Taipei's migration and social polarization have been done. The purpose of this chapter is to provide some answers on migration and the urban labour market within the context of globalization and developmental state regulation. How do globalization and state regulation affect the urban labour market? What are their effects on social transformation? Do the growing clusters of technical and professional workers as well as of low-skill and services oriented labour imply an emerging dual labour market in Taipei City? Does it imply that Taipei City will move towards a dual city – a city of the rich and a city of the urban underclass?

This chapter will explore how economic restructuring and state regulation influence international labour movement, and their effects on the social transformations occurring in Taipei City. The intention is to identify the strategic urban economic process that set the patterns and rhythms for the formation and direction of labour migration and test the social polarization hypothesis. The discussion will be divided into four sections: the first explores economic restructuring as reflected by Taipei's employment changes; the second focuses on the policies of different types of international labour movement – for example, the return of Taiwan transient professionals, contracted foreigner workers, foreign brides and illegal workers – and their profiles; the third discusses the labour market polarization; and the last is a summary and conclusion.

Economic Restructuring and Employment

International labour flows are associated with worldwide trends in capital circulation. There were two directions of capital flow that influenced industrial transformation in Taipei. The first was associated with the transformation of economic structure in old centres of the world economy and the rise of Taiwan's high-tech industry. The Taiwan state adopted a successful outward-orientation to deepen industrialization (see Chapter 1). The second direction was articulated by the relocation of Taiwan's manufacturing sector to selected peripheral areas. Labour shortages and rising wages forced Taiwan firms to import foreign labour and to relocate to Southeast Asian countries or China. As the state lifted border controls on international investment, both direct foreign investment inflow and outflow reached new highs in 2000. Because the outflow capital increased more rapidly than inflow capital, Taiwan has turned from a capital inflow to a capital outflow area. In the past decade, capital flows can be clearly seen to follow three trends (see table 7.1). First, the net capital flow has turned from positive to negative after the 1990s. Second, inflow resources of direct foreign investment into Taiwan are shifting from overseas Chinese to direct foreign investment. Third, China has become the main outflow offshore investment target.

Capital outflow is a harbinger of a new economic crisis, forcing the state to reposition itself in the global economy. The liberal policy of the government has largely done away with geopolitical and economic territory control. In the 1990s, the 'Towards the South Policy' advocated by the state, which encouraged investment in Southeast Asian countries, was replaced by the 'Towards the West' movement of capital, which sought more investment opportunities in the coastal areas of China. The intensive interaction of capital and people has been pushing the relationship across the Taiwan Strait towards economic cooperation.

Capital outflow influences Taipei by decreasing its manufacturing sector and

Table 7.1. Taiwan offshore investment by area and direct foreign investment inflow to Taiwan, 1986–2002.　　　　Unit: 1000 US Dollar; %

| | Taiwanese Offshore Investment | | | | | | | | | Direct Foreign Investment in Taiwan | | | | | Net |
| | Total (a) | U.S. | | ASEAN* | | China | | Other Areas | | Total (b) | Overseas Chinese | | Foreign | | (b)−(a) |
	Number	Number	%	Number	%	Number	%	Number	%	Number	Number	%	Number	%	
1986	56,911	45,967	80.8	8,095	14.2	–	0.0	2,849	5.0	770,380	64,806	8.4	705,574	91.6	713,469
1987	102,751	70,058	68.2	16,088	15.7	–	0.0	16,605	16.2	1,418,796	195,727	13.8	1,223,069	86.2	1,316,045
1988	218,736	123,335	56.4	59,162	27.0	–	0.0	36,233	16.6	1,182,538	121,377	10.3	1,061,161	89.7	963,802
1989	930,986	508,732	54.6	282,082	30.3	–	0.0	140,172	15.1	2,418,299	177,273	7.3	2,241,026	92.7	1,487,313
1990	1,552,206	428,690	27.6	567,382	36.6	–	0.0	556,134	35.8	2,301,772	220,115	9.6	2,081,657	90.4	749,566
1991	1,830,188	297,795	16.3	702,637	38.4	174,158	9.5	655,598	35.8	1,778,419	219,462	12.3	1,558,957	87.7	−51,769
1992	1,134,251	193,026	17.0	288,959	25.5	246,992	21.8	405,274	35.7	1,461,374	312,146	21.4	1,149,228	78.6	327,123
1993	4,829,346	529,063	11.0	275,247	5.7	3,168,411	65.6	856,625	17.7	1,213,476	123,501	10.2	1,089,975	89.8	−3,615,870
1994	2,578,973	143,884	5.6	289,353	11.2	962,209	37.3	1,183,527	45.9	1,630,717	106,790	6.5	1,523,927	93.5	−948,256
1995	2,449,591	248,213	10.1	217,952	8.9	1,092,713	44.6	890,713	36.4	2,925,340	168,554	5.8	2,756,786	94.2	475,749
1996	3,394,645	271,329	8.0	486,789	14.3	1,229,241	36.2	1,407,286	41.5	2,460,836	170,451	6.9	2,290,385	93.1	−933,809
1997	7,228,139	547,416	7.6	555,827	7.7	4,334,313	60.0	1,790,583	24.8	4,266,629	387,463	9.1	3,879,166	90.9	−2,961,510
1998	5,330,923	598,666	11.2	367,416	6.9	2,034,621	38.2	2,330,220	43.7	3,738,758	184,721	4.9	3,554,037	95.1	−1,592,165
1999	4,521,793	445,081	9.8	487,613	10.8	1,252,780	27.7	2,336,319	51.7	4,231,404	132,380	3.1	4,099,024	96.9	−290,389
2000	7,684,204	861,638	11.2	335,400	4.4	2,607,142	33.9	3,880,024	50.5	7,607,739	50,384	0.7	7,557,355	99.3	−76,465
2001	7,175,801	1,092,747	15.2	492,428	6.9	2,784,147	38.8	2,806,479	39.1	5,128,529	47,223	0.9	5,081,306	99.1	−2,047,272
2002	10,093,104	577,782	5.7	155,671	1.5	6,723,058	66.6	2,636,593	26.1	3,271,747	44,960	1.4	3,226,787	98.6	−6,821,357

Source: Department of Statistics Ministry of Economic Affairs, R.O.C., Economic Statistics Annual Taiwan Area, pp. 185, 189, 190, 192–193.

Note: * Asean includes: Sinagpore, Thailand, Malaysia, Indonesia and Philippines.

slowing the growth of the service sector (see Chapter 2). In world cities, the change in urban labour market derived from 'deindustrialization' – the decline of the manufacturing sector, and the rise of the service sector – affecting the urban labour market and employment structure. However, when considering the transformation in employment structure (see table 7.2), Taipei City appears to have a unique trend of decline in both manufacturing and services sectors. Between 1980 and 1990, the growth of Taipei's employment in the service sector was 78.9 per cent. In comparison with 54.3 per cent in Taiwan, and 24.9 per cent in Taipei County, the growth of services successfully transformed Taipei into a centre for management, control and services operations. Taipei City has faced a decrease in the manufacturing sector, –2.9 per cent for the same period. Along with capital outflow to mainland China in the 1990s, Taipei City is experiencing a gradual 'deindustrialization' but unlike Taipei County and Taiwan.

Two reasons may be behind the low level of deindustrialization in Taipei. First, a division of labour between Taipei City and Taipei County set up the City as a service centre, and the county as an industrial region. Industrialization was synchronized with suburbanization producing the spatial division of labour structure (Tsai and Chang, 1997; Wang, 2002). The number of workers in the manufacturing sector in Taipei City was only 58,000, while that in Taipei County was 150,000. Labour in the manufacturing sector of Taipei City decreased by 14,000 from 1990 to 2000, while that in Taipei County increased by 73,000 during the same period. The relatively low level of industry in Taipei is due to the success of the policy of rural industrialization in the 1970s (see Chapter 1). Second, as the discussion in Chapter 2 shows, Taipei City's producer services have some structural constraints and employment in the service sector has reached its limit. Though service workers in Taipei accounted for 78.9 per cent of the labour force, that rate barely increased after the economic restructuring of the 1990s. The share of service workers in Taipei County and Taiwan Area grew much faster than that in Taipei City during the same period.

Taipei's specific economic restructuring process and industrial transformation make the city different from both global cities and cities in the Third World. Taipei was built as a 'regional global city' under the control of a developmental state (Wang, 2003). In 1967, Taipei was upgraded to 'temporary capital' of the Taiwan and it was transformed into the service centre of the state. Because of the concentration of central government institutions with agencies, national media headquarters, Taiwan's corporate headquarters, and universities, Taipei has been a domestic command and control point integrating the central government with banking and financial services. However, Taipei is a primary city unlike those in the Third World countries. The finance, insurance, real estate and business service sectors, which are usually associated with the growth of advanced services and headquarters in

Table 7.2. Employees by industry, by year in Taiwan, Taipei and Taipei County, 1980–2001.   Units: Thousand persons; %

	Taiwan Area							Taipei City							Taipei County						
	1980	1990	2000	Change 1980–1990	% change 1980–1990	Change 1990–2000	% change 1990–2000	1980	1990	2000	Change 1980–1990	% change 1980–1990	Change 1990–2000	% change 1990–2000	1980	1990	2000	Change 1980–1990	% change 1980–1990	Change 1990–2000	% change 1990–2000
Total	6,548	8,283	9,492	1,735	26.5	1,209	14.6	756	1,137	1,136	381	50.4	-1	-0.1	997	1,172	1,542	175	17.6	370	31.6
Agriculture, forestry, fishing & animal husbandry	1,277	1,064	740	-213	-16.7	-324	-30.5	8	3	5	-5	-62.5	2	66.7	74	26	21	-48	-64.9	-5	-19.2
Goods-producing industries	2,784	3,382	3,534	598	21.5	152	4.5	246	236	222	-10	-4.1	-14	-5.9	453	559	632	106	23.4	73	13.1
Mining & quarrying	56	20	11	-36	-64.3	-9	-45.0	2	0	0	-2	-100.0	0	0.0	20	5	0	-15	-75.0	-5	-100.0
Manufacturing	2,152	2,653	2,655	501	23.3	2	0.1	174	169	161	-5	-2.9	-8	-4.7	369	443	476	74	20.1	33	7.4
Electricity, gas & water	27	36	36	9	33.3	0	0.0	6	3	3	-3	-50.0	0	0.0	11	4	6	-7	-63.6	2	50.0
Construction	549	673	832	124	22.6	159	23.6	64	64	58	0	0.0	-6	-9.4	53	107	150	54	101.9	43	40.2
Services-producing industries	2,487	3,837	5,218	1,350	54.3	1,381	36.0	502	898	909	396	78.9	11	1.2	470	587	889	117	24.9	302	51.4
Wholesale, retail & restaurant	1,058	1,621	2,163	563	53.2	542	33.4	219	343	338	124	56.6	-5	-1.5	146	253	361	107	73.3	108	42.7
Transport, storage & communication	332	441	481	109	32.8	40	9.1	73	83	91	10	13.7	8	9.6	61	80	100	19	31.1	20	25.0
Finance, insurance & real estate	87	220	412	133	152.9	192	87.3	41	99	101	58	141.5	2	2.0	32	62	81	30	93.8	19	30.6
Business service	65	148	313	83	127.7	165	111.5		86	81			-5	-5.8			65				
Social, personal & related community service	711	1,098	1,534	387	54.4	436	39.7	169	240	241	71	42.0	1	0.4	231	192	236	-39	-16.9	44	22.9
Public administration	235	308	315	73	31.1	7	2.3		47	57			10	21.3			46				

Sources: Directorate-General of Budget, Accounting and Statistics, Executive Yuan, R.O.C., Yearbook of Manpower Survey Statistics, p. 48; Department of Budget, Accounting and Statistics, Taipei City Government, R.O.C., The Statistical Abstract, pp.136–137.

global cities, were dispersed to Taipei County and other parts of Taiwan from 1990 to 2000.

International Labour Movements

The movements of international labour migration – return migration from advanced countries, emigration to China and immigration from peripheral countries – are embedded in the social context of a developmental state regulation. The state intends both to de-regulate and re-regulate in order to deal with the contradictory relationship between capital flow and employment. The imposition of martial law in Taiwan placed transnational movement under state control. The 'locked' island was opened after 1987. To respond to globalization, the state opened the labour market by relaxing immigration restriction and allowing international labour movement across its borders. In the process of globalization, the opening of the borders to international labour took place in three stages. First, the state opened the door to international labour movement; then it introduced foreign contract workers from Southeast Asian countries; finally, it opened the door to global skilled but excluded low-skilled workers from China. Briefly, the three stages were developed as follows.

The First Stage: The International Labour Movement (1987–1991)

In 1987, the Taiwan state lifted martial law. For humanitarian reasons, the government allowed the veterans, who had migrated to Taiwan following the KMT defeat in 1949, to visit their relatives in China. In 1989, according to the new revised Passport Act, the state abolished the registration requirement for going abroad. Taiwan people were permitted to trade and travel overseas free from any application or registration. As the Taiwan citizens' international movement was freed from state regulation, intensive economic and social interaction between the two sides of the Taiwan Strait began. In 1988, 209,000 Taiwan people visited China, including veterans and tourists. After 1992, the number of Taiwan people going to China was more than a million every year. The number reached 3.1 million in 2000.[1]

The Second Stage: Foreign Contract Workers (1992–1999)

The open foreign labour policy adopted by the state was necessary because of the ongoing labour shortage. Since the 1980s, Taiwan has faced a labour shortage, especially in the manufacturing and construction sectors. Though lifting tight constraints on labour immigration, the state still controls what kinds of employers may hire foreign workers, where those foreign workers may come from, and how many may come from a given country. The state limits the categories that are qualified to hire foreign workers in blue-collar work. The first employers to be allowed to hire foreign workers were those working on major public construction projects, followed by those in the manufacturing sector, and finally, those in the social service sector and in private households. The origin countries of foreign workers also corresponded with the state-led 'Toward the Southeast Policy', which encouraged Taiwan businesses to relocate in Southeast Asian countries. These workers initially came from Thailand, the Philippines, Malaysia and Indonesia. Vietnamese have recently replaced Malaysians while Mongolians have been allowed to work in Taiwan since 2004.

Though willing to accept low wages and sharing a language with the Taiwanese, mainland Chinese workers are still prohibited from entering for reasons of national security. Foreign workers in Taiwan are driven by the market but also controlled by the state which decides who can enter legally. Moreover, the quota of foreign workers responds not only to the needs of the local labour markets, but also to the supply of local labourers. Though the state claims that its foreign worker policy is based on a principle of supplementation rather than replacement, the increase in foreign workers has threatened the employment opportunities of local low-skilled and un-skilled workers. Foreign labour entered the manufacturing and service industries. Capital accumulation has resulted in an overuse of foreign workers which leads to the exclusion of local workers. The rise in the unemployment rate has forced the state to decrease the quota of foreign workers.

Since 2002, the Democratic Progressive Party's new government implemented a policy of reducing the total number of foreign workers by 15,000 or 5 per cent per year. The number of foreign workers was reduced from 304,605 in 2001 to 298,480 in April 2004. In contrast to this initial policy of restricting foreign labour, the number of workers increased to 302,828 in the period between the March 2004 presidential election and July 2004. The expanded foreign workforce is employed in the manufacturing and social services sectors. Policies regarding foreign workers are responsive to labour market demands, but they are also manipulated, when necessary, as an electioneering tactic. Further, the state regulates contracts between Taiwan employers and their foreign workers. The immigration of unskilled labourers is restricted and their short-term migration status is limited to a specific period of time. State intervention in labour contracts determines how long migrant workers can stay in Taiwan, how much they get paid, and even how often they should have health inspections. However, labour protection such as minimum wage and days off are applied to foreign workers in the manufacturing and construction sectors but not in the service sector. Like domestic workers in Singapore, the relationship between a service sector employer and a foreign worker is regarded as a private contract. They have no labour law protection.

Socio-economic policies regarding foreign workers have been highly controversial in Taiwan. Employers in the manufacturing sector asked the government to allow foreign labour not only to fill vacant positions but also to lower labour costs to cope with competition in the international market (Wu and Zhang, 1991). The use of health-care workers and domestic helpers also has generated a debate between humanists and feminists. The policy was criticized as 'a service for the rich class' (Lin, 2000).

The Third Stage: Migration of Global Skilled Labour and Restriction of Low-skilled Chinese Workers (2000 to the present)

In 2000, the DPP's new government adopted an open and flexible policy allowing immigrants to enter the local labour market and de-regulated skilled labour employment. The effects of the open international labour market policy include the following. First, the policy extended the definition of the foreign white-collar class and lessened restrictions on their employment. The revised Employment Law of 1997 opened six areas of employment to foreigners. These included heads of investment firms or other businesses owned by overseas Chinese or foreigners in Taiwan; teachers in public and private colleges, universities or overseas Chinese schools; teachers in extension schools; coaches in sports; cultural workers in religion, art or performance. In 2003, the Employment Law was revised to allow foreigners to teach in high schools as well. The expanding role of foreign workers includes previously illegal foreign teachers, who contribute to Taiwan's educational labour market. Meanwhile, foreign professionals are allowed to work and stay in Taiwan for three years initially, and may request that their employers extend their contracts after that initial period. Second, according to 'Chinese Technical Professional Application for Stay in Taiwan Regulation' of 2001, technical professionals from China are permitted to work legally in Taiwan. The new regulation opened the door to hiring Chinese technical professionals in 18 new industries and technical services firms. Those with higher education degrees and work experience may stay in Taiwan for at least one year.[2] After one year, they are able to request an extension for an additional five years, depending on their performance. Having finished their projects and left Taiwan, they can be invited to come back to work. Third, this policy permitted foreign brides to work legally. Foreign brides used to be defined as household workers rather than formal workers and were not allowed to enter the local market. Becasue a high percentage of Taiwan husbands who belong to the underclass marry foreign brides, in 2001 the work prohibition on foreign brides was lifted for those in low-income families, and in 2002 the restriction was lifted for all families (which included brides from China).

Globalization gave rise to new patterns of urban industrial employment. The international movement of labour includes emigrant and immigrant labourers and both types of migration influence the dynamics of the urban labour market. The issue of emigrant skilled labourers which used to be considered the problem of 'brain drain' – the systematic extraction of talent from developing economies by developed economies – has attracted much attention. Immigrant labour includes two types of migrants: those who migrate for work and long-term settlement, and those contract labourers who are recruited for a specific period of time. Below, a brief profile of urban migrant labour is presented.

Return of Professional Migrants

Return migration in Taiwan was the product of a combination of factors. Initially, local students were sent to overseas universities, and when they graduated, these educated elites were pulled back into the local labour market to assist in industrial development. Economic restructuring and outflow of production plants provided an impetus for skilled labour to move to China. The two trends of return migration and out migration were recently noted in Taipei. The first one – 'brain return' – involves skilled Taiwan labour returning to Taipei from overseas. This happened in the 1980s when old industrial countries dispersed their production to developing countries and the NIEs. The second one – 'brain drain' – involves migration from Taipei to the cities in the coastal areas of China. This happened in the 1990s when Taiwan's firms adopted a relocation strategy to deal with global competition.

Since the 1950s, the Taiwan state has been sending college students abroad for advanced studies. Those sponsored by the government are required to return to Taiwan and work in government-arranged jobs for at least three years.[3] Information made available by the National Youth Mission showed that a high percentage of students studying abroad did not return after they completing their studies. Even if the state-led model of active recruitment attracted more returnees, the overall return rate of skilled workers was still low. However, the rise of high-tech industry attracted overseas skilled labour in the 1980s. The high-tech industry offered opportunities that encouraged Taiwan professionals abroad to develop their careers and build their businesses in Taiwan. Furthermore, changes in returning students' occupational structure reflected that the reverse brain drain initiated by state policy had been replaced by opportunities in high-tech markets. Before 1993, most highly educated returning professionals were assigned positions in the public sector. More than 60 per cent of these returnees were recruited by the government, universities and research institutes, 20 per cent were employed by national enterprises, private enterprises or financial institutes, and only 20 per cent established their own business. In 1995, the percentage of skilled returnees who were self-employed rose to 69.4 per cent. With recent urban economic growth and the expansion of high-tech industry, opportunities for returning professionals to establish their own businesses have attracted a 'brain return' migration.

Although the number of returning professionals in Taiwan is unavailable, Taipei has attracted a high percentage of them. A model of human resource distribution in Taiwan showed that in-migrants favoured highly urbanized areas (Lin and Tsay, 2000). As a centre of finance, education, business and services, Taipei provides opportunities for returning professionals in the public sector and in the commercial and producer services sectors. Thus, returning professionals are likely to be centred in Taipei Metropolis.

Professionals emigrating from Taiwan to China are the most common form of skilled labour migration following capital outflow. This second wave of economic restructuring, the 'reverse brain drain' to Taiwan from developed countries has been replaced by Taiwan emigration to developing China. Due to low labour, land, and environmental costs combined with easy access to a large market, managers and entrepreneurs ignored the Taiwan government's ban on investment in China and chose to build new production sites there as early as the 1980s. Since 1996, the exodus of Taipei's tech-talent has become a deluge to China's shores. Most of them congregate in the cities along the coast of China. Shanghai, the largest city in China, is crowded with Taiwan businessmen, managers and professional persons, and has become a second home for Taiwan traders. The number of Taiwanese emigrants to Shanghai is estimated at 300,000.[4] One survey by *Business Week* in 2001 showed that Taiwan migrants to Shanghai are 31 to 50 years old (73.5 per cent), married and with children (76 per cent), and highly educated (82 per cent with more than a college education). Their positions included: high ranking managers (46 per cent); medium ranking managers (10.5 per cent); entrepreneurs (16.5 per cent); and those looking for an opportunity to establish a business (26 per cent). A special issue of *Time*[5] said, 'If Taipei hadn't lifted many of the restrictions, it was at risk of turning its top executives into a criminal caste'.

Taiwan skilled labourers constitute a part of a global skilled labour market. Some studies on professionals in Taiwan revealed the phenomenon of circular migration among Asian professionals (Kanjanapan, 1992; Tzeng, 1995). The autonomy of professionals across territories and borders shows an unsettling of citizenship in a flowing global economy. Such people are driven by economic motives and no longer settle down in a city or promise allegiance to a single nation-state.

Transient Foreigners

Transient foreigners are those foreigners who enter Taiwan for a short-term stay not for contract work. Despite a substantial increase in direct foreign investment in the 1980s, there are not many professional transient immigrants in Taipei. The number of foreign residents in Taipei was only 10,961 in 1986, and rose to 54,133 in 2001, constituting less than 3 per cent of the city's total population (see table 7.3). The number of employed foreigners in white collar jobs was only 3,260 in 1986 and rose to 11,639 in 2001, while they accounted for only 29.7 per cent of foreign residents in 1986 and 21.5 per cent in 2001. The change of employment for foreigners is presented in table 7.3. First, the numbers of so-called 'global elites' in Taipei has not significantly increased. Trades, teaching and technology are the three major sectors for foreign employment in Taipei. Between 1993 and 2001, the number of employed trades increased by 77.7 per cent, and teachers increased by 46.1 per cent. In contrast, the number of engineers and technicians decreased by 16.6 per cent. Second, though the number of foreign residents increased, many have not entered the formal labour market. These migrants entered Taiwan on tourist or student visas, and they find work as English teachers in extension schools. From 1986 to 2001, the population of foreigners not in formal employment increased from 7,701 to 42,494; increasingly foreigners chose to work in informal occupations, resulting in the 451.8 per cent increase. Part of this increase is dependent on the population of casual workers who have significantly increased over the same time period. These trends are consistent with Kanjanapan's argument (1992) that the non-capital assisted migrants rather than the capital-assisted migrants, constituted the majority of foreign white-collar workers.

Foreign Contract Workers

The number of foreign contract workers in blue-collar jobs rose sharply as the urban services sector grew. Because Taipei is a service-oriented city, foreign workers present different demographic trends from other areas in Taiwan. The number of contract workers in the service industries exceeds that in manufacturing. For example, in 2002, the number of foreign workers in the health-care service was 26,914, or 75.5 per cent of Taipei's total foreign workers; the number of domestic helpers was 2,815, or 7.9 per cent; and the number of construction workers was 3,848, or 10.8 per cent (see table 7.4). Moreover, foreign workers from different countries worked in different industries. Most domestic helpers came from Indonesia and the Philippines. Indonesians made up 70 per cent of foreign health-care workers, with another 21.5 per cent coming from the Philippines. Thai workers congregated in the construction sector.

Whether hired as health-care workers or domestic helpers, female migrant workers from Indonesia and the Philippines clearly support the Taipei household labour force in high-income families, easing the burden of Taipei's career women. These workers' tasks include taking care of the elderly (63.9 per cent), working as domestic maids (42.5 per cent), taking care of the sick (37.4 per cent), taking care

Table 7.3. Alien resident population in Taipei by sex and occupation, 1986–2001.

Year/Population	1986	1990	1991	1992	1993	1994	1995	1996	1997	1998	1999	2000	2001	% change 1993–2001
Total s	10,961	14,903	17,062	19,250	24,088	29,406	22,035	35,497	34,027	37,044	44,139	53,366	54,133	124.7
Alien other than workers s-n	10,961	14,903	17,062	17,583	17,397	17,056	14,220	17,483	18,165	19,304	21,403	23,188	23,630	35.8
%	100.0	100.0	100.0	91.3	72.2	58.0	64.5	49.3	53.4	52.1	48.5	43.5	43.7	-
Employed other than labourers														
labourers	3,260	4,310	5,785	5,349	5,455	5,420	4,433	6,346	6,811	8,632	10,073	11,442	11,639	113.4
%	29.7	28.9	33.9	30.4	31.4	31.8	31.2	36.3	37.5	44.7	47.1	49.3	49.3	316.4
Male	6,009	8,221	9,965	11,474	14,391	17,805	13,434	18,553	15,609	14,837	15,191	16,232	15,439	7.3
Female	4,952	6,709	7,097	7,503	9,697	11,601	8,601	16,926	18,418	22,207	28,948	37,134	38,694	299.0
Labour force a+b	5,735	7,879	10,867	11,878	17,178	22,825	16,373	30,413	29,484	34,940	42,763	52,950	53,661	212.4
The employed a	5,643	7,643	10,655	11,496	16,793	22,395	16,037	29,845	28,853	34,417	42,282	52,467	53,179	216.7
Labour force other than workers a-o	5,735	7,879	10,867	10,211	10,487	10,475	8,558	12,399	13,622	17,200	20,027	22,772	23,158	120.8
Unemployed b	92	236	212	382	385	430	336	568	631	523	481	483	482.00	25.2
Not in labour force c+d+e	6,443	8,601	8,647	9,113	8,810	8,441	6,980	7,797	7,551	7,628	8,435	9,088	9,560	8.5
%	58.8	57.7	50.7	51.8	50.6	49.5	49.1	44.6	41.6	39.5	39.4	39.2	40.5	-20.1
Student c	4,674	6,308	6,252	6,612	6,386	6,127	5,033	5,638	5,309	5,296	5,721	5,601	5569	-12.8
Household workers d	1,721	2,248	2,352	2,454	2,378	2,274	1,908	2,108	2,198	2,292	2,680	3,450	3948	66.0
Other e	48	45	43	47	46	40	39	51	44	40	34	37	43	-6.5
Employees	3,260	4,310	5,785	7,016	12,146	17,770	12,248	24,360	22,673	26,372	32,809	41,620	42,142	247.0
Officer f	0	24	52	3	7	55	32	24	4	6	5	9	9	28.6
Trader g	1,089	1,367	1,678	1740	1661	1,753	1440	1976	2212	2382	2785	2,934	2951	77.7
Engineer and technician h	669	794	1,003	1,038	942	858	631	829	661	674	748	821	786	-16.6
*Professional i	63	65	48	34	45	38	36	37	30	38	49	55	67	48.9
Journal j	15	19	23	21	24	21	12	28	19	24	28	39	41	70.8
Teacher k	335	436	395	730	857	835	635	833	892	980	1,007	1,198	1252	46.1
Missionary l	428	478	407	396	400	429	365	427	401	389	400	415	437	9.3
Crew m	1	1	2	3	2	0	7	8	6	10	10	10	10	400.0
Labour n	0	0	0	1,667	6,691	12,350	7,815	18,014	15,862	17,740	22,736	30,178	30503	355.9
Other o	660	1,126	2,177	1,384	1,517	1,431	1,275	2,184	2,586	4,129	5,041	5,961	6086	301.2

Source: Taipei City Policy Department, Taipei City Government, R.O.C., Police Administration Annual Stastics of Taipei Municipality, pp. 46–47.

* Professional includes doctors, nurses, lawyers and accountants.

of the disabled (23.2 per cent), and taking care of children (8 per cent).[6] Migrant domestic labour is involved in the commercialization of 'the work of everyday life within the intimate domesticity of the home' (Heyzer and Wee, 1994, p. 31).

Foreign Brides

Although foreign brides have constituted an important immigrant group in Taiwan recently, their numbers are not large in Taipei City. There were 11,669 foreign spouses in Taipei in 2002, and 4,191 came from China or Southeast Asian countries. They accounted for 35.92 per cent of the foreign brides in the City.[7] Foreign brides tend to be in low-income areas, such as agricultural counties and the peripheries of cities, rather than urban areas (Hsai, 2000; Wang, 2001).

Illegal Migrant Workers

Workers from Southeast Asian countries and China constitute the major source of illegal workers in Taipei. In the early 1990s, due to local labour shortages, most illegal foreign workers were employed in the manufacturing sector (Abella, 1994). It was estimated that the number of illegal workers from Southeast Asian countries was around 40,000, with workers coming principally from Malaysia (49 per cent), the Philippines (23 per cent), Thailand (23 per cent) and Indonesia (11 per cent) (Tsay, 1992). Some of them would run away from their employers after starting to work in Taiwan. According to the statistics by Council of Labour Affair (CLA), the total number of foreign worker escapees was 48,369 from 1994 to 2001. With the increase of interaction between the two sides of the Taiwan Strait, the current number of illegal migrants has significantly increased. Reliable data for illegal Chinese workers are not available. According to the Census in 2000, the number of Taipei residents from China (Hong Kong and Macao included) was 14,096, but it is obvious that illegal immigrants from China were not included. Most Chinese workers in urban areas are young, female and work in the informal economy, often as prostitutes. Illegal Chinese workers who are caught are first detained in the police station, and then are sent to the Chinese Detention Centre, where they await deportation. The number of stowaways in the Chinese Detention Centre was 2,032 in 2002, in the ratio of about 1 male to 4 females. The migrant female sex workers constitute a new urban marginal group which is in the unprotected urban labour market and excluded from labour law protection.

Social Polarization in Taipei

In the global literature, the social polarization hypothesis is tested by looking at

Table 7.4. The number of foreign workers in Taipei by nationality and Importation Scheme, October 2002.

Importation Scheme	Total persons	Total %	Indonesia persons	Indonesia %	Malaysia persons	Malaysia %	Philippines persons	Philippines %	Thailand persons	Thailand %	Vietnam persons	Vietnam %
Total	35,649	100.0	20,457	57.4	1	–	7,522	21.1	5,701	16.0	1,968	5.5
Major construction projects	3,848	10.8	2	0.1	–	–	37	1.0	3,805	98.9	4	0.1
6 industries and 15 occupations	3	0.0	–	–	–	–	–	–	3	100.0	–	–
Health care workers	26,914	75.5	18,946	70.4	1	–	5,773	21.5	399	1.5	1,795	6.7
Home-maids	2,815	7.9	1,433	50.9	–	–	1,269	45.1	31	1.1	82	2.9
Crewmen	16	0.0	–	–	–	–	–	–	–	–	16	100.0
68 industries	69	0.2	1	1.5	–	–	2	2.9	60	87.0	6	8.7
73 industries	5	0.0	1	20.0	–	–	3	60.0	1	20.0	–	–
Chinaware etc., 6 industries	1	0.0	–	–	–	–	1	100.0	–	–	–	–
New and expanded firms	3	0.0	–	–	–	–	–	–	3	100.0	–	–
* EPZ and SBIP	–	–	–	–	–	–	–	–	–	–	–	–
† 3 K industries	1	0.0	–	–	–	–	–	–	1	100.0	–	–
Big manufacturing investment	327	0.9	1	0.3	–	–	211	64.5	96	29.4	19	5.8
Big construction investent	454	1.3	–	–	–	–	2	0.4	421	92.7	31	6.8
7 industries	–	–	–	–	–	–	–	–	–	–	–	–
‡ Quota relocation	947	2.7	73	7.7	–	–	107	11.3	752	79.4	15	1.6
Non-high technology manufacturing	246	0.7	–	–	–	–	117	47.6	129	52.4	–	–
High technology manufacturing	–	–	–	–	–	–	–	–	–	–	–	–

Source: Unpublished statistical data, from Council of Labor Affairs, Employment and Vocational Training Administration, Executive Yuan, R.O.C.

Notes: * EPZ stands for Export Processing Zones, while SBIP for Science-Based Industrial Park.

† '3 K industries' involve dirty, dangerous and labor-consuming industries.

‡ Quota readjusted two years after initial allocation of manufacturing involve 6 industries and 15 occupations, 68 industries, 73 industries, chinaware etc., 6 industries., New and expanded firms, EPZ and SBIP (1), 3 K industries and 7 industries etc.

earnings and household income. Several groups are left out of such analysis: the unemployed, those working in the informal sector, and foreign contract workers who work illegally are all ignored by the household income variable. The concept of social polarization was re-conceptualized by O'Loughlin and Friedrichs (1996), who use it to refer to a growing antagonism between social groups as their number and composition change, as well as their ethnic status.

The global city can be characterized by a dichotomized labour force: a high percentage of professionals occupying control positions, and a vast army of low-skilled workers engaged in manufacturing, personal service, and the hotel, tourist and entertainment industries. The effects of labour polarization in Taipei should be considered in the context of specific local circumstances. Globalization in Taipei resulted in the rise of two urban classes. On the one hand, the 'global elites' – returning students, transient foreign professionals – build a global network for financial, commercial, technological, and cultural flows. On the other hand, the new migrant urban underclass – foreign contract workers, foreign brides and illegal workers – enters households as a replacement family force or the low-level urban services, but brings cross-cultural contact with people, private families and communities in the host country. In official statistics, this category of workers is excluded. The analyses below first discuss the changes in occupational structure. Second, salary disparities between the global elite class and the underclass, as well as household income distribution are reviewed.

The transformation in the occupational structure in Taipei from 1993 to 2001 is illustrated in table 7.5. Except rural workers in agricultural and animal husbandry, forestry and fisheries, six statistical categories are organized into three groups: (1) the upper class: including legislators, government administrators, business executives and managers as well as professionals; (2) the middle class: including associate professionals, technicians, as well as service workers, and sales workers; (3) the lower class: including clerks as well as craft and related workers, plant and machine operators, assemblers, and labourers. The data illustrate that both the numbers of the upper class and the lower class proportionately decreased over time, while the middle class increased. Rather than the polarized structure of a typical global city, Taipei City presents a growing middle class. From 1993 to 2001, the upper class decreased from 254,000 to 245,000 people, decreasing by 3.5 per cent, while the lower class also decreased from 388,000 to 345,000 people, decreasing by 11.1 per cent. In contrast, the middle class increased from 461,000 to 517,000 people, growing by 12.1 per cent. Labour differentiation, statistically, has tended toward an inverted-shaped distribution: both the population of the upper class and the lower class are shrinking, but that of the middle class is expanding.

The decrease of the lower class is misleading. Official statistics on Taipei's employment exclude all foreign employees. The contract blue-collar workers and the illegal migrants together might have made up the loss of lower class employment (43,000 workers between 1993 and 2001 as calculated from table 7.5). Taking the data in table 7.4 into consideration, the number of lower class workers, 35,649 in 2002, in reality, was probably stabilizing rather than decreasing. Similarly the decrease of upper class employment (9,000 over the same period as calculated from table 7.5) was made up by the transient foreign employment, 11,639 in 2001 (see table 7.3). By including the foreign white-collar workers, there may be a slight increase in the upper-class employment. Taking into account these statistical omissions, this suggests that the present labour structure has a stable upper and lower class, while the middle class is gradually expanding.

The emigration of the elites is the reason for the stabilization of the upper class. While the number of professionals increased from 107,000 to 131,000, the number of legislators, government administrators, business executives and managers decreased from 147,000 to 114,000 between 1993 and 2001. Since neither the central government nor the city government have actually increased their employees, the stabilized upper-class employment is made up by the reduction of managers and professionals in the private sector,[8] as employment in the public sector has had a slight increase. In the process of globalization, industrial transformation should have increased the professionals. The decrease of executives and managers is because many Taipei companies have relocated to China, reducing the number of business executives and managers. Furthermore, the outflow of capital induced many Taiwan executives and managers to settle in China. This new brain drain has significantly influenced the occupational structure in Taipei.

Moreover, industrial relocation and replacement by foreign workers contribute to the stabilization of the lower class. While the number of clerks increased from 133,000 to 167,000, the number of craft workers decreased from 225,000 to 195,000. Meanwhile, there are over 30,000 foreign contract workers and illegal immigrants who, accepting lower wages, filled vacant low-wage positions, replacing low-skilled local labour from the urban labour market.

State regulation of the urban labour market controls the earning disparity between local blue-collar workers and foreign contract workers. Wage disparities over the past decade are illustrated in table 7.6. According to Labour Standard Law, foreign workers' earnings include a regular monthly salary and overtime pay in the manufacturing and construction sectors. The minimum wage regulation set for foreign workers' average monthly salary, equalled 76 per cent of local workers' regular salaries in 1993. It was reduced to 74 per cent in 2002. In 1999, despite these pay-rate differentials, foreign contract workers earned almost as much as local workers in junior positions due to their high incidence of overtime pay. In 2000, protest by local labour organizations forced the state to reduce the quota of foreign contract workers and to decrease the real wages by excluding meals

Table 7.5. Number and percentage in emloyment by ocupation in Taipei,1993–2001.   Unit: Thousand person

		1993	1994	1995	1996	1997	1998	1999	2000	2001	% change 1993–2001
Legislators, government administrators, business executives and managers (A)	number	147	147	145	127	127	122	113	113	114	-22.4
	%	13.2	13.0	12.6	11.3	11.5	11.0	10.0	9.9	10.3	
Professionals (B)	number	107	105	114	113	108	109	117	126	131	22.4
	%	9.6	9.3	9.9	10.0	9.8	9.8	10.4	11.1	11.8	
Technicians, and associate professionals (C)	number	300	311	316	294	308	328	340	353	357	19.0
	%	27.0	27.4	27.5	26.1	27.8	29.5	30.2	31.0	32.2	
Clerks (D)	number	133	145	154	164	162	158	168	173	167	25.6
	%	12.0	12.8	13.4	14.6	14.6	14.2	14.9	15.2	15.0	
Service workers, shop and market sales workers (E)	number	161	170	179	184	176	176	177	173	160	-0.6
	%	14.5	15.0	15.6	16.3	15.9	15.8	15.7	15.2	14.4	
Agricultural, animal husbandry workers, forestry workers and fishermen (F)	number	7	8	7	6	4	4	4	3	3	-57.1
	%	0.6	0.7	0.6	0.5	0.4	0.4	0.4	0.3	0.3	
Craft and related workers, plant and machine operators and assemblers, and labourers (G)	number	255	248	236	239	222	216	205	195	178	-30.2
	%	23.0	21.9	20.5	21.2	20.1	19.4	18.2	17.2	16.0	
Top class (A+B)	number	254	252	259	240	235	231	230	239	245	-3.5
	%	22.8	22.3	21.1	21.7	21.3	19.8	18.6	17.4	16.3	
Middle class (C+E)	number	461	481	495	478	484	504	517	526	517	12.1
	%	41.5	42.5	43.0	42.4	43.7	45.3	46.0	46.3	46.6	
Underclass (D+G)	number	388	393	390	403	384	374	373	368	345	-11.1
	%	35.0	34.7	33.9	35.8	34.7	33.6	33.2	32.4	31.1	

Source: Department of Budget, Accounting and Statistics, Taipei City Government, R.O.C., The Statistical Abstract, pp.140–141.

Table 7.6. Average monthly earnings between foreign workers and local workers

	Foreign worker*			Local Worker†		Share of F.W. to L.W.	
	Average salary (A)	Regular earning (C)	Overtime pay	Average salary (B)	Regular earning (D)	Average earning (A)/(B)	Regular earning (C)/(D)
1993	17,603	14,100	3,503	20,751	18,674	0.85	0.76
1994	18,211	14,737	3,475	21,125	18,790	0.86	0.78
1995	19,530	15,487	4,042	21,997	19,930	0.89	0.78
1996	20,080	15,540	4,539	21,477	19,080	0.93	0.81
1997	20,892	16,059	4,833	21,761	19,123	0.96	0.84
1998	21,193	16,352	4,841	21,864	19,676	0.97	0.83
1999	20,919	16,507	4,412	21,116	19,405	0.99	0.85
2000	20,959	16,470	4,490	24,533	21,505	0.85	0.77
2001	19,502	16,353	3,149	24,681	22,227	0.79	0.74
2002	20,536	16,353	4,183	24,815	22,119	0.83	0.74
change % 1993 to 2000	16.7	16.0	19.4	19.6	18.4		

Sources: Council of Labor Affair, Executive Yuan, R.O.C., Report on the Use and Management of Foreign Workers in Taiwan Area, p. 3.

Notes: * Foreign worker's average monthly earning is limited to those who are working in the manufacturing sector and construction.
† Local workers' average monthly wage is compared with those who are working in the manufacturing sector and construction for less than two years.

and accommodation. The regular earning of a foreign contract worker gradually reduced from NT$16,507 in 1999 to NT$16,353 in 2001. The wage difference between local workers and foreign contract workers allows Taiwan firms to lower their labour costs. By setting the foreign contract workers' wages low, they become the standard by which the increase of local workers' wages is suppressed.

The state intervention in the labour market has stabilized the earnings gap between local blue-collar workers and foreign contract workers. The domestic workers are the exception. The local domestic workers are protected by state labour relegations, but foreign domestic workers and their employers negotiate individual private contracts determined by the market. The low wages for the foreign contract workers allow many of Taipei's families to hire foreign domestic workers as household maids. Housework, essential to the survival of the family and society, is mainly concerned with the process of reproduction of labour rather than production. The state rationalizes that, by not directly contributing to production, domestic workers' wages are thus denied protection under the labour law (Eviota, 1992; Noriel, 1993). As domestic labourers working and living in their employers' homes, foreign workers are isolated in the work place and living place, and are most vulnerable in wage negotiations.

The statistical data support the trend of growing household income inequality between 1993 and 2000. The income of a household in the upper class increased faster than that of a lower class household (see table 7.7). Income inequality in Taipei is increasing, as the ratio of the income share of the highest-earning 20 per cent to the lowest-earning 20 per cent rose from 3.6 in 1993, to 4.3 in 2000.

Wacquant (2000) reminded us that one way to measure the deteriorating life chances at the bottom of the class structure lies in evaluating social polarization from 'below'. The number of people living in poverty in Taipei doubled in the past decade. The number of people living in poverty rose from 13,768 to 27,184 between 1990 and 2002, while the number of households living in poverty also increased from 5,464 to 12,073 in the same period. A significant growth in the urban poverty accompanied globalization in Taipei. The unemployment rate in Taipei has also risen in the past decade. In 1990, it was only 1.8 per cent, but increased to 4.6 per cent by 2002.

Summary and Conclusion

This chapter attempts to illustrate the consequences of globalization for social polarization and income inequality in Taipei City. The effect of globalization on social polarization is analyzed within the context of the developmental state, in which the state mediates the process of globalization through migration and labour policies. Due to the strategic importance in the national economy, Taipei became

Table 7.7. Average disposable income by the head household's occupation in Taipei, 1993–2001.

		1993	1994	1995	1996	1997	1998	1999	2000	% change 1993–2000
Legislators, government administrators, business executives and managers (A)	surveyed households	429	166,636	132,150	157,547	151,110	145,185	149,430	136,977	
	average disposable income (A)	1,212,232	1,365,020	1,577,442	1,561,802	1,623,625	1,690,721	1,774,021	1,780,674	46.9
Professionals (B)	surveyed households	324	96,636	109,492	104,116	87,464	98,252	89,264	99,091	
	average disposable income	1,178,826	1,344,685	1,365,946	1,448,158	1,572,491	1,545,761	1,594,576	1,644,708	39.5
Technicians, and associate professionals (C)	surveyed households	390	125,228	136,861	124,910	149,364	154,968	165,504	172,351	
	average disposable income	1,026,489	1,146,317	1,221,470	1,209,357	1,280,581	1,302,003	1,298,780	1,316,990	28.3
Clerks (D)	surveyed households	255	82,398	83,185	72,345	66,820	70,784	71,602	72,320	
	average disposable income	839,691	958,297	1,002,564	1,023,246	1,035,390	1,082,767	1,133,275	1,118,261	33.2
Service workers, shop and market sales workers (E)	surveyed households	415	120,669	125,979	134,627	133,843	125,591	118,150	121,698	
	average disposable income	854,444	903,960	1,028,234	985,191	1,024,979	1,042,617	1,026,759	1,063,764	24.5
Agricultural, animal husbandry workers, forestry workers and fishermen (F)	surveyed households	5	5,839	2,298	1,678	5,392	348	684	2,689	
	average disposable income	448,990	781,452	1,021,410	1,036,705	1,357,224	626,102	951,460	1,287,632	186.8
Craft and related workers, plant and machine operators and assemblers, and labourers (G)	surveyed households	498	67,718	67,869	72,709	72,114	72,886	71,731	49,940	
	average disposable income	755,966	670,843	943,894	976,799	1,024,255	990,256	594,542	973,831	28.8
Ratio of income share of highest 20% to that of lowest 20%		3.6	3.8	4.4	4.2	3.9	4.3	4.5	4.3	

Source: Department of Budget, Accounting & Statistics, Taipei City Government, Report on the Family Income & Expenditure Survey, p. 8; pp.164–165.

a local service and finance centre in the 1970s. However, in the 1990s, a new crisis – the continuous exodus of the manufacturing sector and a standstill in the service sector – has had an impact on Taipei's employment structure.

There are two causes which influenced international labour movement in Taipei City. The first was the rise of Taiwan's high-tech industry. National industrialization policy (see Chapter 1) resulted in a geographically decentralized production accompanied by a sharp spatial division of labour. The inflow of direct foreign investment and the return of overseas educated labour contributed to the rapid growth of Taiwan's high-tech industry in the 1980s. The second was the industrial response to the intensive global competition, which led to Taiwan firms having to relocate abroad in lower production cost locations and to introduce cheaper foreign contract workers.

The movement of international labour in Taiwan has changed from a state-initiated 'brain return' to a market-initiated 'brain drain' for white-collar labour in the past five decades. Although the state has been forced to open its borders to migration, it keeps a close control on selective immigrant labour. In the first wave of economic restructuring, the state kept tight control on migration but attracted the return of skilled and educated emigrants with employment in the public sector. In the private sector, the return of Taiwanese professionals – rather than foreign experts who dominated economic development in the Third World – played a pivotal role in Taiwan's high-tech industry. The network they built to connect Taipei with the global electronic industry has created successful high-tech development.

In the second wave of economic restructuring, the demand for low-wage workers forced the state to allow service labour migration. The majority of Taipei's foreign white-collar migrants are traders and teachers. Contract migrant workers, foreign brides and illegal migrant workers constitute a source for low-level services and the sex industry. Female migrant workers are an important source of domestic labour for the urban middle class. Illegal Southeast Asian and Chinese workers are emerging as a new underclass in the urban economy. Migrant domestic workers and sex workers in the urban service sector have become the most disadvantaged group.

This chapter has discussed polarization from the point of view of occupational change and income distribution. The upper class and the lower class have stabilized over time in Taipei. Instead of social polarization, there is a growing middle class. The 'global elite' began to emigrate while the urban underclass was dispersed to the peripheries or shifted to services or was replaced by migrant blue-collar labour.

An analysis of income distribution in Taipei took two factors into consideration: the migrant workers who constitute the low earning class of the urban economy, and household disposable income. State regulation for the labour market contributes to the disparity in earnings between migrant workers and their local counterparts. In the urban production sector, as in the manufacturing and construction, foreign contract workers' earnings stand at lower than 80 per cent of local workers'. In the urban reproduction sector, foreign domestic workers' wages are only one-third or half of local workers' earnings. The household disposable income gap between global professionals and low-wage labourers has gradually increased. Along with globalization, the income inequality is rising in Taipei.

At least three factors may help to explain why socio-economic polarization, though occurring in Taipei, is not as significant as in the global cities. The first is the economic link across the Taiwan Strait. With increasing capital outflow to China, a corresponding outflow of business executives and managers occurs. This population flow has built a new network between Taipei and China's southeast coast. The second factor is Taipei's industrial restructuring. Taipei is not a typical post-industrial city. It has a contracting manufacturing sector and an expanding service sector. The decrease in the manufacturing sector of the 1980s was not as significant as the increase in the service sector between 1980 and 1990. The expanded service sector then gave rise to the growth of the middle class which kept social polarization in check. The third factor is the relatively low number of recent migrants to Taipei City, as manufacturing jobs are relocating overseas. Migrant foreign contract workers, while contributing less to the urban labour force, highlight the conditions of ethnic bias and income inequality.

Taipei has been classified as a secondary city in the Asian sub-global system centred on the Tokyo-Singapore axis (Friedmann and Wolff, 1982). Directed by the developmental state, Taipei, under state regulation within the context of globalization, emerges as a regional city with selective migrant labour rather than a global city with international migrant labour.

Notes

1. The original source was from *China Monthly Statistics*, published by the China Statistical Information and Consulting Company. The citation was from *Cross-Strait Economic Statistics Monthly*, January 2001, p. 35, published by the Mainland Affairs Council of Taiwan. Because Taiwan's statistics do not record visits to mainland China, Taiwan tends to underestimate these figures. In 2001, for example, the number of registered Taiwan nationals going to mainland China was 548,764, while mainland Chinese entering Taiwan was 155,001.
2. The qualifications include:
   (1) PhD degree and more than two years work experience;
   (2) Master's degree and more than three years work experience;
   (3) Bachelor's degree and more than five years work experience;
   (4) Special achievement in research.
3. The Regulation of Education Department, International Education, pp. 555–556.
4. *China Times*, September 4, 2000.
5. Forney, Matthew, *Time*, 21 May 2001, Volume 157, Number 20, p. 30.
6. Population Affairs Administration, and National Policy Administration, Department of Interior, Taiwan, http://moi.tw/W3/stat/home/asp.
7. Secret China, http://www.secretchina.com/news/.

8. The number of government employees in Taiwan was 209,212 in 1993, and it rose to 237,765 in 2002. The number of government employees did not decrease after the elimination of the Taiwan Provincial Government in 1998 (http://www/exam.gov.tw/). Moreover, the Taipei City government employed 80,930 people in 1993 which increased to 81,756 in 2002 (Statistical Abstract of Taipei City, pp. 166–169).

References

Abella, M. (1994) Turning points in labour migration. *Asian and Pacific Migration Journal*, **3**(1), pp. 1–7.

Abella, M. and Mori, H. (1996) Structural change and labour migration in East Asia, in O'Connor, D. and Farsakh, L. (eds.) *Development Strategy, Employment and Migration: Country Experiences*. Paris: OECD, pp. 35–62.

Athukorala, P. (1993) International labour migration in the Asian-Pacific region: patterns, policies and economic implications. *Asia-Pacific Economic Literature*, **7**(2), pp. 28–57.

Baum, S. (1999) Social transformation in the global city. *Urban Studies*, **36**(7), pp. 1095–1117.

Chang, S.L. (1992) Causes of brain drain and solution: the Taiwan experience. *Studies in Comparative International Development*, **27**(1), pp. 27–43.

Casteles, S. and Miller, M.J. (1993) *The Age of Migration: International Population Movements in the Modern World*. London: Macmillan.

Castells, M. (1992) Four Asian tigers with a dragon head, in Appelbaum, Richard P. and Henderson, Jeffrey (eds.) *States and Development in the Asian Pacific Rim*. Thousand Oaks, CA: Sage.

Cheng, L. and Yang, P.Q. (1998) Global interaction, global inequality, and migration of the highly trained to the United States. *International Migration Review*, **32**(3), pp. 626–653.

Cheng, S.J.A. (1996) Migrant women domestic workers in Hong Kong, Singapore and Taiwan: a comparative analysis, in Battiste, Graziano and Paganoni, Anthony (eds.) *Asian Women in Migration*. Quezon City, Philippines: Scalabrini Migration Center.

Eviota, E.U. (1992) *The Political Economy of Gender: Women and Sexual Division of Labour in the Philippines*. London: Zed Books.

Fainstein, S., Gordon, I. and Harloe, M. (1992) *Divided Cities: New York and London in the Contemporary World*. Oxford: Blackwell.

Findlay, A.M., Jones, H. and Davidson, G.M. (1998) Migration transition or migration transformation in the Asian Dragon economies? *Internaitonal Journal of Urban and Regional Research*, **22**, pp. 643–663.

Friedmann, J. (1986) The city in global context. *Development and Change*, **1**(17), pp. 69–83.

Friedmann, J. (2001) World cities revisited: a comment. *Urban Studies*, **38**(13), pp. 2535–2536.

Friedmann, J. and Wolff, G. (1982) World city formation. *International Journal of Urban and Regional Research*, **6**, pp. 306–344.

Hammnet, C. (1994) Social polarization in global cities: theory and evidence. *Urban Studies*, **31**(3), pp. 401–424.

Hannerz, U. (1993) The cultural roles of world cities, in Cohen, A.P. and Fukuo, K. (eds.) *Humanizing The City?* Edinburgh: Edinburgh University Press.

Henderson, J. and Castells, M. (1987) *Global Restructuring and Territorial Development*. Thousand Oaks, CA: Sage.

Heyzer, N. and Wee, V. (1994) Domestic workers in transient overseas employment: who benefits, who profits? in Heyzer, N., Lycklama à Nijeholt, G. and Weerakoon, N. (eds.) *The Trade in Domestic Workers: Causes, Mechanisms and Consequences of International Migration*. London: Zed Books.

Hill, R.C. and Kim, W. (2000) Global cities and developmental states: New York, Tokyo and Seoul. *Urban Studies*, **37**(12), pp. 2167–2195.

Hill, R.C. and Kim, W. (2001) Reply to Friedmann and Sassen. *Urban Studies*, **38**(13), pp. 2541–2542.

Hsai, H.C. (2000) Transnational marriage and internationalization of capital – the case of the 'foreign bride' phenomenon in Taiwan. *Taiwan: A Radical Quarterly in Social Studies*, No.39, pp. 45–92.

Iredale, R. (2000) Migration policies for the highly skilled in the Asia-Pacific region. *International Migration Review*, **34**(3), pp. 882–906.

Kanjanapan, W. (1992) Immigration of Asian professionals to the U.S. *International Migration Review*, **9**(4), pp. 7–32.

Lim, L.L. and Abella, M. (1994) The movement of people in Asia: internal, intra-regional and international migration. *Asian and Pacific Migration Journal*, **3**(2/3), pp. 209–250.

Lin, C.J. (2000) The state policy that divides women: rethinking feminist critiques to 'The Foreign Maid Policy' in Taiwan. *Taiwan: A Radical Quarterly in Social Studies*, No. 39, pp. 93–151.

Lin, J.P. and Tsay, C.L. (2000) Labour migration and allocation of human resources in Taiwan: return and onward cases. *Asian and Pacific Migration Journal*, **9**(1), pp. 1–31.

Massey, D.S. (1988) International migration and economic development in comparative perspective. *Population and Development Review*, **14**, pp. 383–414.

Noriel, C.C. (1993) Labour rights in selected Asian countries. *Asian and Pacific Migration Journal*, **2**(2), pp. 147–160.

O'Loughlin, J. and Friedichs, J. (1996) *Social Polarization in Post-Industrial Metropolises*. Berlin: Walter de Gruyter.

Salt, J. and Findlay, A. (1989) International migration of highly-skilled manpower: theoretical and developmental issues, in Appleyard, R.T. (ed.) *The Impact of International Migration on Developing Countries*. Washington, DC: OECD Publications and Information Center.

Sassen, S. (1988) *The Mobility of Labour and Capital*. Cambridge: Cambridge University Press.

Sassen, S. (1991) *The Global City*. Princeton, NJ: Princeton University Press.

Sassen, S. (1994) *City in a World Economy*. Thousand Oaks: Pine Forge Press.

Sassen, S. (2001) Global cities and developmentalist states: how to derail what could be an interesting debate: a response to Hill and Kim. *Urban Studies*, **38**(13), pp. 2537–2540.

Skeldon, R. (1997) *Migration and Development: A Global Perspective*. Harlow: Addison Wesley Longman.

Stahl, C.W. (1995) Theories of international labour migration: an overview. *Asian and Pacific Migration Journal*, **4**, pp. 211–232.

Stahl, C.W. and Appleyard, R.T. (1992) International manpower flows in Asia: an overview. *Asian and Pacific Migration Journal*, **1**(3/4), pp. 417–476.

Tai, P.F. (1994) Who are vendors? The historical formation of vendors in Taiwan. *Taiwan: A Radical Quarterly in Social Studies*, No. 17, pp. 121–148.

Tsai, Y.M. and Chang, Y.H. (1997) *Taiwan's Urban Society*. Taipei: Ju liu Publishment.

Tsay, C.L. (1992) Clandestine labour migration to Taiwan. *Asian and Pacific Migration Journal*, **1**(3/4), pp. 637–655.

Tsay, C.L. (2001) Urban population in Taiwan and the growth of the Taipei Metropolitan Area, in Lo, Fu-chen and Marcotullio, Peter J. (eds.) *Globalization and the Sustainability of Cities in the Asia Pacific Region*. Tokyo: United Nations University Press.

Tzeng, R. (1995) International labour migration through multinational enterprises. *International Migration Review*, **29**, pp. 139–154.

Wacquant, L. (2000) Logics of urban polarization: the view from below, in Crompton, Rosemary, Devine, Fiona and Scott, John (eds.) *Renewing Class Analysis*. Oxford: Blackwell, pp.107–119.

Wade, R. (1990) *Governing the Market: Economic Theory and the Role of Government in East Asian Industrialization*, Princeton, NJ: Princeton University Press.

Wang, C.H. (2003) Taipei as a global city: a theoretical and empirical examination. *Urban Studies*, **40**(2), pp. 309–334.

Wang, H.Z. (2001) Social stratification, Vietnamese partners migration and Taiwan labour market. *Taiwan: A Radical Quarterly in Social Studies*, No. 41, pp. 99–127.

Wang, J.H. (1996) *Who Governs Taiwan? State Apparatus and Power Structure*. Taipei: Ju liu Publishment.

Wang, J.H. (1997) Governance of a cross-border economic region: Taiwan and Southern China. *Taiwan: A Radical Quarterly in Social Studies*, No, 27, pp. 1–36.

Wang, J.H. (2002) Different routes towards world city formation in East Asia: Seoul and Taipei compared, *Taiwan: A Radical Quarterly in Social Studies*, No. 47, pp. 85–131.

White, G. (1988) *Developmental States in East Asia*. Brighton: University of Sussex.

Wu, H.L. and Zhang, Y. (1991) *Labour Shortages and Foreign Worker's Problem in Taiwan*. Taipei: Chung Hua Institute of Economic Research.

Chapter Eight

Daily Consumption in a Globalizing City: Food Markets at the Crossroads

Peter Cheng-Chong Wu

Contemporary urbanization in the global context, as earlier chapters have illustrated, has two faces: the global flows of people, money, commodities, and information, on the one hand, and the localized economic, political, social and cultural disparities, on the other. Mainstream research on urbanization and globalization, therefore, tends to focus on the global cities as control centres of the world economy. In the regional context of the Asia-Pacific, this is closely related to regional cities' changing roles in the processes of global economic restructuring (Smith, 2001). For others, notably urban sociologists and geographers, attention has been paid to such issues as employment, housing, transportation, crime, consumption, and education as discrete local problems. In reality these two worlds closely interweave with each other in the course of everyday urban life.

While Taiwan in general and Taipei in particular are moving from the back regions of global production systems to the front stages of global consumption networks, it requires a more balanced treatment of the relationships between the global and the local in the processes of production and consumption. The contemporary city, as Bromley and Thomas (1993, p. 2) note, 'is to a substantial degree articulated in relation to retail facilities, and this has important consequences for the nature of city growth and associated opportunities and constraints for urban planning'. Because the vast majority of the urban population is involved in some direct or indirect way with shopping activities and because retailing provides a necessary channelling between the daily consumption of individuals and the production system on the whole, this chapter examines the interplay between local consumption processes and global production networks by looking at the changing structures of food retailing and the associated market development in Taipei.

The focus on food retail can be justified on several grounds. As Counihan and van Esterik (1997, p. 1) argue, 'food is the foundation of everyday economy . . . a central pawn in political strategies of states and households'. To quote Belasco's (2002, p. 2) words, 'There is in fact nothing more basic. Food is the first of the essentials of life, the biggest industry . . .'. Food and other retailing has been an increasingly important source of employment and national income in both developed and developing countries. Moreover, as Lefebvre (1991) articulated in *Critique of Everyday Life*, things as simple as buying ordinary foodstuffs in a local market could involve very complicated interrelations of global economic-political restructuring and the related local socio-cultural connections. However, Crewe (2000, p. 276) observes that traditional retail geography focuses almost without exception on the food system by considering food retailing as a piece of the economy at the expense of more culturally sensitive accounts. This chapter, therefore, attempts to explore Taipei's food retailing in a more dynamic way by viewing the active production and transformation of various kinds of food markets as the product of economic, political and socio-cultural activities. The need to look at Taipei's markets in the globalizing context lies in the fact that throughout history, as Bestor (1999, p. 203) notes, 'cities and markets have sustained each other in ways that the former provide location, demand, and social context for the latter, while the latter provide substance, profit, and cultural verve to the former'. This city-market relationship is especially registered in the globalization era on the grounds that cities are no longer just playing their roles in organizing production activities but they are also major locales of consumption, entertainment and education (Hannigan, 1998).

Here 'markets' literately mean 'marketplaces' (*shichang*) or 'food markets' (*cai shichang*) where fresh and cooked food as well as a variety of household necessities are bought and sold. Via the market lens, we can get at the interwoven characteristics of Taipei's involvement in the complex networks of global and local production, distribution, exchange, and consumption of basic foodstuffs. It will then be possible to bring out the global-local connections in production and consumption, while casting a new light on the future of Taipei's role in both global and regional contexts.

The rest of the chapter is divided into three sections. The first section highlights the overall market structure in Taipei, with special reference to four types of market forms. They are traditional retail markets, supermarkets, hypermarkets (or superstores), and dusk markets (*huanghun shichang*). This is followed by a brief account of the major forces behind the market structure, notably the market tradition of street vending, the market intervention from the state, the market innovations of modern Western retailing, and the changing market needs related to changing household lifestyles. The chapter concludes by recasting Taipei's market development into a wider socio-cultural context of globalization from a living city's point of view. It stresses the need to take a fuller account of people's life and living experiences in the increasingly fragmented world of a globalizing city, while safeguarding the diversity of retail in order to assure a vibrant city for all.

A Pluralistic, Hybrid Market Structure: When the East Meets the West

Food markets in Taipei are not only passive intersections of demand and supply of foodstuffs, but also active contested landscapes for production, representation, and consumption. They are characterized by a pluralistic and hybrid development with distinctive features – unlike many large cities in developed societies where modern retail corporations, such as supermarkets and hypermarkets, dominate the urban market landscape; nor is it like many Third-World cities where small, independent food stores/vendors and traditional markets occupy the lion's share of the market; Taipei has a more balanced and diverse market structure.

In 2003, for example, Taipei had 82 traditional retail markets, 117 chain supermarkets, 8 hypermarkets and at least 10 major dusk markets. Traditional retail markets are the gathering of stallholders in purpose-built market buildings, selling daily foodstuffs such as vegetables and fruit, livestock and poultry, fish and shrimp, sun-dried foodstuffs, drinks, and other groceries. Supermarkets, by contrast, are self-service food stores of less than 2,500 square metres sales area (Cai, 1992; Department of Commerce, Ministry of Economic Affairs, 1994; Guy, 1994; Bowlby, 1997). Hypermarkets refer to self-service stores offering a wide range of food and non-food merchandise with at least 2,500 square metres net floor space and supported by car parking.[1] Dusk markets in Taipei are street markets comprised of small vendors operating in the late afternoon until early evening near residential areas selling food and household items similar to traditional retail markets.[2] Such a market structure involves not only the private retail sector but also the public and the informal sector. Moreover, these markets have very different business hours. Traditional retail markets open at normal business hours as day markets, especially in the morning. Most supermarkets and hypermarkets open longer hours from 8 o'clock in the morning to midnight; but an increasing number of supermarkets and some hypermarkets open 24 hours a day. Dusk markets, by contrast, only appear in the late afternoon and early evening (between 3 and 7 pm).

As far as their spatial distributions are concerned, different kinds of markets distribute quite evenly across Taipei. Because food markets in Taipei are local shopping facilities serving the communities in the neighbourhoods, their distribution is by and large in proportion to the distribution of Taipei's population.

Even the hypermarkets, which tend to be located in freestanding locations in the outer suburbs in Western countries, are sometimes found in the inner rings of Taipei. Accordingly, one can easily get access to a variety of markets within walking distance or a very short car trip.

There are, however, some variations in the distribution of the different kinds of markets. For example, there are more traditional retail markets in the inner parts of Taipei, especially in the older districts like Wanhua, Zhongzheng, Zhongshan, and Datong districts (figure 0.3 in Introduction). Supermarkets are as popular in the inner parts of Taipei as in suburban Taipei. Hypermarkets, by virtue of their large scale and nature of bulky shopping, tend to be distributed in the outer rings of Taipei, such as Beitou, Neihu, Nangang, and Jingmei districts (figure I.3 in Introduction), and in the outer suburbs of Taipei, Taipei county and Taoyuan county. More recently, some of the leading hypermarkets began to concentrate in the newly developed enterprise zones in Neihu where over 250 hectares of land became suitable for development following the straightening of the Keelung River in the mid 1990s. One of the most interesting phenomena in Taipei's market development, however, is the emergence of dusk markets in the streets of many residential areas. Together these different kinds of market create a diverse shopping environment that offers households a wide range of choice between different forms, times, and locations of markets. While Taipei is gradually becoming globalized, the question is: will this pluralistic market structure continue or will it move towards a monotonous market landscape dominated by large retail chains? Before answering this question, let us take a closer look at the development patterns and processes of different market forms.

Traditional Retail Markets: A Market Tradition in Decline

According to their legal statuses, traditional retail markets in Taipei can be divided into three categories: public retail markets, private retail markets, and temporary retail markets. Public retail markets are built by the government at places designated for market use in city plans (figures 8.1 and 8.2). Sales areas in the markets are divided into small units, or stalls, to lease to individual small traders, but the administration is directly under the city government. Private retail markets, in contrast, are built by private investors, usually the landowners, on private land (figure 8.3). They recruit small traders to organize a market and apply for permission from the city government. Moreover, in order to solve traffic and environmental problems created by street vendors, in 1985, the city government agreed that street vendors could have temporary legal status if they stayed in certain locations, the temporary retail markets. Very often these marketplaces are unused or underused public land, and in some cases, they are street or road spaces. As might be expected,

Figure 8.1. Public retail market building.

Figure 8.2. Public retail market.

Figure 8.3. Private retail market.

the quality of the shopping environment is much better in public retail markets than in private and temporary retail markets.

Traditional retail markets have been, and still are, the most important market institutions in Taipei. In 2003, Taipei had a total of 82 traditional retail markets, including 53 public retail markets, 11 private retail markets and 18 temporary retail markets. In urban planning, they are designated as neighbourhood public facilities; among others are parks, schools, hospitals, police stations, fire brigade, and so on. In other words, food markets are considered to be an important part of collective consumption in city life that requires constant monitoring and/or direct intervention from the state. This market policy, which makes traditional retail markets a historically important retail sector, can be traced back to the time of Japanese rule at the turn of the twentieth century. For the sake of hygiene, public order, and tax considerations, in 1900, the Japanese colonial government in Taiwan passed a law banning street vending, which was the most common form of food trading in Taiwan at that time, while using public retail markets as a measure of institutional control over food retailing. Not only were public markets carefully designed to meet the highest hygiene standards at that time, but also market regulations were stipulated to regulate trading practices in the markets, including the details of trading and the qualifications for stallholders (Zeng, 2000; Lin, 2002a, 2002b). In 1908, the first public retail market in Taiwan, Ximending Retail Market, opened in, the then, downtown Taipei. The number of public retail markets increased steadily thereafter. Among those retail markets set up in the Japanese ruling period, some were smaller private retail markets mainly serving Taiwan people. At the end of the Japanese ruling period (1949), there were 20 public and private retail markets in Taipei, and the island as a whole had over 200 retail markets.

During the period of Japanese rule, markets opened from 12 noon until the early evening. Most of the shoppers in the public retail markets were Japanese housewives who tended to go to the market in the afternoon around 3 or 4 pm, when they finished their housework. In the private retail markets a considerable number of the shoppers were men instead of women. This was partly because Taiwanese women at that time tended to have more children and the task of childcare and other housework made it difficult to go out, and partly, because many Taiwanese women had bound feet that made shopping trips rather difficult. So buying from street peddlers on the doorstep was very common for Taiwanese housewives, and this has much to do with the market culture of street vending.

At the end of World War II when Taiwan was handed back from Japan to China, the public market policy was adopted by the Nationalist government. It remains the guiding rule of the government's market policy today. The number of traditional retail markets increased substantially in the post-war years. It grew four times from 20 to over 80 in the years between 1950 and 1970. The 1970s was the heyday of traditional retail markets in Taipei. In the 1980s, traditional retail markets moved into a period of revitalization and modernization. Many markets built in the Japanese period were becoming old and dilapidated after several decades of use, and modern Western supermarkets were gradually becoming popular after a decade of development since their introduction into Taipei in the late 1960s. The need for a cleaner, brighter, and more pleasant market environment has become an overriding goal of traditional retail market renewal, especially in the socio-economic context of rising standards of living in Taipei. This was especially the case for public retail markets. Not only were the old single-level market buildings refurbished or rebuilt as modern three- or four-storey buildings, but also other facilities, such as, community centres, senior citizen clubs, and community libraries, were incorporated into the markets. It was believed that a multiple use of the traditional retail markets would maintain their central role in the neighbourhood.

Traditional retail markets, however, did not continue to revitalize, but turned to a steady, though slow, decline. In 2002, nearly 40 per cent of the stalls in public retail markets were vacant (figure 8.4) (Department of Budget, Accounting and Statistics, Taipei City Government, 2003). They are facing strong competition from supermarkets and other forms of market. Nevertheless, the decline of traditional retail markets may have more to do with their inability to accommodate the time-space changes of households' shopping practices than with the quality of the shopping environment. The business hours of most traditional retail markets are simply unsuitable for most career women, except during weekends. Moreover, the time may be suitable to housewives who do not have to work during the day, notably more senior ones, but the multi-storey design of the markets makes it difficult for them to walk up and down stairs while carrying heavy shopping bags.[3] As might be expected, traditional retail markets in general, and public retail

Figure 8.4. Vacant stalls in a public retail market.

markets in particular, are gradually losing their market share while other kinds of markets have expanded quickly in the last few decades.

Supermarkets: Supermarket Chains and 'Super Corner Shops'

The time when Taipei's traditional retail markets began to decline was also the time when modern supermarkets were in fast growth. Nevertheless, it was not until very recently that routine shopping in the supermarkets became a common experience for Taipei households. By 2003 a great majority of supermarkets in Taipei were the outlets of large supermarket chains. But the supermarkets in Taipei are different from the large, car-dependent supermarkets in the Western world, especially those in the suburbs of North American cities, in terms of location, scale, and ways of operating. This can be illustrated by the three development periods of Taipei's supermarkets.

1. The Emergence Period and Department Store Supermarkets

In 1969, the first supermarket in Taiwan, *Ximen* supermarket, opened in Ximending, traditional downtown Taipei. However, it was nothing more than a large self-serviced grocery store selling Western merchandise, such as, bread, canned and packaged food, and some frozen food. In 1971, *Dinghao* supermarket (figure 8.5), a bigger supermarket with a larger sales area and a wider range of merchandise, especially fresh and frozen foods, opened in Zhongxiao East Road, the eastern part of traditional downtown Taipei. Later the area was known as Dinghao shichang (market), one of the most fashionable places in town. In 1972, a then newly opened

Figure 8.5. Dinghao supermarket.

department store, *Xinxindazhong*, incorporated a supermarket in the basement of the department store. This was immediately followed by other department stores around the island. In the 1970s and the first half of the 1980s, department store supermarkets were the norm of Taipei's supermarket operation (Huang, 1989, 1993; Department of Commerce, Ministry of Economic Affairs, 1993). Nevertheless, the items and prices of the merchandise sold in department store supermarkets were very different from those sold in traditional retail markets. Supermarkets during this period were luxury consumption spaces representing the display window of the affluent Western lifestyles rather than the practical daily shopping places accessible to ordinary people.

2. *The Growth Period and Public Supermarkets*

Entering the 1980s, the market structure in Taipei began to change when the first public supermarket, *Yanji* supermarket had a grand opening on Yanji Street near the Dinghao shichang area. It was first planned as a public traditional retail market for the local street vendors. The street vendors, however, considered the planned market location was unsuitable and refused to move in. Later, Taipei City Government negotiated with some leading department stores which had successful supermarket experiences to take over. Again, these department stores thought that it was too risky to open an independent supermarket on the edge of the central commercial area and were unwilling to take over. Finally, a then national enterprise, Taipei Agricultural Marketing Corporation, which ran the wholesale markets in Taipei, was invited to run the market. Without any supermarket experience, Taipei Agricultural Marketing Corporation used their experience in the wholesale markets and the advantages of their commodity networks to open the very first public supermarket in 1980. Because the market provided a wide range of fresh vegetables and fruit at affordable prices, it was a great success. In the next few years, more public supermarkets were opened in different districts of the city as a part of the revitalization and modernization policy for public retail markets.

In the meantime, the private sector also responded actively by joining the supermarket war. In the 1980s, a variety of supermarkets, large and small, independent and chained, mushroomed in Taipei. Supermarkets were no longer the jewel in the crown. They gradually moved into communities all over the city and began to compete with traditional retail markets. However, a considerable proportion of the supermarket expansion in the 1980s was from the growth of mini-marts, i.e. larger grocery stores mainly selling packaged food and household necessities but with a very limited range of fresh food, instead of from the growth of large modern supermarkets. It was not until the 1990s that large, modern supermarkets, especially supermarket chains, became popular in Taipei.

3. *Supermarket Chains and Community Supermarkets*

In the 1990s, fierce competition in food retailing and advances in distribution systems led supermarkets to move into the period of chain operation. It was characterized by a fast expansion of a few large supermarket chains and the closing down of many others, mainly independent supermarkets and mini-marts. In 2003, the three leading supermarket chains, Wellcome, Taipei Agricultural Marketing Corporation and Songqing accounted for more than 85 per cent of the number of supermarkets in Taipei.

However, unlike many large supermarket chains in the United States and other European countries, most of the outlets of Taipei's supermarket chains are located in communities in both downtown and suburban areas (figures 8.6 and 8.7). Their average sales area is relatively small, about 800 square metres. Many of the supermarkets are opened in the basement of residential or commercial buildings. That means these supermarkets are local, community supermarkets within walking distance. They open longer hours from 7 am to 11 pm, and an increasing number of them are now opening 24 hours a day. Most of the community supermarkets do not

Figure 8.6. Community supermarket

Figure 8.7. Community supermarket in a basement.

have any, or only have a limited space for, cars to park. Moreover, the merchandise sold in the supermarkets is, generally, in smaller packages and the prices of fresh food are slightly higher than those sold in traditional retail markets. Therefore, people tend to use the community supermarkets for packaged food, frozen food, household necessities, and, less often, for fresh food, on a more frequent but smaller quantity basis. Most of such shopping trips are made on foot or by motorcycle. They are very different from those weekly or fortnightly major shopping trips made by car to free-standing supermarkets in Western countries. In other words, to a certain extent the community supermarkets in Taipei are more like 'super corner shops' that supplement, rather than substitute, traditional retail markets in the provision of foodstuffs and daily necessities.

Hypermarkets: Shopping Baskets on Wheels

In the 1990s, the competition between different kinds of markets in Taipei became more intense. One important factor that contributed to the fierce competition in Taipei's market development was the introduction of the hypermarkets (*da'aichang*). Here hypermarkets and superstores (*liangfandian*) are used interchangeably with the understanding that hypermarkets are large general superstores, and sometimes superstores are used to describe non-food stores of the retail warehouse type, or specialty superstores. But in the United States and Britain, hypermarkets and superstores are slightly different in terms of their scale and type of merchandise. Superstores mean single-level, self-service stores offering a wide range of food and non-food merchandise, with at least 2,500 square metres sales area and supported by car parking, while hypermarkets refer to general superstores of at least 5,000 square metres sales area (Guy, 1994, p. xvi) (figure 8.8).

Figure 8.8. Hypermarket with car park.

Although hypermarkets have undergone a long period of development in Western countries, it was not until 1989 that the first hypermarket in Taiwan, Makro (a joint venture of a local investment group, Fengqun Group, in association with the Dutch retail giant SHV Group and Thai food retailer, Charoen Pokphand Enterprise), opened in the warehouse/light industrial zone in Taoyuan, an outer suburb of metropolitan Taipei, 40 minutes by car from central Taipei. It was a great success that dramatically changed the retail environment in Taiwan. Although originally targeted at business customers as a wholesale warehouse, Makro also attracted many household customers who considered the wholesale packages better value for money. In the same year, the French hypermarket retailer Carrefour joined the market by cooperating with a local food retail giant, the President Group (also a market leader in convenience store chains, the 7-Eleven). Again, Carrefour chose to locate in the outer suburb of northeast Taipei near Xizhi, some 30 minutes by car from central Taipei. But unlike Makro, which was a wholesale warehouse targeted at business customers, Carrefour defined itself as a general hypermarket providing services to ordinary customers.

In 1990, Makro opened their second outlet in a warehouse/industrial zone in Niehu, in eastern Taipei. It was also the first hypermarket opened in Taipei City. In the next few years, a lot more hypermarkets joined the market, including both foreign and local names, such as, Costco from the United States (figure 8.9), Géant-Casino from France, Tesco from Britain, and many other local firms (Teng, 2001; Kelly, 2000). In 1995, a local hypermarket, RT-Mart, acquired another two local hypermarkets, Save & Safe and APIC, and became one of the largest hypermarket brands in Taiwan. Since then, hypermarkets have been playing an increasingly important role in the food retailing sector. In 1994, for example, hypermarkets as a whole had annual sales of NT$50.5 billion, compared to NT$51.1 billion for the

Figure 8.9. Costco hypermarket.

supermarkets. But in 2000, while the sales of supermarkets in Taiwan increased to NT$75.7 billion, the sales rose to NT$151.2 billion for hypermarkets (Ministry of Economic Affairs, 2001).

In 2003, there were a total of 8 hypermarkets in Taipei (Carrfour (2), RT-Mart (2), Géant-Hyper (2), Costco and Tesco).[4] Several of them are concentrated in the newly developed warehouse/industrial zone near the Keelung River shoreline in Niehu. Together with other specialty superstores, such as, Hola (home centre), B&Q (DIY), Cankun 3C (computer and electronics), Lili (furniture), and Autobacs (automobile specialties), they have created a new retail landscape similar to a retail park in Western countries. And this has profound implications for both the market structure and the associated shopping practices in Taipei. By virtue of hypermarkets' large scale and their out-of-centre locations, shopping trips to hypermarkets made by car on a less frequent, bulk buying basis are very different from those local shopping trips made on foot or by riding motorcycle to traditional retail markets or community supermarkets more frequently and for small quantity purchases (figures 8.10 and 8.11). Moreover, unlike most local shopping practices, which are mainly undertaken by women, a considerable proportion of the shopping trips to hypermarkets are made by men. Partly because most households in Taipei have only one car in the household that is used mainly by the men for their daily commuting, thus it is more difficult for women to have access to the car during the day. Also, partly because men are better able to carry the bulk shopping following trips to the hypermarkets, though women may still be the major shoppers in the households. It is apparent that a trend of new gender division of household labour is taking place in the hypermarkets. Food shopping is no more merely a household chore relegated to women but is increasingly incorporating leisure elements shared by household members. In these hypermarkets, food shopping is often combined with other

Figure 8.10. Bulk buying in a hypermarket.

Figure 8.11. Modern Shopping in a hypermarket.

shopping for personal items or household goods. This is especially apparent in the Neihu enterprise zone where the variety of hypermarkets and specialty superstores makes the out-of-centre location an increasingly important retail space in Taipei in contrast to local markets and downtown department stores.

Dusk Markets: Cancer of the City or Light of the City?

Apart from the three main kinds of markets mentioned earlier, there also exists one more inconspicuous market form, the dusk market, which is an important contributor to the diversity of Taipei's market structure. Dusk markets represent the manifestation of a traditional market culture of individual traders and street vending. The number of street vendors continues to grow even when they face strong suppression from the government and fierce competition from other market institutions. Moreover, some street vendors have gradually become institutionalized, thought not in the sense of a formal market organization, and developed into different market formats. Dusk markets and night markets are two of the most important types of informal street markets in Taipei. The major differences between dusk markets and night markets lie at the kinds of goods they sell. Night markets are leisure and tourist oriented markets selling snack food and drinks, clothes, and a wide variety of goods (figures 8.12 and 8.13). They are located in central or nodal locations with larger catchment areas and longer business hours, normally from early evening until midnight. Dusk markets, in contrast, are local food markets selling daily foodstuffs and household necessities in the neighbourhood areas. As far as daily food shopping is concerned, the discussion here is restricted to dusk markets.

Dusk markets have existed in Taipei for 20 years. One of the most distinctive features of Taipei's dusk markets is their spread along streets, mainly in smaller

Figure 8.12. Night market.

Figure 8.13. Night market stalls.

streets or wider lanes in residential or mixed-use areas where traffic is less busy than on main roads (figure 8.14). Because dusk markets use the sidewalks or road space on the street, they are open-air markets rather than roofed ones. This is different from those dusk markets in other towns and cities in Taiwan, where dusk markets are concentrated in enclosed private land at off-road locations. Dusk markets are nicknamed 'garbage markets'. Many goods sold there are either inferior in quality or cheaper in price because they are unsold items from traditional retail markets in the morning and are to be cleared at lower prices in the afternoon.

The spatial arrangement and the development processes vary from one dusk market to another, and each dusk market has a very different scale and organization from the next. For example, some dusk markets only gather a dozen vendors on a small lane of a residential area, while others are large clusters of more than 200 stands, sprawling hundreds of metres and crossing several blocks. Some dusk markets do not have any formal agreement between vendors but there is a clear understanding between them as to the division of territories, while others have formal arrangements to organize the market, such as, assignment of stand locations to individual vendors, collecting money to install water and electricity, and hiring people to clean the streets when the markets are closed. Moreover, some dusk markets even attempt to move a step farther by petitioning the Taipei City Government and the City Council for legal status as traditional retail markets. Notwithstanding, because dusk markets are neither formally organized nor legally recognized, they are under-theorized and largely neglected in retail literature. Very often they are indiscriminately mingled with other types of street trading characterized as the informal sector of street vending, and almost no official statistics or market surveys are available about their locations, scale, composition and sales. It is estimated that in Taipei there are at least 10 large dusk markets which

Figure 8.14. Dusk market along the streets.

have 50 or more stands. The number may be doubled or even tripled if the smaller and less established ones are taken into account. They represent one of the most important market landscapes in Taipei. For many people, dusk markets are the most accessible shopping facilities in terms of time and space – they are right in the neighbourhood at a suitable time. Therefore, dusk markets must be understood in the context of the changing time-space configurations of everyday household lives and the associated changing shopping needs in Taipei.

First and foremost, the business hours of dusk markets, typically from late afternoon to early evening (figure 8.15), suggest that the time-space arrangements of modern urban households have undergone some dramatic changes in the last 20 years. This is especially apparent for career women who have to reorganize their schedules to accommodate the more fragmented moments between work, leisure and housework. Second, the higher proportion of prepared and cooked foods sold in dusk markets implies that the eating and cooking habits of many urban households have shifted to more convenient and/or more efficient ways of meal preparation (figure 8.16). In the dusk markets, people can buy cooked food for main dishes, vegetables for a quick stir-fry, plus some steamed buns, if they do not have time to cook rice at home – and a dinner to serve a family of four can be ready in half an hour, with fresh fruits and deserts. Third, the appearance of dusk markets in the neighbourhood areas brings back a vibrant street life to a city that has seen car traffic dominate road space for many years. Now in the afternoon, housewives, children and the elderly can walk safely on the street to browse and do the food shopping, while career women can have a quick shop on their way home in the early evening. Last but not least, the vibrant street life created by dusk markets is accompanied by some negative side effects, namely, litter, traffic congestion, an environmental amenity problems, and the like. However, the dusk markets as a

Figure 8.15. Dusk market in the early evening.

Figure 8.16. Food stalls in a dusk market.

daily consumption space do trigger a force of resistance from the prevailing formal retail and predominantly Western modes of modern retailing.

Dominance and Resistance:
Forces behind the Market Development

The patterns and processes of Taipei's market development suggest that the market structure in Taipei, as in other Southeast Asian cities, has undergone a dramatic change in the last few decades (Othman, 1990; Chen, 1999; Lau and Lee, 1988; Li, 2000; Tan and Teoh, 1988). It is characterized by a process of retail modernization involving a dynamic relation of dominance and resistance between different market forms. This is exemplified by the growth of supermarkets in the last 30 years and, more recently, the rise of hypermarkets along with the decline of traditional retail markets and the emergence of dusk markets. It seems that Taipei is facing a sweeping 'retail revolution' in food retailing akin to what happened in North America half a century ago, or what Britain experienced a quarter of century ago (Huang, 1996; Huang, 1989; Kaynak, 1988; Worpole, 1992; Wrigley, 1993; Wrigley and Lowe, 1996; Benson and Ugolini, 2003). But the pluralistic and hybrid nature of Taipei's current market structure also suggests that Taipei may take a different route of retail development in the course of globalization. There are several factors contributing to such market dynamics, among the most important are the market culture of stall trading, intervention from the state, the influence of retail innovations, and changes in shopping needs.

One of the most important characteristics of contemporary food retailing in Taipei is the market culture of stall trading. It consists of the basic units in the markets: the stalls. The history of stall trading dates back long before the rise of cities. Gradually, it has developed into different forms, including street peddlers, hawkers, dusk markets, night markets, traditional retail markets, and even formal retail markets. This 'market culture' is in contrast to the 'store culture' of Western food retailing. The latter has been the vanguard of modern food and grocery retailing (Alexander and Akehurst, 1999; Benson and Shaw, 1999; Crossick and Jaumain, 1999; Benson and Ugolini, 2003). Although modern Western retail stores, like convenience stores, supermarkets and hypermarkets, are now popular in Taiwan, the lion's share of their sales is concentrated in packaged food and other household items. In supermarkets, for example, fresh food only accounts for one-fifth of the sale areas, and the percentage of sales is even lower. It was not until very recently that food stores have gradually become common in Taipei. But the types of stores are limited to greengrocers selling fresh vegetables and fruit, and other types of food stores such as butchers and fishmongers are hardly seen. In other words, the market culture of stall trading still holds a strong position in Taipei's market structure; and a very important part of the history of Taipei's market development is centred on the suppression, accommodation, and resistance of stall trading.

On the one hand, stall trading on the street constitutes one of the most important retail sectors, the informal sector, of Taiwan's urban economy. It is considered to be a product of less developed economies, providing employment opportunities for the disadvantaged groups; and its importance will diminish when the economy and national income grow to a certain level (Hart, 1973; Button, 1984; Chen, 1986; Feng and Xu, 1986; Portes *et al.*, 1989; Dai, 1994; Maldonado, 1995; Chen, 1997; Williams and Windebank, 2001; Chang and Zhou, 1997). However, with the increase of national income in the past few decades, the number of street vendors has not decreased; in contrast, it has increased substantially (Directorate-General of Budget, Accounting and Statistics, Executive Yuan, 1989; 1999). On the other hand, many street vendors are incorporated into the formal market organizations through strong state intervention. The market culture of stall trading, both in the markets and on the streets, creates a vibrant shopping environment in Taipei that can hardly be replaced by large-scale, self-service retail.

Apart from the market culture of stall trading, in the history of Taipei's market development over the century, the state has been playing a key role in shaping the overall market structure in Taipei. From the designation of marketplaces in planning, the construction of public market buildings, the involvement in the operations of public supermarkets and wholesale markets, to the suppression and incorporation of street vendors, the government has interfered in food retailing to an extent that seems to run against the logic of a free economy. The policy of strong intervention in the market might justify itself as a measure to secure appropriate food supply in the post-war years. However, this market intervention has increasingly become a 'market failure' on the grounds that public retail markets are gradually losing their market share when faced with strong competition from the private sector. Shabby market buildings, deteriorating shopping environments, and inappropriate business hours are but a few symptoms of the decline of public retail markets. After a series of attempts to revitalize public retail markets, such as rebuilding and/or refurbishing the markets, modernizing the shopping environments in the markets, providing consultancy services to individual markets and stallholders, initiating promotion campaigns, and so on, the trend of decline continues, but merely at a slower pace.

Public supermarkets, by contrast, are doing slightly better than traditional retail markets. Because of their close relationship with the wholesale markets and the scale of economies of quantity purchasing, public supermarkets sell fresh food at lower prices than individual stallholders in traditional retail markets.[5] Nevertheless, public supermarkets are gradually losing their competitive advantage to private supermarket chains and large hypermarkets that are supported by international capital and advanced management. The tradeoffs between public and private supermarkets are illustrated by the growth in the number of private supermarkets. In 2003, for example, private supermarkets accounted for 80 per cent of the supermarkets in Taipei. Most importantly, an increasing number of the public supermarket buildings are now leased to private supermarkets (10 out of 27 in 2003). Even with diminishing importance, public supermarkets still play an important role in stabilizing the price levels for agricultural products in typhoon seasons.

While the government is heavily involved in the operation of different kinds of markets in Taipei, the lack of clear market policies is a major threat to a healthy retail environment in the capital city, especially as Taipei moves rapidly towards a globalizing city. The policy ambiguities between suppressing and encouraging street trading and between safeguarding public markets and protecting private retailers are just two cases in point. This suggests that a vision of the overall market structure is crucial to a vital and viable retail environment for a globalizing Taipei.

While the interplay between the market culture of stall trading and market intervention from the state has set the tone for Taipei's market structure, the introduction of modern Western retail practices also triggered an institutional transformation of Taipei's market structure from traditional modes of market operation to a modern retailing industry. This market transformation is closely related to the retail innovations that characterized the 'retail revolution' sweeping through Western countries. These retail innovations supported by modern computerized stocking systems, advanced freezing and transportation technologies, and state-of-the-art marketing techniques have fundamentally changed the retail landscape that is manifested in the concentration of retail capital in the hands of a relatively small number of corporations and the continuing growth of large multiple chains in out-of-centre locations, usually at the expense of small, independent stores in both central and local locations (O'Brien and Harris, 1991; Worpole, 1992; Wrigley, 1993; Burke and Shackleton, 1996; Lowe and Wrigley, 1996).

The pace and patterns of Taipei's market transformation are very different from the 'retail revolution' observed in Western countries. Rather than a direct 'import' from the United States, where most of the modern retail innovations originated, many of the modern market practices adopted in Taipei were introduced into the capital city via very different routes and indirect sources from other areas, such as, England, France, Holland, Hong Kong, and especially, Japan (Huang, 1989; Department of Commerce, Ministry of Economic Affairs, 1993). As might be expected, although these modern markets share the same names as supermarkets or hypermarkets and do business in similar ways, with large sales areas, a wide range of merchandise, self-service, single checkout, and so on, in effect they connote very different social and cultural meanings in Taipei than in Western cities. This is exemplified by the three phases of Taipei's modern retail development discussed earlier.

Before the 1980s, supermarkets were a luxury food shopping environment serving a small group of the well-off population in downtown areas, especially in the department stores. The 1980s was a watershed for Taipei's market structure change, shifting from predominantly traditional modes of market operation towards modern forms of Western retailing. There was a mushrooming of large and small supermarkets in the capital city, including the opening of several public supermarkets and the launch of Taiwan's first hypermarket in the outer suburb of metropolitan Taipei in 1989. In the 1990s, the process of market transformation moved into a period of fast expansion. On the one hand, a few large chain supermarkets dominated the supermarket sector through acquisition and the opening of more new outlets in the neighbourhoods. On the other hand, hypermarkets sought to open larger outlets in free-standing locations selling merchandise at lower prices. In this period the conventional market logic of 'mass production' was replaced by the logic of 'mass retailing'. On the grounds of economies of scale in purchasing and marketing, these retail giants began to dominate the chains of commodities through horizontal expansion and vertical integration.

The net results of the market transformation affected by modern retail innovations are the decline of traditional market practices and the associated changes in food shopping and consumption, that is, from a relatively local food system to a national and, to an increasing extent, a global uniformity. Not only are more agricultural products grown farther away, the final products also take many forms and may be under very different names that have more to do with the ways or the forms of processing than with the raw materials themselves. Even the foodstuffs in their raw forms can have distinctive 'brand names' associated with the location of production, special treatment in the growth processes, the ways products are packaged, or simply by a marketing slogan on the wrapping. This phenomenon has been described by Goody (1982, p. 154) as the 'industrialization of cuisine', referring to a complicated relationship between the processing, mechanization, wholesaling, retailing, and transport of foodstuffs (see also, Bestor, 1999, p. 206). These changes have profound implications not only for the competition between different kinds of markets, which shapes Taipei's market structure, but also for the daily practices of food shopping and consumption that affect millions of the urban population. In turn, these routinized daily shopping experiences are crucial to the future of Taipei's market development.

Changing Household Lives, Changing Shopping Needs

The transformation of Taipei's market structure towards modern retail organizations and the associated shopping and eating practices are not taking place solely because of technological advances in food production, transportation, distribution, and marketing; rather, they are also closely related to the lifestyle changes of households. In the last 40 years, the economic development in Taiwan has, by and large, raised per capita income and living standards. As a consequence, the need for more and better food supply increased, including a wider choice of foodstuffs and an improved shopping environment. The economic factor partly explains why the supermarkets in Taipei have taken 20 years to develop since they were introduced into the capital in the late 1960s, while the hypermarkets needed just a few years to become popular in the 1990s.

Moreover, the changes of Taipei's market structure should be understood in a wider socioeconomic context of the changing time-space configurations of household lives, especially in the time-space conflicts between paid employment and housework for career women. As might be expected, modern women have always been the major shoppers in the households. It has changed little when more and more housewives go out to work. Most household work, such as, cleaning, childcare, cooking and food shopping, remains to be women's work. The paid employment, including what work, when to work, where to work, and the mode of transport, has imposed considerable constraints on women's time and household work. The work hours of 9 am to 5 pm make it difficult, if not impossible, for most career women to shop during the day, except at weekends or during holidays. Given that nearly 60 per cent of the female workforce in Taiwan is in paid employment (Directorate-General of Budget, Accounting and Statistics, Executive Yuan, 2003), it is not surprising that the daily shopping practices of two-earner households have changed considerably to accommodate the time-space constraints of the changing home-work relation.

A lack of time due to paid employment, the popularity of time- and labour-saving home appliances (such as, rice cookers, gas ranges and microwave ovens) and larger storage spaces in the home (large fridges and freezers) for fresh and prepared/cooked food, the isolated residential locations (for suburban households), considerations of the economies of bulk shopping, and the availability of a wide range of small bistros and restaurants as well as snack stalls near residential areas, all contribute to the changing needs in cooking and food shopping. In many a household, not only are breakfasts and lunches bought from shops or simply eaten out, but also an increasing number of dinners are treated in similar ways. It is common for a household to cook only a few meals a week and these meals tend to be simple, requiring less labour in preparation, and include instant noodles, microwave foods, takeout, pizza delivery, and so on.

As a consequence, the changing and diverse shopping needs can no longer be met by any single market organization in terms of suitable times, convenient locations, and appropriate varieties. In a sense, the rise in variety of market forms is a market response to the changing social and consumption needs. Given the complicated interplay between the traditional market culture of stall trading, the market policy of state intervention, the introduction of Western retail innovations, as well as the changing household lives and changing shopping needs, what is unclear is whether such a diverse market development will continue, or whether it will move from traditional small market practices towards modern large retail operations. This has profound implications for Taipei when the capital city is moving towards a globalizing city.

Summary and Conclusion

To sum up, there have been some persistent trends of dominance and resistance in the processes of Taipei's market development. The first trend is the ongoing struggle between formal and informal markets. In the past, there were frequent confrontations between street vendors and traditional retail markets. In recent years, the situation has risen to an institutional level of market competition between informal dusk markets and other formal markets such as traditional retail markets and supermarkets/hypermarkets. The second trend is the market conflict between public and private sectors, especially between public and private retail markets in traditional retail markets and between public and private supermarket chains in modern food retailing. In a sense, the interference of the state in food retailing and its slow accommodation to market change has hindered the adjustment of Taipei's market structure in the global era. The third trend is the continuing trade-off between traditional and modern modes of market operation which is characterized as a persistent shift from small, individual market traders towards large, chained, and predominantly Western-style retail enterprises. As a consequence, these market trends create a unique retail environment in Taipei that exhibits a pluralistic, hybrid nature – a market structure that is neither a defence for conventional market practices nor an unthinkable duplication of Western retail operations.

For example, while most large supermarket chains choose to open smaller outlets in basements of tower buildings in the residential areas around Taipei, some hypermarkets are moving from the outskirts of Taipei metropolitan area into the edge of the inner rings. Moreover, different types of market practices increasingly mingle with each other. Supermarkets and hypermarkets, for instance, have incorporated traditional market ingredients of personal services such as small stalls (butcher, baker, fishmonger, and the like) and sales information (not called out by a vendor but broadcast from a tape). Traditional retail markets and dusk markets, in contrast, have included more imported foodstuffs and adopted similar packaging and pricing tactics to those used in modern supermarkets and hypermarkets. Behind these pluralistic and hybrid market scenes, it seems that the market development in Taipei is at the crossroads between formal and informal market organizations, between public and private market sectors, between traditional and modern market operations, and between small market traders and large retail enterprises.

The experiences of Western retail development suggest that a pluralistic development could be a short-term phenomenon in the middle of a process of moving towards a monolithic retail landscape dominated by large retailers at the expense of small, individual traders. This is illustrated by the dynamics of retail development in North America in the 1950s and 1960s, and a similar story in England, in the 1970s and 1980s (see Gayler, 1984; Burke and Shackleton, 1996; Longstreth, 1997; Ruston, 1999; Smith, 1997; Wrigley, 1993). In like manner, while the introduction of modern, Western retail practices into Taipei has provided more choice and better services to customers, the retail landscape in Taipei may become a blight of monotony if the same trend prevails. There is no lack of examples in this retail trend. In the last 20 years, for instance, international and national convenience store chains, such as, 7-Eleven, Family, Life, and OK, have swept the island, first in the metropolitan areas and later in small towns and cities, and forced independent, small corner shops and grocery stores to close. These standardized brands have reduced the personal social connections of daily shopping and consumption to anonymous and impersonal commodity relations of market exchange in a highly standardized environment, changing a community activity into a pure economic exchange.

As far as food markets and daily shopping and consumption are concerned, the issue is that they are not only commercial activities, but also create demand and shape the ways of life that have significant social and cultural meanings. In this sense, traditional retail markets represent a trading culture based on face-to-face contact. Here personal services play an important role in the process of exchange. Customers are dealing with the shop/stall keepers rather than with the commodities over the counter. This is in contrast to the modern retail practice in supermarkets or hypermarkets where consumers directly interact with the commodities in the processes of browsing, choosing, carrying and checking out. Likewise, the crowd in the dusk markets can largely reduce the traffic flows in the streets; that is what the concept of pedestrianization attempts to achieve, but hardly realizes. The vibrant street life in the late afternoon and the early evening reclaims the once lost community life in cities, and brings people back to the street in a congenial shopping environment. Moreover, the opening of large hypermarkets at out-of-centre locations signifies a lifestyle change in daily food shopping to an enjoyable community activity, more equally shared by both genders, than simply an isolated housework chore.

While Taipei is moving from a back region to the forefront of global networks of production and consumption, the change in Taipei's market structure involves not only the economic restructuring of retail industry, but also a more complicated social and cultural transformation. It could be argued that an urban policy with an overriding emphasis on the productive role of a city, but without care for the reproductive needs of local population, can have only a limited degree of success because such a city cannot be socially attractive to people to work and live in. In contrast, what is fundamental for a globalizing city like Taipei is, among other things, to assure a vital and viable market environment of retail diversity and conviviality able to accommodate diverse shopping needs for households in different situations. As Jacobs (1961) reminds us in *The Death and Life of Great American Cities*, 'commercial diversity is, in itself, immensely important for cities, socially as well as economically'. The presence of retail/market diversity will attract many other kinds of diversity, such as, a variety of cultural opportunities, social arenas and, most importantly, urban population. It is the material foundation of a living and liveable city. Accordingly, the future of Taipei as a globalizing city in the Asia-Pacific region is, apart from its economic role, its social and cultural significance, distinctive from other Asian cities, particularly in terms of the aesthetic value of the urban landscape and the diversity of city life. The authenticity and the liveability of a city derives from the life and living experiences of its urban population, thus, a living city of retail diversity, will be the most valuable asset that Taipei should create and treasure.

Notes

1. Here hypermarkets and superstores are used interchangeably with the understanding that on some occasions a finer distinction is made between them by defining hyper-

markets as larger superstores with over 5,000 square metres of net floor space, while superstores are also used to describe non-food stores of the retail warehouse type.
2. In other towns and cities in Taiwan, dusk markets are located in off-road sites on enclosed private land rather than sprawling along the streets.
3. A great majority of the multi-storey markets do not have escalators or passenger elevators.
4. Though being the first hypermarket in Taiwan, *Makro* finally pulled out of the Taiwan market in February 2003.
5. Two-thirds of the public supermarkets are run by Taipei Agricultural Marketing Corporation, a state corporation which also controls the wholesale markets in Taipei.

References

Alexander, N. and Akehurst, G. (eds.) (1999) *The Emergence of Modern Retailing 1750–1950*. London: Frank Cass.
Belasco, W. (2002) Food matters: Perspectives on an emerging field, in Belasco, W. and Scranton, P. (eds.) *Food Nations: Selling Taste in Consumer Societies*. London : Routledge, pp. 2–23.
Benson, J. and Shaw, G. (eds.) (1999) *The Retailing Industry*. London: I.B. Tauris.
Benson, J. and Ugolini, L. (eds.) (2003) *A Nation of Shopkeepers: Five Centuries of British Retailing*. London: I.B. Tauris.
Bestor, T. C. (1999) Wholesale sushi, in Low, S.M. (ed.) *Theorizing the City: The New Urban Anthropology Reader*. New Brunswick, NJ: Rutgers University Press, pp. 201–242.
Bowlby, R. (1997) Supermarket futures, in Falk, Pasi and Campbell, Colin (eds.) *The Shopping Experience*. Thousand Oaks, CA: Sage, pp. 92–110.
Bromley, R.D. & C.J. Thomas (1993) Retail change and the issues, in Bromley, R.D. and C.J. Thomas, C.J. (eds.) *Retail Change: Contemporary Issues*. London: UCL Press, pp. 2–14.
Burke, T. and Shackleton, J.R. (1996) *Trouble in Store? UK Retailing in the 1990s*. London: Institute of Economic Affairs.
Button, K. (1984) Regional variations in the irregular economy: a study of possible trends. *Regional Studies*, **18**, pp. 385–392.
Cai, C.H. (1992) Urban society and retail markets: the case of Miaoli City. *Journal of United College*, **9**, pp. 245–273.
Chang, S.Q. and Zhou, Y.R. (1997) The creation of alternative livelihood space: a case study of street vendors, in Lou, Yong-Sheng (ed.) *Whose City? Civic Culture and Political Discourse in Postwar Hong Kong*. Oxford: Oxford University Press, pp. 141–160.
Chen, G.Y. (1999) The successful cases of Singapore's vendors. *Dian Huo Qiu Zi*, **4**, pp. 32–33.
Chen, X.H. (1997) The informal sectors in cities, in Cai, Yong-Mai and Chang, Ying-Hua (eds.) *The Urban Society of Taiwan*. Taipei: Juliu, pp. 287-312.
Chen, Y.F. (1986) The informal sector in cities: the case of Taipei's vendors. Master's Thesis, Graduate Institute of Urban Planning, National Chunghsing University.
Counihan, C. and van Esterik, P. (1997) Introduction, in Counihan, C. and van Esterik, P. (eds.) *Food and Culture: A Reader*. London: Routledege, pp. 1–7.
Crewe, L. (2000) Geographies of retailing and consumption. *Progress in Human Geography*, **24**(2), pp. 275–290.
Crossick, G. and Jaumain, S. (eds.) (1999) *Cathedrals of Consumption: The European Department Store, 1850–1939*. Aldershot: Ashgate.
Dai, B.F. (1994) Who are the vendors? A historical perspective on the formation of vendors in Taiwan. *Taiwan: A Critical Quarterly in Social Studies*, **17**, pp. 121–48.
Department of Budget, Accounting and Statistics, Taipei City Government (2003) *The Statistical Abstract of Taipei City*. Taipei: Department of Budget, Accounting and Statistics, Taipei City Government.
Department of Commerce, Ministry of Economic Affairs (1993) The history and trend of supermarket development in Taiwan. *Services Business Report*, **35**, pp. 1–46.

Department of Commerce, Ministry of Economic Affairs(1994) The impacts of the rise of supermarkets and convenience stores on traditional retails. *Services Business Report*, **51**, pp. 189–211.

Directorate-General of Budget, Accounting and Statistics, Executive Yuan (1989) *Report on the Survey of Vendors in Taiwan Area: 1988*. Taipei: Directorate-General of Budget, Accounting and Statistics, Executive Yuan.

Directorate-General of Budget, Accounting and Statistics, Executive Yuan (1999) *Report on the Survey of Vendors in Taiwan Area: 1998*. Taipei: Directorate-General of Budget, Accounting and Statistics, Executive Yuan.

Directorate-General of Budget, Accounting and Statistics, Executive Yuan (2003) *National Statistics: Labor Force*. http://www.stat.gov.tw/bs2/stat/labor.htm.

Feng, X.M. and Xu, G.C.(1986) The vendor problems and their solutions in urban Taiwan. *Bank of Taiwan Quarterly*, **37**(3), pp. 175–204.

Jacobs, J. 1961 (1961) *The Death and Life of Great American Cities*. New York: Random House.

Gayler, H.J. (1984) *Retail Innovation in Britain: The Problems of Out-of-Town Shopping Centre Development*. Norwich: Geo Books.

Goody, J. (1982) *Cooking, Cuisine, and Class: A Study in Comparative Sociology*. Cambridge: Cambridge University Press.

Guy, C. (1994) *The Retail Development Process: Location, Property and Planning*. London: Routledge.

Hannigan, J. (1998) *Fantasy City: Pleasure and Profit in the Postmodern Metropolis*. London: Routledge.

Hart, K. (1973) Informal income opportunities and urban employment in Ghana. *Journal of Modern African Studies*, **11**, pp. 61–89.

Huang, Q.R. (1989) Supermarket development in Taiwan, USA and Japan, and its impact on the marketing of agricultural products in Taiwan. *Taiwan Land and Finance Quarterly*, **26**(3), pp. 1–31.

Huang, Q.R. (1993) Supermarkets in Taiwan: their market position and development trend. *Journal of Agricultural Marketing*, **94**, pp. 1–6.

Huang, Z.H. (1996) Current development and future trend of the retailing industry in Taiwan. *Taiwan Economic Research*, Volume **19**(5), pp. 32–38.

Kaynak, E. (1988) Global retailing: integrative statement, in Kaynak, E. (ed.) *Transnational Retailing*. Berlin: Walter de Gruyter, pp. 3–19.

Kelly, J. (2000) Every little helps: an interview with Terry Leahy, CEO, Tesco. *Long Range Planning*, **33**, pp. 430–439.

Lau, H.F. and Lee, K.H. (1988) Development of supermarkets in Hong Kong: current status and future trends, in Kaynak, E. (ed.) *Transnational Retailing*. Berlin: Walter de Gruyter, pp. 321–329.

Lefebvre, H. (1991, 1958) *Critique of Everyday Life*, Vol. 1. (trans. J. Moore). London: Verso.

Li, D.X. (2000) Singapore can, we can, too: a report on the management of vendors in Singapore. *Dian Huo Qiu Zi*, **12**, pp. 4–8.

Lin, Z.Z. (2002*a*) The establishment of the public traditional markets in Taiwan under Japanese ruling period. Part One. *Dian Huo Qiu Zi*, **32**, pp. 34–41.

Lin, Z.Z. (2002*b*) The establishment of the public traditional markets in Taiwan under Japanese ruling period. Part Two. *Dian Huo Qiu Zi*, **33**, pp. 36–43.

Longstreth, R.W. (1997) *City Center to Regional Mall: Architecture, the Automobile, and Retailing in Los Angeles, 1920-1950*. Cambridge, MA: MIT Press.

Lowe, M. and Wrigley, N. (1996) Towards the new retail geography, in Wrigley, N. and Lowe, M. (eds.) *Retailing, Consumption and Capital: Towards the New Retail Geography*. Harlow: Longman, pp. 3–30.

Maldonado, C. (1995) The informal sector: legalization or laissez-faire? *International Labour Review*, Volume **135**(6), pp. 704–728.

Ministry of Economic Affairs, Executive Yuan, Republic of China (2001) *Commercial Statistics Monthly*. Taipei: Ministry of Economic Affairs, Executive Yuan.

O'Brien, L. and Harris, F. (1991) *Retailing: Shopping, Society, Space*. London: David Fulton.

Othman, K. (1990) Patterns of supermarket use in Malaysia, in Findlay, Allan M., Paddison, Ronan and Dawson, John A.(eds.) *Retailing Environments in Developing Countries*. London: Routledge, pp. 205–214.

Portes, A. *et al.* (eds.) (1989) *The Informal Economy: Studies in Advanced and Less Developing Countries*. Baltimore: Johns Hopkins University Press.

Ruston, P. (1999) *Out of Town Shopping: The Future of Retailing*. London: British Library.

Smith, A. (1997) *Retailing and Small Shops*. Edinburgh: Scottish Office Central Research Unit.

Smith, D.W. (2001) Cities in Pacific Asia, in Paddison, R. (ed.) *Handbook of Urban Studies*. Thousand Oaks, CA: Sage, pp. 419–450.

Tan, C.T. and Teoh, J. (1988) Retailing system in Singapore, in Kaynak, E. (ed.) *Transnational Retailing*. Berlin: Walter de Gruyter, pp. 309–319.

Teng, S.F. (2001) Carrefour, Costco, Tesco and RT-Mart: hypermarkets in comparison. *Taiwan Journal*, Volume **26**(1), pp. 40–47.

Worpole, K. (1992) *Towns for People: Transforming Urban Life*. Buckingham: Open University Press.

Wrigley, N. (1993) Retail concentration and the internationalization of British grocery retailing, in Rosemary, D.F. and Thomas, C.J. (eds.) *Retail Change: Contemporary Issues*. London: UCL Press, pp. 41–68.

Wrigley, N. and Lowe, M. (eds.) (1996) *Retail, Consumption and Capital: Towards the New Retail Geography*. Harlow: Longman.

Williams, C.C. and Windebank, J. (2001) The growth of urban informal economies, in Paddison, R. (ed.) *Handbook of Urban Studies*. Thousand Oaks, CA: Sage, pp. 308–322.

Zeng, H.M. (2000) Market consumption in early days: a review of the market consumption in Japanese ruling period. *Dian Huo Qiu Zi*, **17**, pp. 4–11.

Chapter Nine

Modernization Ideoscape: Imaginative Geography and Aesthetic Landscape in Taipei Rapid Transit System

Chih-Hung Wang

A man wanted to fulfil his deceased mother's will to donate her organs, but he failed to get an ambulance or help from any hospitals. He decided to put her body in a wheelchair with a towel covering her face, and take the Taipei Rapid Transit System (TRTS) line to the hospital. There were other passengers who talked with the man in the transit carriage, but no one discovered that he was transporting a corpse. As this story was reported by newspapers, the general manager of Taipei Rapid Transit Corporation said he would check surveillance video records to verify whether it was true. He also noted that this kind of situation had violated the 'social customs' article in the 'Rules for TRTS Passengers', as the transit corporation does not allow the carrying corpses. If the corpse was disguised, however, he admitted that it would be difficult for the operation staff to detect (*China Times*, 22–23 November, 2000).

This urban legend of death taboo, involving official images of mass rapid transit, traffic norms, and surveillance, is an epitome of concern: the globalization of Taipei is not only an economic process and one of social change, but also a cultural imagination that imbues specific values into the urban space, as the mass rapid transit system is a concrete expression and material support for this globalization imagination. However, cultural imagination is not a pure fantasy, but anchors on ideas with material expression, which have normative and exclusive effects. The efficient, technological, clean, and high cultural images of TRTS reside in spatial designs that selectively exclude those who do not fit the modern cityscape. As the corpse-in-TRTS story illustrates, aberrant behaviour and repressed or forgotten episodes will appear now and then, disturbing the modernization landscape and confusing the homogeneous surface of globalization imagination.

Therefore, Taipei mass rapid transit system can be analyzed in the light of Appadurai's concept of ideoscape as 'concatenations of images, but they are often directly political and frequently have to do with the ideologies of states and the counter-ideologies of movements explicitly oriented to capturing state power or a piece of it' (1996, p. 36). Thus, the TRTS is not only a response to urban traffic crisis, but also one of the main symbolic spaces of imagination which centre on the ideology of modernization, enforcing an aestheticized mechanism of exclusion. The aim of this chapter is to discuss how the TRTS transformed from a huge engineering project under an authoritarian/developmental state to an imaginative geography of globalization in urban cultural governance.

Urban Crisis, Spatial Transformation and New Cultural Landscape

In 2000, Taipei was named the fifth best Asian Business City by *Fortune* magazine and the second best city among the region's forty major cities by *Asiaweek*. For a city government that emphasizes city competitiveness, these honours were taken as administrative achievement. For Taipei citizens who have suffered a long period of traffic gridlock, the transformation was an experience that means something much deeper. The so-called 'Dark Age of Traffic' started from 1988 when the TRTS construction began, and lasted until 1996 when the system opened for operation (the present length of lines in operation is about 60 kilometres). Therefore, the above mentioned honours mean more than a global competitive game for capital and state, but a timely recognition eagerly needed for the citizens who are still uncertain about the city's new experience.

For the past 20 years, major cities in the Asia-Pacific, including Seoul, Singapore, Shanghai, Bangkok, Guangzhou and Kuala Lumpur, have all earnestly engaged in the construction of rapid transit systems, which have the significance of modernization and nationalism. Under globalization, the TRTS is the key for Taipei's entrance to the club of first-class international cities, and has become the symbol of vitality and competitiveness.

The construction project for a mass rapid transit system was first proposed by the central government during the 1970s. Later, Taipei City Government, facing a worsening traffic problem, drew up its own version of a transit system plan. On the surface, the two plans were complementary, but in reality they were in competition. Both plans were targeted at solving the worsening traffic crisis. The difference was that the plan proposed by central government was mainly 'demand oriented', aimed at easing the congested radial transportation corridors, and thus reinforcing the established city centre. The Taipei City Government's plan, in contrast, was relatively inexpensive, required less construction time, and was basically 'supply oriented', intended to connect the new Xinyi Centre District and Taipei Zoo.

Although there were disputes, rapid transit plans proposed by central and city governments were eventually integrated and the Taipei Rapid Transit System plan was completed. In 1987, the Department of Rapid Transit Systems (DORTS) was formally established as a task-force unit under the jurisdiction of the Taipei City Government to implement the project. In the first stage, the project laid out a TRTS network with a total route length of 88 kilometres with 79 stations. Attached to the project were three-stage special funds, totalling some US$13 billion. Later, a budget of about US$4.7 billion was added for the extended construction project of new lines that will not be in operation before 2010. Major projects for future networks include extensions to outer urban areas; two new routes across the central area; an orbital route in Taipei County; and a Chiang Kai-Shek Airport Line (see figure 9.1). Due to the heavy demand placed on the government budget, a change to the light railway system or other less expensive systems were proposed.

When construction started in 1988, the TRTS received overwhelming support from the government, which was willing to provide both administrative and financial support. The project also met with enthusiastic expectations from the general public. Nevertheless, the TRTS project was soon overshadowed by the excessive budget spending, rumours of corruption and illegal bidding activities, poor management and delays to the schedule, frequent accidents during construction and test periods, and a lawsuit against France Metro Corp. These incidents seriously damaged the image and public relations of DORTS, and the TRTS became a subject of frequent criticism by the media. Two Director Generals of DORTS resigned because of poor work performance during this period (Liu and Lü, 1994). In 1990, hoping to find a way out of the traffic crisis, the government launched a 'Keep Taipei Moving' campaign, pleading with citizens to 'go hand-in-hand through the transition stage of transportation' and laying out plans for improving the situation. Unfortunately, the completion schedules of TRTS kept being postponed. For example, the first route was originally scheduled to be completed in December 1991, only to be completed in March 1996. As a consequence, the 'Dark Age of Traffic' became a common expression of the painful experience for Taipei citizens (Wang, 1990).

As the first few routes of the TRTS were completed in succession from 1996, the long anticipated impacts of the rapid transit system on the urban structure and processes, such as, modes of transportation, real estate prices and population distribution, gradually became evident. Not all the impacts were positive, the Taiwan's real estate market, after reaching its peak in the late 1980s and early 1990s, was in a prolonged downturn. The completion of the TRTS did not boost the price of real estate or the demand for the joint development projects along the TRTS lines as expected.

A research project commissioned by the Taipei City Government (Feng, 2001, pp. 179–180) indicated that the impact of TRTS after 5 years of operation could be divided into three categories. First, the impact on the distribution of population was manifold. The trend of Taipei's population outward movement had slowed down, and the population of suburban areas was on the increase. Population growth tended to concentrate along the TRTS lines and centred on stations in residential

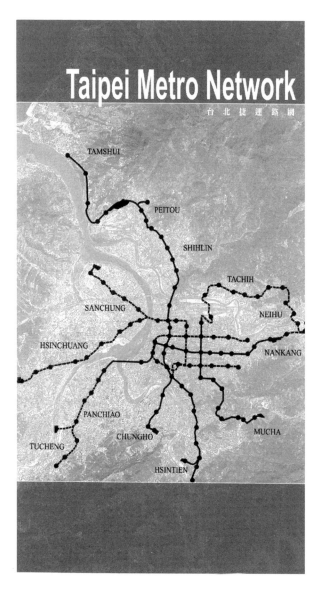

Figure 9.1. Map of the Taipei Rapid Transit System network. *Source*: Department of Rapid Transit System website.

or residential-commercial combined areas. The downtown and commercial areas, however, did not witness an obvious population growth. Second, the impact on real estate was obvious. The TRTS had a very real effect on the price of real estate, i.e., the closer to the station, the higher the price, but it had little effect on the price in downtown areas. Third, the impact on transportation and public activities is that TRTS improves the scope of daily activities of all citizens. Although still not obvious at this stage, TRTS had an effect in creating new development centres. As the TRTS network extended, the use of public transportation increased. The TRTS had more impact on bus transportation than on automobiles and motorcycles. However, the drastic increase of automobiles and motorcycles in the 1980s slowed down in the late 1990s (see table 9.1).

Table 9.1. Taipei traffic statistics.

Year	Daily average number of bus passengers	Growth rate %	Daily average number of TRTS passengers	Growth rate %	Number of registered cars	Growth rate %	Number of registered motorcycles	Growth rate %
1975	1,952,013	–	–	–	58,625	–	188,487	–
1980	2,319,575	18.83	–	–	131,474	124.26	350,921	86.18
1985	2,603,053	12.22	–	–	222,824	69.48	586,272	67.07
1990	2,163,496	–16.89	–	–	426,957	91.61	597,586	1.93
1995	1,753,829	–18.94	–	–	548,447	28.45	735,015	23.00
1998	1,919,315	9.44	166,524	–	607,205	10.71	904,232	23.02
2000	1,856,135	–3.29	733,847	340.69	595,742	–1.89	959,013	6.09
2002	1,773,647	–4.44	888,814	21.12	606,839	1.86	971,568	1.31

Source: Department of Rapid Transit Systems and Department of transportation, Taipei City Government.

According to statistics provided by the Department of Transportation of Taipei City Government, the city's transportation experienced a structural change after the opening of the TRTS. Passenger traffic on buses decreased by 10 per cent and vacant taxies increased from 33 per cent to 52.5 per cent in the period from the mid 1990s to 2000. Trips by automobiles and motorcycles both decreased by 100,000 person-times per day, while bicycle trips increased slightly (see table 9.2). However, the

Table 9.2. Most frequently used mode of transportation of Taipei citizens.

Mode	TRTS	Bus	Car	Motorcycle	Taxi	Bicycle	On foot	Other
Ratios	12.6%	27.7%	21.9%	25.6%	2.9%	2.5%	4.8%	2.0%

Source: The Annual of Department of Transportation Taipei City Government (2000) (http://www.dot.taipei.gov.tw/annual/89/8.htm). Interviewed by phone, 12/28/2000.

TRTS attracted mostly bus commuters who were mainly women (more than 70 per cent) with some students and senior citizens.

The TRTS is not only a new infrastructure that improves the mobility within the city and causes a transformation of urban spatial structure, but also a spatial representation complex which carries and stimulates imagination – that is, it acts as sites of the production and delivery of urban culture. In addition to the impact of the TRTS on the urban spatial structure, the effect of TRTS on urban culture is a key to the understanding of Taipei city development.

The most obvious new development brought about by the TRTS occurred mainly around TRTS stations. New stores mushroomed, old ones were remodelled (especially restaurants and coffee shops) and public areas around the stations were redesigned and renewed, creating relatively clean and neat consumption centres for the city. This happened to the stations within downtown commercial areas as well as those in the suburban commercial areas. Taking account of spatial design and users' experiences of TRTS stations, these consumption centres are in fact playing a major role in creating a new urban cultural landscape.

Starting from the 1970s, Taipei City has engaged in incessant construction projects. Early ones included major streets and tunnels connecting to the suburban areas. In the 1980s, the government started to move the railway underground, and initiated various construction mega-projects, such as a city express highway, Xinyi Centre District, Keelung River, and redevelopment of old Wanhua District, in addition to the TRTS. These constructions constantly altered the spatial texture of Taipei City. Parallel to these projects, a trend of the 'city beautiful movement' emerged, stressing the visual quality of city landscape. The early stages of this trend were evidenced by the regulation of street billboards, open space award policy, promotion of public art, new parks and plazas, and waterfront green belt. The efforts later extended to the preservation of historic sites and community renewal projects, culminating in the establishment of the Cultural Affairs Bureau of Taipei. Its policies emphasized multiculturalism, popular memory, place identity, and community cultural activities. The most important trend, however, was the newly emerging middle-class aesthetics of consumption. The TRTS was the manifestation and paradigm of this new trend.

In order to understand the role of the TRTS in the transformation of Taipei's new cultural landscape, it has to be placed in the wider context of social change. The planning and construction stages of the TRTS happened at a period of transformation of Taiwan's state apparatus. After long years of martial law, Taiwan was then moving away from authoritarian repression, and rapidly moving towards democracy. Long suppressed local culture began to regain ground and localization prevailed (including the revival of once repressed local dialects, enhancement of ethnic consciousness, and emphasis on a sense of place and community). After almost 30 years of official designation, the first direct election of a Taipei Mayor was held in 1994, and in 1996, the first presidential election of Taiwan. At the same time, manipulation of political image supported by competing media became a critical playground for the emerging nationalistic politics which required a more sophisticated mode in various symbolic and cultural dimensions.

The TRTS project was initiated during the period of authoritarian regime, and it would work well as long as it followed certain implicit rules imposed by the central bureaucracy. In response, the design of all stations corresponded to the prescribed double themes of modernization and Chinese nationalism. The TRTS was basically a belated rational policy in face of an urban crisis. The emergence of the critical social and media forces during the construction stage, however, entrapped the TRTS in a predicament. The disclosure of government corruption typified the kind of social complaint in the state transformation period. The operation stage of the TRTS coincided with the takeover of the position of City Mayor by the opposition party, the Democratic Progress Party. The newly empowered party, based on its success in advocating democratization and localization, tried to consolidate its still fragile social support through cultural governance, and promoted the vision of internationalization as the new policy focus.

As the industrial structure changed and family income grew in the 1980s, Taipei became a consumption-oriented city, characterized by the appearance of modern department stores and shopping centres, fashionable restaurants, and cultural activities as well as green consumption, all of which was a sign of cultural change. The aesthetic taste of the middle class was being formed, reflecting an increasing demand for high-quality consumption and living environment. These leisure oriented cultural expressions featured appropriate international modernist styles and images, but they also included vernacular elements which had been suppressed under Chinese nationalism. These were indicators revealing a new pattern of social distinction through selective social exclusion.

The cultural rhetoric in the state transformation period and the cultural performance of the new middle class converged on the TRTS, the largest public space reticulum which reshaped the imagination and reality of public culture. The following sections will discuss the features of the TRTS as a new cultural space in greater detail. The discussion will focus on two aspects – the 'imaginative geographies of globalization' and the 'aesthetic landscapes of exclusion'.

Imaginative Geographies of Globalization

Mass transit systems, just as super highways, airports and sea ports, are global spaces in themselves. The basic designs are almost the same everywhere with similar technology, standard spatial arrangement, aesthetic style, and guiding systems with English signs, so even foreign travellers with some mass rapid transit experience will find the mass rapid transit in another city user-friendly. The global space of mass rapid transit is both functional and imaginary.

'Globalization', which regulates contemporary economic and social development, contains its own dimensions of symbolic culture. As Western colonialism has been intertwined with the imaginative geography of Orientalism (Said, 1978) globalization has its own imaginative geography that shapes the cultural dimension. This imaginative geography and its encounter with local culture can be understood from different aspects – the spectacle of technology, the symbolic language of space, image engineering, and the connection with global consumption.

Spectacle of Technology: Merging with Machines

The TRTS is a product of an international endeavour, a hybrid of international capital and technology. From the planning stage, companies from many countries were involved in different stages of this project. The British (BMTC) and United States (ATC) consulting companies were involved at the planning phase. In the construction stage, many international firms participated, including railroad construction from Japan, procurement of mechanical and electrical systems and train carriages from France, Britain, United States, Germany and other European companies. In fact, the import of new technology and its transfer were among the major goals of the project. Although criticized as being too dependent upon foreign technology, the introduction of highly advanced and automatic technology by the TRTS was still viewed as a much welcomed feature by local media and residents. It has, in other words, become a generally accepted link to the imaginative geography of modernization, internationalization and globalization.

The TRTS was full of all kinds of technological spectacles. The Muzha line employs an automatic driving system with no driver on the train. This is quite a different experience for local passengers who may feel unsafe to be on an 'abandoned' high speed train. On the other hand, it may provoke the excitement of a futuristic driving experience as depicted in science-fiction movies. Standing on an elevated platform surrounded by large pieces of glass and steel frames, or on the underground platform, feeling the chill air, and a gale of strong wind with the train approaching, induces a kind of fantastic futuristic sensation. There are all kinds of omnipresent automatic machines (elevators, escalators, ticket vending machines, coin changers, ATM, and vending machines) as well as screens and monitors. The images of highly advanced technology embedded in these technological spectacles and automatic machines combine to project a hi-tech fantasy.

An electronic monitoring system, including video cameras and terminals, is the basic element of the hi-tech setting. With justification on grounds of security and safety, the monitoring system in the TRTS stations closely watches the movements inside the station. On 14 May 1999, a train hit a five-year-old boy on the rail. In order to prevent a similar tragedy in the future, the Taipei Rapid Transit Corporation decided to install another 300 monitors, and upgraded the video equipment along higher capacity lines. Moreover, all stations have been designated a 'night waiting zone for women' on each platform with enhanced monitoring cameras for the safety of unaccompanied female passengers at night, forming a protective 'gender enclosure'.

In Taipei metropolitan area, it is common to see surveillance equipment installed near banks, post offices, convenient stores, ATMs, gas stations, and even in selected neighbourhood locations. Residents are quite used to the existence of video cameras. Instead of provoking anxiety, the installation of monitors is justified by the 'ideology of safety', and it is claimed as a major achievement needing the minimum level of local administration. When a criminal event takes place, the videotape is a convenient source for media broadcasting. This is a spectacle of an urban 'witness', a kind of voluntary electronic panopticism (Lyon, 1994; which extended the surveillance theme developed by Foucault, 1977). Electronic surveillance combines the function of safekeeping and the image of technology, and it conforms to the modern urban resident's anxiety over personal safety and the new middle class's expectation for progress and security.

Dealing with programmed automatic machines caters to the new middle class's expectation for independence and free choice – the freedom of not being bothered by other human beings. Nevertheless, entering the TRTS with a whole range of automatic machines and electronic surveillance systems is actually an experience signifying the enclosure of human subjects into a mechanized network and rhythm. During confrontation with machines, the hidden desire is to manipulate them, or to become a machine, or even to be controlled by machines. The effective performance of the TRTS requires cooperation between human beings and machines. The smoothness of cooperation presupposes an acceptance of the machine tempo without fear and reflection, and when this is the case, the human becomes a part of the machine.

Symbolic Language in Space:
Modernity, Nationalism and the Vernacularism

Most of the TRTS stations are characterized by gigantic constructions and spacious interiors, and naturally become the key objects of cultural expression. The language of spatial design includes the image of modern technology created by the use of steel frames and transparent materials, and symbols of the vernacular (referring to both Taiwanese and Chinese vernacular that contrast with the 'West').

Of all stations, the most impressive and expensive one is the elevated Jiantan

Station of the Tamsui line (see figure 9.2). The design of the station is unique with a roof styled as a dragon boat supported by pillars and steel ropes. The station, together with the traditional Chinese style of the nearby Grand Hotel, Jiantan Overseas Youth Activity Centre, and a newly built ferroconcrete bridge, comprise a vivid and striking sculpture-like urban landscape. Most of the stations along Tamsui line are built in a traditional Chinese architectural style with tilted roofs, *dougong*, and lattice windows (see figure 9.3). The intention of the design is obvious: to give a distinctive national characteristic. The Tamsui Station also contains a flavour of local architectural style as a reminder that the district was an old trading port (see figure 9.4). Contrasting with the traditional style, many other stations deliberately create an impression of advanced technology. The use of truss and glass for the wall and roof of Beitou Station (see figures 9.5 and 9.6), the transparency of the exits of most Nangang line stations, the stretching hallway and glass brick wall of the Xiao Nanmen Station, and the large transparent wall outside the elevated station of Muzha line (see figures 9.7 and 9.8) all help to shape the TRTS space as a symbolic landscape of technology.

Spatial symbols can also be found in the design and building materials of specific stations, the most distinct of which is the Chiang Kai-Shek Memorial Hall Station. Unlike other underground stations, there are no advertisement billboards on either side of the island platform, and the wall of the station is made of expensive slates

Figure 9.2. Jiantan Station of the Tamsui line in the image of a dragon boat. Photo by Meng-Ying Shen

Figure 9.3. Lattice windows of a typical Tamsui line station. Photo by Meng-Ying Shen

Figure 9.4. Tamsui Station of Tamsui line in the traditional Minnan style. Photos by Meng-Ying Shen

Figure 9.5. The truss and glass for the wall and roof of Beitou Station. Photo by Meng-Ying Shen

Figure 9.6. The truss and glass for the wall and roof of Beitou Station. Photo by Meng-Ying Shen

Figure 9.7. A typical Muzha line station. Photo by Meng-Ying Shen

Figure 9.8. An elevated station of the Muzha line. Photo by Meng-Ying Shen

rather than the regular aluminium sheets as in other stations. The exit which leads to the National Theatre and National Concert Hall adopts a Chinese style design similar to that of Chiang Kai-Shek Memorial Hall (see figures 9.9 and 9.10) and the nameplate of the station is in black rather than green (the standard colour used in all other stations on the same line). Such specific design reflects the unique symbolic status of this location, though its significance has changed from a monument of the authoritarian ruler to a symbol of cultural consumption.

Other than architectural design, the denomination of each station has its representative meaning too. Since the TRTS system has become a powerful force in reshaping the urban image, its stations have naturally turned into centres of urban population flows, and thus, have become powerful place names for the surrounding area. An important principle of station denomination is to combine the names of the two intersecting streets where the station is located in the city grid. Contrasting with this functional method, selected stations have names that are deliberately traced back to the historical origins of the locality, or emphasize their connection to the vernacular culture. The two principles are divided between stations located in the urban centre and those in suburban areas – the former use intersecting streets, the latter use historical origins. This distinction highlights the division of function and meaning between urban centre and periphery.

The importance of the spatial symbols regarding modernity, nationalism and the local/vernacular is manifested through the design history of the TRTS logo which shifts from Chinese nationalism to local/vernacular and modernization. According to the DORTS, the concept behind the original blue hexagonal logo is as follows:

The logo is a hexagon consisting of two interdependent parts, symbolizing the two powers [Ying and Yang], the Heaven, the Earth, and four directions within one universe. Two reversing Chinese characters 'human' represent the to and fro of passengers as well as the transportation function of TRTS. The outward form of the logo is that of a flying bird which

Figure 9.9. The Chiang Kai-Shek Memorial Hall Station. *Note:* The entrance adopts a Chinese style design similar to that of Chiang Kai-Shek Memorial Hall. Photo by Meng-Ying Shen

Figure 9.10. The Chiang Kai-Shek Memorial Hall Station entrance (right) and the National Theatre (left). Photo by Meng-Ying Shen

Figure 9.11. Logo of TRTS. *Source*: Department of Rapid Transit System website.

means 'as swift as flying'. Blue and white colours indicate calm, clean, and swift. (see figure 9.11) (DORTS, http://www.dorts.gov.tw/brief/dortslogo/dortslogo.htm)

The Taipei Rapid Transit Corporation which is now in charge of the operation of TRTS adopts the original logo of DORTS with some modification (figure 9.11). On the one hand, the new logo omits the two parts that symbolize the two powers and six directions, representing the abandonment of the traditional Chinese elements. On the other hand, it emphasizes the meaning of internationalization, modernization, technology, and globalization. This change coincides with the change of cultural symbols accompanying the transformation of the Taiwan state and society – from Chinese nationalism to localization as well as modernization, internationalization, and globalization – as can be seen in the following quotation:

The logo of the new enterprise inherits the original 'human-bird logo' to symbolize a continuity of the fundamental spirit . . . The two circles outside the human-bird logo represent the smooth operation of TRTS. The strokes of the circles start from thin to thick, displaying the uniqueness of its rhythm, movement and speed, symbolizing the image of efficiency and service. Moreover, the colours of green and blue represent grassland and blue sky respectively, which means that the TRTS belongs to the land where we all live. Under the premise of 'internationalization, modernization, and technology', the circle tilted slightly toward the right enhances the image of energy, speed, and motion, demonstrating its ambitious goal of 'globalization'. (Taipei Rapid Transit Corporation website, http://www.trtc.com.tw/magzine/mag38/mag3801.htm)

Nevertheless, the Taipei Rapid Transit Corporation selects Chinese 'dragon' as its mascot. The main reason is:

Dragon implies leadership which in turn represents the status of the TRTS as the leader of Taiwan rapid transit systems. It also symbolizes the way trains shuttle back and forth in the greater Taipei area, connecting the different districts of the city, and bringing a new lifestyle. This three-dimensional and lively design is not only unique, but also conforms with current trend of international style. (Taipei Rapid Transit Corporation website)

Image Engineering: Museum Ambience and TRTS Culture

Raised ceilings, chilled air, shimmering flagstones, metal and glass, illumination, and works of art in the underground stations all help to create a grandiose and clean image, constructing a gallery or museum ambience and a sense of monumentality. Symbolic expression of space not only conveys a unique aesthetic taste, but also generates an implicit code of conduct: the museum ambience anticipates placid and orderly manner.

Indeed, the city government plans to make the TRTS a cultural and artistic showcase (see figure 9.12). In many countries, expensive mass rapid transit systems serve various symbolic functions to convey the cultural achievements of the country or the city. From the station to the train, interior display to the ticket, all become objects of exhibition (Yang, 1998; 2002a). The TRTS is no exception. The city government openly invites art works for permanent exhibition, designates areas for performing arts and activities, and organizes various cultural events (see figure 9.13). The most famous include Taipei Easy Mall, Performance Zone, Taipei Jazz Station, and events like 'Mass Rapid Transit Tea Break', 'Top Ten Mass Rapid Transit Readings', 'Wedding in Mass Rapid Transit', and issuing of special one-day tickets as promotion for exhibitions such as the Le Corbusier Exhibition in Taipei Art Museum. Additionally, the Department of Information and the Cultural Affair Bureau of Taipei jointly hold contests every year to select poems and short prose. These works are posted inside buses and TRTS trains. Drawings from the picture book *Sound of Colors* (2001) by famous local artist Jimmy were selected as the design patterns on TRTS tickets which later became collectable memorabilia.

Public art, cultural events and exhibitions combine to achieve the goal of 'image-engineering', and create a new form of genteel urban culture of which the TRTS is the focus. Most of the passengers do not pay much attention to these artistic works or exhibitions that often emphasize speed, change, travel, and encountering. The cultural messages, though accidentally and occasionally, create an elegant taste which belongs uniquely to the new middle class. Moreover, the image engineering is not exclusively on modernity and internationalization, for it also promotes local characteristics, and the combination becomes the signature of the region.

TRTS public arts should properly express the characteristics of local cultural and natural specialty. They should help to rebuild the space quality, provide pleasant scenery and environment, express local culture and historic background, and integrate and reinforce citizens' mental images . . . For instance, the cross patterns outside Shipai Station symbolize the medical connection to a nearby hospital and the bright colours at Mingde Station are an acknowledgement of 'foreign flavours' of the multicultural Tianmu neighbourhood. (Taipei Rapid Transit Corporation website, http://www.dorts.gov.tw/artnet/PublicArt/PA-main.htm#pa-2)

One phenomenon reveals the aesthetic limitation of the TRTS culture. The various

Figure 9.12. Taipei City Hall Station (at the Xinyi Center District). Photo by Meng-Ying Shen.

Figure 9.13. Public art works on the platform of Taipei City Hall Station. Photo by Meng-Ying Shen.

styles of coloured drawings on the shop doors within the Easy Mall remind us of 'graffiti' which represents the spirit of resistance, mobility, boldness, swiftness and youth. Although these coloured drawings of the counter culture do not seem to conform with the dominant style of TRTS cultural activities and displays, they are, by subtle manipulation, absorbed into mainstream artistic codes. For example, a photo of each drawing is posted right next to the shop door with illustration of its theme and painter. In this way, the drawings are legitimized as formal art and divorced from the radical context of 'graffiti', thus rid of any implication of radical politics.

Global Consumption Connections: New Middle-Class Taste

In addition to the obsession with technology, the painstakingly created symbolic space, public art, and cultural events, the TRTS also displays a global connection with fashionable consumption.

First, popular culture, fashionable products, and advertisements abound acting as an intermediary and interpretation of citizens' rapid transit experiences. These rapid transit scenes constructed citizens' image and imagination even before the opening of the TRTS. The scene of a running train appears often in films and television, mostly about New York or European subways in Hollywood movies, or railway commuters depicted in popular Japanese TV programmes. These scenes from advanced countries help to reinforce the system's images as being advanced, technological, metropolitan, clean, fashionable, and futuristic. Under such circumstance, transit users' cognition structure is gradually influenced by these images that mediate between travelling experience and the imagination of globalization and modernization.

After the opening of the TRTS, its stations and trains have increasingly become the background of local TV commercials. Books about subways catch onto the 'train fashion', such as *Mass Rapid Transit Love Stories* (1997) by local writers, which depict love affairs taking place in the trains, the translation of Japanese writer Murakami Haruki's book *Underground* (1998) and a writer who pioneered criticism of the TRTS from a political economy approach (Yang, 1989) later published a number of books celebrating the beauty of mass rapid transit (Yang, 1998; 2002*a*; 2002*b*). Moreover, bookstores are well stocked with all types of publication regarding travelling and recreational experiences. There are books giving information along the TRTS lines with detailed information of routes, restaurants and scenic spots. It seems that the TRTS not only plays an important role in leisure and consumption, but the system itself has become an object of consumption.

The TRTS is also an important channel that connects consumption activities around Taipei metropolitan area. In recent years, the city government has regularly held public parties on downtown plazas during Christmas and New Year holidays. Hundreds of thousands of people, mainly teenagers, travel between the Presidential Hall Plaza and the City Hall Plaza by the TRTS to attend these parties. Several thousand take part in the New Year countdown on trains. The TRTS lines link consumption centres for teenagers with those of the white-collar class, namely

Ximending Shopping Area, Eastern District and Xinyi Centre District, as well as famous suburban scenic areas. Department stores provide a bus to pick up customers from TRTS stations. The volume of passenger traffic can easily go over a million on major holidays such as Christmas, Mother's Day and St Valentine's Day.

Finally, the TRTS has become a consumption space itself. In and around several stations, underground malls are located as the main consumption centres of the city. The most common stores in these malls are clothing stores, restaurants, convenient stores and bookstores. For instance, the opening of Eastern District Underground Shopping Mall, in July 2002, attracted nearly one million people during its first month, and generated US$1.5 million in revenue. As the crowds kept rushing into the mall, many shops were unable to close at closing time.

Aesthetic Landscape of Exclusion

The spectacle of technology, symbolic spatial design, museum ambience, image engineering, and consumption taken together construct the imagination of globalization. The substantial content is the modernization ideoscape – with progress, efficiency, cleanliness, safety, and civility as the core values embedded in the material form and symbolic meaning of the TRTS. However, behind the international/modern images and middle-class taste, there is a powerful command of prohibition and exclusion, demonstrating that the access to public space and public culture is selective (Sibley, 1995). This aesthetic landscape of exclusion is the hidden side of the modernization ideoscape.

There is a code of inclusion and exclusion, 'Be a Good Citizen', embedded in the space-time of the TRTS. As a mass transport system, the TRTS will include as many people as possible, covering the needs of the elderly and the disabled. The TRTS also attempts to regulate and control passengers, excluding those with inappropriate behaviour. The signs (for example, notices, warnings, and prohibitions) of the TRTS system are not only symbols of reason, efficiency and safety, but also the rhetoric of control and norm that dominate the rhythm of flows within the TRTS space-time.

From a professional viewpoint, the space and equipment layout and the route arrangement inside the station have to follow rational principles, which place emphasis on safety, facility and efficiency. But if viewed differently, these principles presuppose a knowledge and acceptance of rational, abstract and total control. The TRTS anticipates passengers to act rationally according to the social norms it prescribes, but at the same time forces each individual to obey and follow the norms through prohibition, surveillance and penalty.

Inside the TRTS, passengers are told when, where and what to do – and what not to do. Signs are everywhere to ensure everything is in order, and are further enforced by a penalty clause (for example, a fine of US$45 for eating and drinking) and supervisors (including police). In other words, the system is supported by authoritative institutions. In many cases, the dominant code is as strict and detailed as military training. For example, a sign at the gate says 'When exiting the station, please: (1) Hold the ticket in your right hand; (2) Front side upward; (3) Point the arrow forwardly; and (4) Pass through the left side of the gate'. The constant rehearsals of 'stand on the right side of the escalator, left side for passing' through various media establish a new 'ethics of movement' when taking the escalator, which gradually extends its influence to railway stations and department stores. On the station platforms, passengers will follow the signs on the ground and wait orderly in lines, an uncommon scene in Taipei outside the TRTS stations.

These rules turn the space of the TRTS into a disciplinary space, and people internalize these rules through repetitive performances to the point that rules have become the 'natural' elements of their value judgments and practices. People cultivate a mentality of speed and accept the ideology of efficiency while obeying the regulations of space, adapting to the driving acceleration of the TRTS train and its regular rhythm of opening and closing train doors.

The rule that is most difficult to become immediately accustomed to is the prohibition on eating and drinking. People in Taiwan are accustomed to eating and drinking in railroad trains and other vehicles, so there is a conflict between the new discipline and social habits. Statistics show that in 2000, there were more than 400 cases of rule violation per month, about 70 per cent of which were cases of smoking and eating in stations and trains (*China Times*, 11 September, 2000, p. 18). Another record shows that within a four month period in 2000 more than 1,300 people were warned for violating the code prohibiting eating and drinking, and the total fines exceeded US$58,000. Seventy per cent of the violators came from areas other than Taipei City (*United Evening News*, 18 May, 2000, p. 12). Notices of prohibition and punishment warnings are seen all around, and information and warning messages are broadcast repeatedly from loud speakers, forming an inextricable disciplinary space-time mode of visual-audio signs in the TRTS. Like the new ethics of taking escalators, regulations on eating and drinking have recently extended to some buses as well.

These guidelines, prohibitions and warning messages are not only rules of performance that passengers must obey, but also require passengers to possess a specific mode of recognition, such as the ability to read all kinds of TRTS maps. Usually there are three maps in the entrance or station lobby, illustrating the TRTS route network, nearby streets and buildings, and the layout of the station. These maps require a 'panoramic view' of spectators who must project themselves onto the 'your position' marks on these maps. Since the orientation of the map is not always consistent with the viewers' actual position, map readers need to 'turn or reverse' the map in their minds to find the right directions. Moreover, they have to recognize and connect the relationship between places, and project three-dimensional spatial experiences from the two-dimensional map. All these abilities involve abstract spatial perception. As for the strip maps of the TRTS routes located on the upper side of sliding doors, ticket vending machines, and platform walls, which are stretched to fit into limited space, distorting the actual relation and distance between places, requires people to adjust again by using their abstract spatial perception capability.

Certainly, there is rhetoric of globalization and localization within the rhythm of guidance and prohibition. English is appended to virtually all the signs in the TRTS, testifying to the declared goal of globalization. The station names are broadcast inside the trains in Mandarin, Minnan, Hakka and English in turn to cater for the principle of ethnic balance in vernacular and international terms.

In brief, on entering a TRTS station – going through to buy tickets, passing through gates, taking escalators, waiting for trains on the platform, stepping into the carriage, ultimately leaving the station – passengers immerse themselves into a complex and message-filled dominant rhetoric. They have to possess the decoding capacity and the ethics of obeying rules in order to present an appropriate body performance. The ideal situation is for individuals to take the position of 'properly behaved passenger', and become themselves signs in the dominant rhetoric, as practitioners, carriers and 'models' of this disciplinary system of representation.

The exclusive regulation of TRTS space-time also appears in rental rules for performing and exhibition. There are specific regulations about the use of open space, and for the design of brochures and posters on the TRTS stations. For example, the following types of exhibition in an artistic salon are forbidden: works that reveal the naked body, obscenity, or are below the general level of artistic performance, or violate social order, customs and laws; displays that refer to political positions, business interests or violate intellectual property rights. Items on display should cover at least two-thirds or more of the length of salon; the quality cannot be poor or rough in design; works on display must be framed; and works cannot degrade the reputation of the Taipei Rapid Transit Corporation. These regulations aim to maintain a specific style and the TRTS as a 'decent' cultural space.

What is the nature of 'public' in the TRTS as the main public space for public art and display? The 'public' in public art and public space is never a simple and clear topic, but refers to processes of social production and conflicting power relationships residing in established social order. For example, in the challenge to the air shaft construction in one underground TRTS shopping mall, public art becomes the medium of solving dispute. By reducing the noise volume, changing the location and 'beautifying' the contentious air shaft design and the TRTS entrances, the protest of local businesses and the community were converted into expectation for public art. There remains the conflict between professional elites and different interests in the community (Wu, 1998, chapter 4). As another example, there was once a freely distributed periodical entitled 'Pots' in TRTS stations which was welcomed by the youth for its alternative perspectives, strange but cool aesthetic style, and plentiful cultural messages. The Taipei Rapid Transit Corporation unilaterally announced an end to the contract with Pots on the grounds of pornographic advertisements in it, which raised social protest and disagreement.

These disputes about public art and periodicals reveal that the TRTS public space is neither open to everyone nor to all values, but saturated with a dominant rhetoric of differentiation and selected values exemplified in the symbolic expression of TRTS space and the regulation of behaviour.

In addition, there is an obvious commercial connection involved in the 'public', which is controlled and disciplined by officials and entrepreneurs. For instance, painted carriages such as the 'Cola train' and 'McDonald train' are provided by enterprises that use the carriages as space for promoting their image. The Taipei Rapid Transit Corporation obtains huge profits from providing spaces for advertisement (including light boxes and billboards on walls and columns). In one case, a bid of over US$2 million was offered for more than one hundred advertisement light boxes in Taipei Central Station, and it was almost thirteen times the price for Taiwan Railroad (China Times, 31 July, 1998, p. 18). The annual advertising revenue in seven stations of the Xindian-Zhonghe lines came to US$5 million (China Times, 29 December, 1998, p. 19). These advertisements now occupy public space originally designed for the TRTS, and cover up and modify the spatial symbols. Thus, advertisements inaugurate an era of commodification of public space, and the inserted public art surpasses and often confuses the original symbols shaped by state bureaucracy. The 'commodity aesthetic' becomes another symbolic coordinate for the TRTS experience.

The prohibition of eating and drinking, as inscribed in the yellow lines on the entrance of TRTS stations, has been relaxed and withdrawn. This rule change of the 'good citizen' behaviour was a concession to business practice. The space leading to the gates towards the platforms offered an excellent business opportunity. It was originally reserved for books and newspapers. These small businesses are intended to cultivate the 'good habit' of reading on the trains, but, the book stand enterprise failed. To fill the vacated stores, food and drink retail were allowed to replace the lost revenue, and the zones forbidding eating and drinking shrank accordingly.

In short, the public space of the TRTS is no guarantee of universal access. Many people and values are excluded through the space-time regulation of guidance and prohibition, specific standards of morality and aesthetics, but all these can be conceded for commercial rationale. The TRTS constructs a cultural paradigm for citizens to follow, to respect with rhetoric of high-tech and modernization. However, the aesthetic exclusive landscapes cannot assure citizens of well-ordered and perfect behaviour. The aesthetic landscapes of exclusion do not necessarily secure the desired social order or work perfectly, instead, there are many situations for deviance within the space-time of the TRTS. The encounter of diverse values brings up troublesome ethical questions and conflicts in urban space.

Deviating Performances

Smoking is prohibited here,
But you can smoke your imagination and emotion as you wish.
Eating and drinking are not allowed here,
But your slowness and easiness of mind will not be forbidden.
Please confirm the direction and route of trains;
Taking escalator of dreams, waiting for broadcasting station of hope, and watch your belongings, emotions and memories;
Be careful, your feeling might be stolen away.
Zhao-Huang Ge (1998) 'Rules for Taking Rapid Transit'

In spite of surveillance and punishment, the regulation of the TRTS space-time is still full of loopholes. Therefore, the procedure in dealing with various deviating behaviours has to be set up by the TRTS. A 'station controlling' course in the training programme is introduced for the operations staff. The most critical situations include 'controlling flows of people', 'evacuating the station', and 'dealing with incidents of protest'. In addition, there is a 'passengers services' course including treatment of 'lost property', 'passengers' complaints', 'passengers' safety', etc., and subjects such as 'malfunction elimination', 'operation delay', 'operation in emergency', 'accidents treatment', 'identifying counterfeit money', 'first aid training', 'prevention of crime and coping with criminals', etc. (Wang, 1997, pp. 35–40). The Taipei Rapid Transit Corporation has to minimize the possibility of disorder from the massive gatherings of several hundred thousand people, and the uncertainty of mistakes caused by complicated technological systems. For instance, one passenger complained there were no lockers in the TRTS, and the Taipei Rapid Transit Corporation replied that 'there is no plan to set up lockers at this stage, for there may be bombs installed or pets abandoned inside the lockers' (Shen, 1999, p. 48).

Various 'deviations' do occur frequently, such as emergency stops because four junior high school students were sitting on the rail side of a platform or a drunken woman wandered into the rail zone (both cases were fined US$1,470); also the case mentioned in the opening paragraph of a corpse in a wheelchair. There are incidences of high school students and lovers acting 'improperly' with intimate behaviour on the platform and in the carriages. More regular events are violations against the prohibition of eating and drinking, often causing disputes and complaints (Shen, 1999, pp. 32, 70).

Wrong direction journeys are most common as the passengers are unfamiliar with the TRTS and confused by the new strange space, different from their usual framework of recognition – they are the improperly disciplined subjects. There are many passengers who deliberately challenge these signs of prohibition as lures for adventure and transgression.

These deviations can become a matter of life and death, and expose the fallibility and malfunction of the TRTS surveillance/discipline system. On 1 July, 1998, a woman committed suicide by lying on the track of one TRTS line, causing tremendous mental pressure for drivers and staff, and casting a shadow on the TRTS image of high-tech efficiency, safety, and cleanliness. The previously mentioned accident of a running train hitting a five-year-old boy also generated much criticism from the public. If the fatality becomes the cause for more strict surveillance and more video cameras, barriers and alarm bells, but not for the positive concerns for human and social well being, then the spirit of 'safety ideology' will constantly reappear.

Summary and Conclusion

We glance at each other, our gestures and bodies, while travelling by train, with a proper distance, a constant perspective – so rare, this relationship between strangers in the public sphere. And the height of the seat, angle of the backrest, and the brightened sense of space, maintains decency for people without losing kindness. Then, you are able to develop your own 'living physiognomy'. (Lei, 2001, p. 73)

The TRTS is still under construction and the future complete network has not been determined, so it requires continuous observation of its spatial and social impact on Taipei City. Using the framework of 'globalization politics of identity, state transformation, and civil society', the trends and features of the TRTS can be summarized in its social context.

In regard to state transformation, the authoritarian regime, at the planning stage of the TRTS, facilitated the integration of the two different projects of rapid transit systems proposed by the central government and the Taipei City Government, and the passing of a large special budget by avoiding public supervision. Whereas at the constructing stage, the state apparatus went through radical transformation when martial law was abolished and long suppressed social protests erupted. At this stage, the corruption in the Taipei City Government and Department of Rapid Transit Systems was exposed, and citizens questioned the legitimacy of the TRTS. In the meantime, the financial burden drove the state to consider private-public partnership as the way out of financial shortfall. As to the present stage of operation, the TRTS has become the site of cultural governance in the context of populism and image engineering politics. Accompanying the rise of a new middle class, the TRTS constructs an imaginative geography of globalization and aesthetic landscape of exclusion. Responding to the change in political and cultural climate, the 'traditional' language of architecture with Chinese nationalism inscribed in spatial form has gradually turned into a vernacular style in the movement towards localization. However, the dominant theme, globalization, is internationalization and modernization.

As for globalization, the TRTS itself is a dreamscape for joining the first-class international cities, which materialized in the flow experiences of high-tech and automation, cultural activities, image engineering and the global consumption connection. In the context of international competition between cities, the declaration of city government aspires to achieve a global city status, but with little evidence in economic terms. The TRTS space follows that of the developed countries, thus weaving the imaginary geography of globalization into the social consciousness. In pursuit of modernization, an aesthetic landscape of exclusion emerges out of the ideoscape in order to eliminate the 'non-modern' social elements.

In the sphere of identity politics, although the discourse of a new Taiwan nationalism has been fuelled by cross-Strait confrontations, the politics of identity in the space-time of the TRTS is overwhelmingly shaped by the middle-class landscape of exclusion and consumptive culture. Traces of ethnic politics exist in multi-lingual broadcasting in the TRTS trains. Local ethnic identities are overtaken by middle-class identity, conforming to the imagination of globalization citizenship. The fictitious 'public', commodification, and the nearly universal acceptance of an aesthetic landscape of exclusion (with occasional deviation) reveal that the developing civil society is still fragile, lacking public consciousness and social awareness that go beyond individual benefits.

In face of the strong and homogeneous global imaginary geography and middle-class aesthetic landscape of exclusion embedded in the TRTS, what are the alternatives? The 'politics of interpersonal identification', in the quotation at the beginning of this section, may be relevant to raising questions. Interpersonal encounter in the crowded TRTS is inevitable. Would these encounters develop new kinds of spatial ethics in the necessary coexistence amongst differences? In what way will these interpersonal encounters engender interactive dialogue, and not passivity and alienation? How will the excluded and ignored respond to the aesthetic landscape of power once the aesthetic landscape of exclusion is socially recognized? These are some of the questions that would advance the imaging of the TRTS beyond the ideoscape of globalization.

References

Appadurai, A. (1996) *Modernity at Large: Cultural Dimensions of Globalization*. Minneapolis: University of Minnesota Press.
Feng, Z.M. (2001) *Taipei zonghe fazhan jihua: jieyun luwang fazhan dui Taipei dushi kongjian jiegou*

yingxiang zhi guihua zongjie baogaoshu (*The Comprehensive Plan of Taipei City: The Final Report of the Impact of MRT Network Development to Taipei's Urban Spatial Structure*). Taipei: Department of Urban Development Taipei City Government.

Foucault, M. (1977) *Discipline and Punish: The Birth of the Prison* (translated by Alan Sheridan). New York: Pantheon Books.

Jimmy (2001) *Sound of Colors*. Taipei: Locus Publishing.

Lei, X. (2001) *Taipei xieshengtie* (*A Sketch Book of Taipei*). Taipei: Department of Information Taipei City Government.

Liu, B.J. and. Lü, S.W. (1994) *Jieyun baipishu: 4444 yi de jiaoxun* (*The MRT White Book: A Lesson Cost 444.4 Billions*). Taipei: China Times Publishing.

Lyon, D. (1994) *The Electronic Eye: The Rise of Surveillance Society*. Cambridge: Polity Press.

Murakami, H. (1988) *Dixiatie shijian* (*Underground*).Taipei: China Times Publishing.

Said, E. (1978) *Orientalism*. New York: Vintage Books.

Shen, Y.R. (1999) Jieyun xitong lüke shensu anjian fenxi ji chuli zhi jiantao (Analysis and examination of the treatment of petition: cases from MRT passengers). Master's Thesis, Graduate Institute of Transportation, National ChiaoTung University.

Sibley, D. (1995) *Geographies of Exclusion*, London: Routledge.

Wang, C.H. (1990) Dushi liudong weiji de lunshu yu xianshi (The reality and discourse of urban flow crisis). *Taiwan: A Radical Quarterly in Social Studies*, l(2/3), pp. 105–182.

Wang, C.H. (2002) Liudong dijing yu shikong caoyan: Taipei jieyun xitong yu xin dushi jingyan (Landscape of flows and spatial-temporal performances: new urban experiences through Taipei MRT) *Dili Xuebao* (*Journal of Geographical Science*), **31**(June), pp. 83–115.

Wang, Y.J. (1997) Taipei jieyun gongsi yunwu renyuan zhuanye xunlian zhi yanjiu (Research on professional training of TRTC operation staff). Master's Thesis, Graduate Institute of Transportation, National ChiaoTung University.

Wu, S.H. (1998) Gonggong yishu shengchan de gonggong guocheng yu gonggongxing Jiangou (Public structuring and public process in the production of public art). Master's Thesis, Graduate Institute of Building and Planning, National Taiwan University.

Yang, Z.B. (1989) Taiwan dushi jiaotong zhengce de zhengzhi jingjixue fenxi: Taipei duhuiqu dazhong jieyun xitong jihua zhi ge'an yanjiu (The political economy of urban transportation policies in Taiwan: a case study of Taipei Metropolitan Area MRT System). Master's Thesis, Graduate Institute of Civil Engineering, National Taiwan University.

Yang, Z.B. (1998) *Ke yidong de wenhua xiangyan* (*A Movable Cultural Feast*). Taipei: Meta Media International.

Yang, Z.B. (2002a) *Jieyun gonggong yishu pintu* (*Metro, Art, Life*). Taipei: Marco Polo Press.

Yang, Z.B. (2002b) *Milian jieyun* (*Obsession with MRT*). Taipei: Garden City.

Young, I.M. (1990) The ideal of community and the politics of difference, in Nicholson, L.J. (ed.) *Feminism/Postmodernism*. London: Routledge, pp. 300–323.

Chapter Ten

Commentary on the Marginalized Society: The Films of Tsai Ming-Liang

Kuang-Tien Yao

The new Taiwan cinema movement attracted world attention in the early 1980s, led by the first wave of filmmakers, such as, Hou Hsiao-Hsien and Edward Yang (Yang Dechang), who successfully constructed and developed an indigenous Taiwanese cinema that reflects Taiwan's history, colonial past, social transformation, and contemporary cultural growth. Their narratives often dealt with the struggle of the working and peasant classes against deprivation and misery. In the 1980s, almost every film tried to reconstruct images of the past to some extent – namely, the transformation of Taiwanese society between the 1940s and 1970. These new directors, partially influenced by identity politics, were also moved to return to native and regional cultures and languages. As a result, multiple dialects – Mandarin, Taiwanese and Hakka – are often incorporated in their films.

In the 1990s, the first wave of filmmakers was followed by a new group of 'Second Wave' filmmakers. However, the Second Wave developed a different form. These directors were no longer interested in Taiwan's past history; they were mostly concerned with their present-day capitalist globalized metropolitan culture. Taipei became a major thematic concern prevalent in Taiwanese films in the 1990s. It played a key role in the construction of contemporary Taiwanese experiences rather than simply serving as a narrative background.

The most representative director during this period is Tsai Ming-Liang who often paints a very critical picture of Taipei. In his first five feature films, Taipei is portrayed mostly as an alienating, superficial, disjointed and impersonal modern globalized city, where people care only for money and are emotionally starved. Tsai said in production notes to *The Hole* (*Dong*, 1998):

The image of the 21st century that drifted out of my eyes was one of unending rain . . . I think the world environment, particularly that of Asia, was destroyed in the 20th century. Whether I am in Taiwan or in the country of my birth, Malaysia, I feel that the situation is at its most serious in these two developing countries. Why am I so pessimistic? If you live in Taiwan, you will naturally feel pessimism. We paid a heavy price for the take-off of Taiwan's economy over the past ten years. People have to live with crime and violence, political conflict and corruption, the serious pollution of the environment, alienation and growing friction in personal relationships. All these are almost permanent fixtures of people's lives. The most serious problem, I believe, is the sense of anxiety and insecurity in people and their loss of confidence and trust in the government. Therefore I think the future will be fraught with suspicion and tragedy. (http://www.cs.mu.oz.au/~peteg/zine/toto/tsai.htm)

As Tsai often admits, his films demonstrate his 'observation of the society, which closely relates to the economic prosperity and environmental changes in Taipei' (Jiao, 1997, p. 55). Tsai's production notes, indeed, express his great concerns for the social, cultural and environmental changes in the postmodern society of Taipei in the aftermath of the economic miracle. Particularly, he is concerned about Taipei's under class and marginalized people, those who are left out or underprivileged by globalization.

Tsai's films are portraits of marginalized people who live in an over crowded metropolis. Their physical being and mental consciousness are imprisoned in the city and are unable to rise above the fast pace of modernization – accompanied by heavy economic pressures resulting from globalization and the island's economic success. Consequently, they choose to live in isolation and meaninglessly in the city. They exhibit pain and anguish amidst sexual pleasure, while the acquisition and consumption of modern luxuries do not bring them any contentment. These are portraits of aimless Taipei youths, who either live alone or in disconnected families with parents – likewise dysfunctional – in Taipei's low-income, marginalized community. Young people, who are lonely, some even homeless, are incapable of communicating with others, and can barely subsist, whether by selling urn space in a columbarium, peddling watches in the busy Ximending District, or selling designer Hong Kong clothes illegally in Taipei night markets. And also, portraits of parents who are either unemployed or making their living by driving a taxi or operating a restaurant elevator.

I.C. Jarvie, author of *Movie as Social Criticism*, states that 'Popular movies are a rich source of ideas about, information (to be sure, misinformation also) concerning, and criticism of, society' (Jarvie, 1978, p. iv). Through his films, Tsai Ming-Liang documents, informs, criticizes and exposes the lives of those marginalized people with whom he is familiar and shares concern. Moreover, in recent years, the ever-increasing recognition of academic Chinese film studies in universities and colleges has confirmed that scholars perceive film as a social commentary and a medium that reflects the reality and exposes truths of society. Through the study of stories and imageries of films, students explore how Chinese films have reflected and responded to radical social, economic, and political changes in China, Taiwan, and Hong Kong. They tackle issues as broad as globalization, as personal as family relationships, and as intimate and controversial as sexuality. Tsai Ming-Liang's films should be required screening on lists and syllabuses for Chinese film studies. For Tsai's films connect with the society – particularly in the way he portrays the views and values of the culture in Taiwan – and are viewed as a rich source of ideas and criticism of Taipei society. Though Tsai's films often focus on changes happening in Taiwan, especially Taipei, it is evident his concerns extend far beyond the island as he understands that, with economic progress and globalization, Taipei is not alone in suffering from crime and violence, alienation and growing friction in personal relationships, and growing environmental pollution.

A brief history of Taiwanese film and the emergence of New Taiwan Cinema, in the 1980s, prior to Tsai's arrival in Taiwan, will be provided as a background to how he became one of the most promising directors in the 1990s. This chapter, then, discusses the most significant recurrent themes in Tsai's films and his social critiques, which have been recognized by many critics as his unique style and trademark. While discussing these recurrent themes, how his films observe and evaluate human relations and reflect on pressing social issues in the postmodern society of Taipei in the aftermath of the economic miracle of the 1990s will be discussed.

Contemporary Evolution of Taiwanese Films

Prior to Taiwan New Cinema of the 1980s

The history of Taiwan film began shortly after the Japanese took over the island. In July 1900, a Japanese timber import merchant in Taipei invited a projectionist from Japan to show French documentary films, which was the first time Taiwanese people in Taipei saw any type of film (Ye, 1995, p. 3). For the first 20 years, only Japanese documentaries and Japanese feature films were produced and allowed to be shown in Taiwan. The restriction of producing only Japanese language film in Taiwan is seen as one of the measures taken by the Japanese government to assimilate the Taiwanese. In order to keep the colonial structure intact, no Taiwanese actor was allowed in films produced in Taiwan until 1922, when Liu Xiyang, a Taiwanese bank clerk, was given a leading role in a Japanese feature film called *The Eyes of the Buddha* (*Da fo de tong kong*) and became the first Taiwanese actor in the history of Taiwanese film.

Beginning in 1925, an integrated film industry gradually formed using Taiwanese talent and capital. The Taiwanese made ten feature films in collaboration with the Japanese. The content of these movies focused predominately on propagating Japanese militarism. The film industry was interrupted in 1937 by the Sino-Japanese war; consequently, virtually nothing was produced until after the Nationalist government took over Taiwan in 1945.

With the end of the civil war, Chiang Kai-Shek and his government retreated to Taiwan in December 1949 and established Taipei as the provincial capital of the Republic of China. Shanghai filmmakers sympathetic to the Nationalist government also followed Chiang to Taiwan. As Taiwan's economy and society became stabilized in the 1950s, exiled filmmakers from Shanghai, subsidized by the Nationalist government, formed the nexus of a new film industry that produced Mandarin and low-budget Taiwanese dialect films. Mandarin films propagated the development of Taiwan as a free China, and were used as a political tool for the nationalist government to denounce the communist regime of mainland China.

As economic prosperity, industrialization and modernization swiftly expanded in Taiwan from the 1960s through the early 1970s, a genre of 'Healthy and Realistic' melodramas (*Jiankang xieshi pian*), introduced by the government-owned Central Motion Picture Corporation (CMPC), gained popularity. 'Healthy and Realistic' films advocated a positive attitude towards traditional moral values, easing the conflict between socio-economic restructuring and moral-ethical values of the traditional agrarian society. Two other popular genres of the 1960s are Huangmei Tune Musical Operas (*Huangmei diao*) and Knight-Errant (*Wuxiao* a.k.a. *Gongfu*) movies. Although these popular genres reaped great profit for the film industry in the 1960s, their audiences quickly lost interest – due to the films' repetitiveness and lack of originality.

As Taiwan embarked on its economic miracle in the 1970s, its film industry seemed primed to gallop ahead toward the proverbial *cinematic* sunset. By the end of the 1970s, audiences became tired of escapist romance movies, while Gongfu action films fell out of favour overseas, especially in Southeast Asian theatres, because of its sloppy production. Consequently, Taiwan's yearly total production in films slipped from triple to double digits and the industry began to lose its competitiveness, enabling Hong Kong to take over film markets in Taiwan and Southeast Asia. Furthermore, with the advent of home video in the early 1980s, the number of Taiwan films released in theatres dwindled further.

A Changing Society and Taiwan New Cinema in the 1980s

For the people of Taiwan, 1979 through 1989 was a stifling era characterized by unparalleled economic and social progress amidst frequent political change. The most eventful political change came when the United States, in order to extend diplomatic recognition to China, ended its long-standing political relation with

Taiwan on 1 January, 1979, nine months after Chiang Ching-Kuo became president of the Republic of China. Yet in this difficult period, the Taiwanese people stood firm and created an 'economic miracle'. In 1985, due to successful economic reforms in the 1950s and 1960s, Taiwan took its place alongside Singapore, South Korea and Hong Kong as one of the region's four 'dragons'.

In 1987, shortly before his death in January 1988, Chiang Ching-Kuo lifted the Emergency Decree, putting an end to four decades of martial law in Taiwan. Also in November 1987, the ban on travel into mainland China was lifted. As a result, freedom of speech and political activity expanded. Taiwan society became progressively more open and vocal, and its people more actively asserted their unique identity. For Hou Hsiao-Hsien and Edward Yang, directors of Taiwanese New Wave Cinema, who were both born in the 1950s and reached adulthood under socio-political liberalization, the restoration and re-examination of Taiwan's 'forgotten' historical experience became a critical theme (Lu, 1997).

Unexpected economic success had considerable bearing, too, on social and environmental change in Taiwan. Towards the end of the 1980s, though people in Taiwan enjoyed freedom of speech and wealth never before envisioned, they also faced numerous problems – crises in faith and identity emerged, and a sense of insecurity permeated throughout society.

Amidst the economic and social progress, and political changes, the film industry underwent monumental change in the 1980s. In the early 1980s, the Central Motion Picture Corporation hired a group of young directors and screenwriters, who were well educated in film schools in Taiwan and the United States, to work for them. Hou Hsiao-Hsien and Edward Yang were hired and trained to be directors, and Tsai Ming-Liang was hired as screenwriter (Li, 1997, p. 188). In 1982, the Corporation backed these two young and unknown directors in two films: *In Our Time* (*Guangyin de gushi*, 1982), directed by Edward Yang, and *Sandwich Man* (*Erzi de dawanou*, 1983), one of the four episodes of which was directed by Hou Hsiao-Hsien. Although these two films were not box-office hits, they were well received and have been regarded as two of the forerunners of 'Taiwan New Cinema'.

At the time Taiwan New Wave films began entering the international market, the production of local Taiwan films was at a nadir. Hong Kong films dominated the market. In the 1990s, even though the Government Information Office, the agency responsible for overseeing the film industry, began offering grants to promote film production in Taiwan, actual production remained low because filmmakers were not willing to invest capital to shoot films in Taiwan. Instead, investments flowed out to Hong Kong and mainland China. Films like *Farewell My Concubine* and *Raise the Red Lantern* have all been made under the model of 'Taiwan money, Hong Kong skills, and mainland locations'. By the late 1990s, only about 30 films a year were being produced in Taiwan (*Sinorama*, 1 November, 1999), even fewer of which were actually released in theatres in Taiwan. Films that did play on the big screen typically fell into two categories, either cheap comedies thrown together by the Central Motion Picture Corporation, or serious art films directed by Tsai Ming-Liang, Hou Hsiao-Hsien and Edward Yang.

Era of Tsai Ming-Liang's Films in the 1990s

In the 1980s, prior to Tsai's era, the first wave of filmmakers presented a rather uniform aesthetic tradition in their films. While recollecting and reconstructing their memories of Taiwan's past and culture in their films, they have reflected an impartial view of the reality. They painted a warm and caring agrarian society in which people abided by Confucian ethics and respected traditional family values and life. In the late 1980s, some directors, including Hou and Yang, began exploring themes based on observance and evaluation of modern urban life in Taiwan, rather than dwelling on the nostalgia of the past. Consequently, a city-based film, also known as *Chengshi dianying*, set in a metropolitan centre, particularly in Taipei, became the main feature and context for the majority of films from Taiwan. Taipei is the genuine protagonist, where marginalized individuals live scattered in every corner of the city. Understanding the contours of Taipei, its social and economic changes, and how its people reside in this society have become an essential function in deciphering the Taiwan films of the 1990s. On the subject of contemporary Taipei and its marginalized people, Tsai Ming-Liang has been considered its key director of the 1990s.

Identity Politics: Mainlanders and Taiwanese

Before reviewing Tsai Ming-Liang's emergence as a key filmmaker, one critical social-political issue that permeates Taiwanese society should be discussed. Taiwanese identity is an extremely complicated subject, often causing taunting arguments, particularly when the sensitive political issue of unification or 'One China, Two Systems' is mentioned. The subject of 'Taiwan identity' is fraught with sensitive political implications, and was taboo until the late 1970s. Closely related is a crucial distinction between native Taiwanese and immigrant Mainlanders – the latter referring to those Chinese exiled to Taiwan at the end of the civil war between the KMT and Communist parties. In Taiwan, the Nationalist government employs administrative procedures requiring identification of one's hometown based on one's father's place of origin. This information is a requisite item on identification cards carried by all persons aged fifteen and over (Rubinstein, 1994, p. 92). Under this policy, children born in Taiwan after 1945 to mainland parents or to mixed parentage are registered as a 'Mainlander'.

Classification, either as Mainlander or Taiwanese, was less problematic in the years immediately following the KMT retreat to Taiwan, as distinctions were fairly obvious, and criteria for labelling a person was rather simple. However, with time, intermarriage, and the births of second and third generations, these distinctions became more difficult to draw and the criteria became increasingly questionable. For the second and third generations of Mainlander offspring, their identities have become an emotional and agonizing issue to deal with. This group complains of exclusion from Taiwanese society because one, or both, of their parents are mainland Chinese. Some even fear that because they are considered by Taiwanese as second generation Mainlanders, they may be persecuted and deprived of their present social standing, if Taiwan-independence advocates ascend to power. Other offspring of Mainlanders, who consider Taiwan their home and espouse belonging via birthright, experience difficulty receiving acceptance as 'Taiwanese' in the eyes of some native Taiwanese people.

No matter how emotional and sensitive the issue is, the so-called Mainlanders and Taiwanese, through living on the same island, breathing the same air, and eating the same foods, for more than 50 years, together have inspired a very unique Taiwanese popular culture, particularly noticeable in the area of language, one of the most common markers of identity. Before 1987, speaking the Taiwanese dialect was a primary marker of being native Taiwanese. To prevent language from becoming a focus for opposition, the Nationalist government promoted Mandarin as the official language in the 1960s and 1970s, and prohibited the teaching of the Taiwanese dialect in schools.

With the passing of time and increasing intermarriage, offspring of Mainlanders were often raised in a bilingual environment. Taiwan, as a society, has become increasingly bilingual, but the Mainlander-Taiwanese conflict, as a social dilemma, has not escaped the attention of filmmakers. Hou Hsiao-Hsien's films provide many examples of these bilingual families. The best example is *City of Sadness* (*Beiqing Chengshi*), which confronts the 28 February Incident of 1947[1] head-on in an unsentimental fashion, bringing out the violent clash of distinct ways of life through the use of Taiwanese, Shanghainese, Mandarin and Japanese languages. Thus, Hou's films set a tradition of using films for social observation and commentary.

Tsai Ming-Liang and His Life in Taiwan

Tsai Ming-Liang, in fact, is not even a Taiwanese. He is an ethnic-Chinese, born and raised in Malaysia, where his grandfather, and later his father, settled. Tsai was born in 1957 in Kuching, Malaysia. A small town meaning 'cat' in Malay, Kuching was a peaceful town with a slow pace of life, where the only leisure activities people had were cinema or radio. Tsai came from a fairly humble family; his father was a farmer and had a little street-corner stall where he sold noodles to ordinary people in the evenings. When Tsai was little, he had also lived with his maternal grandparents who also owned a noodle shop. One grandparent would take Tsai to movie theatres in the evenings, while the other worked, alternating regularly. For this reason, Tsai often went to the same movie twice. Later, Tsai's grandmother operated a small casino when his grandfather became ill and could no longer provide for the family. Tsai often recalled his grandmother as a small, but very strong-willed, and extremely tough woman.

Spending his free time accompanying his grandparents to the movies, Tsai's cinema education began at a very young age by watching Hollywood-style films, Hong Kong films in Cantonese, and Taiwan films in Taiwanese. After graduating from high school, Tsai became a bit of a gigolo, with long hair and flared trousers. Tsai's father, worried about his education in Malaysia, decided to send him to Taiwan to ensure that his son would turn out 'all right', because the education system there was known to be disciplined and strict.

Tsai arrived in Taiwan in 1977, when martial law was still in force. While he was pursuing a degree in drama and cinema at the Chinese Culture University of Taiwan, society in Taiwan was in the midst of political, economic and social change. Although Tsai was enrolled to study in the theatre department, most of the time he did not go to classes. Instead, he spent much of his time in the film library viewing videos, exploring and studying European films and auteur films. He had also collected a library of pirated videotapes of auteur films before the Taiwan government prohibited illegal copying of videos and films. Today, he continues to hunt for auteur films in video shops selling pirated videos.

When Tsai was still a student, he lived in various low-income districts of Taipei, where he mingled with people who lived marginal lives in a big city. He experienced a flood in his little room. Tsai saw a couple, who lived under his floor, fight three times in one night – and almost kill each other. He also owned and ran an eatery and prepared take-out foods for customers. After graduating from film school, for about 10 years he worked as a theatrical producer, television producer, and screenwriter. In the early days of his film career in the 1980s, Tsai often went to the district called Ximending, the displaced traditional city centre where teenagers particularly liked to loiter, now famous for its inexpensive shopping, movie theatres, and film production houses. Besides going there to watch movies, Tsai also spent time walking the streets to meet ordinary people like teenagers, small street-corner vendors, and old Chinese soldiers. Ximending became the central location for his TV series and Tsai's first film, *Rebels of the Neon God* (hereafter *Rebels*). Today, he still walks around the streets there and even considers the district his film studio (Rehm *et al*,, 1999). That Tsai is neither a Mainlander nor Taiwanese, an immigrant brought up with Chinese cultural tradition, and has a lower-class origin, make him a unique and objective observer. Tsai's esoteric film-making, his years of training, his chosen student life and his preference for the urban district, allow him to understand and become an acute commentator of Taipei's under-class society.

Rebels (see figure 10.1), a study of disaffected Taiwan teenagers in Taipei, was Tsai Ming-Liang's debut feature film, which won him numerous international prizes, including the First Prize at the Turin International Film Festival in 1992, the Bronze Prize at the Tokyo International Film Festival in 1993, and a Special Jury Prize *ex aequo* at the Singapore International Film Festival in 1994. Following this highly successful debut, Tsai made another four films that have won him further international recognition. His second film, *Vive L'Amour* (*Aiqing wansui*; see figure 10.2), won the Golden Lion award for best film at the 1994 Venice Film Festival. In 1997, his third film, *The River* (*Heliu*; see figure 10.3), won the Special Jury Prize at the Berlin Film Festival and Best Film at the Singapore Film Festival. In 1998, his fourth film, *The Hole* (*Dong*; see figure 10.4), commissioned by a group of French TV producers as part of their end-of-the-millennium series, won the Golden Hugo Best Film award at the Chicago Film Festival. In 2001, Tsai made his fifth film, *What Time*

Figure 10.1. *Rebels of the Neon God. Source:* http://mongrelmedia.com/films/ RebelsOfTheNeonGod.html

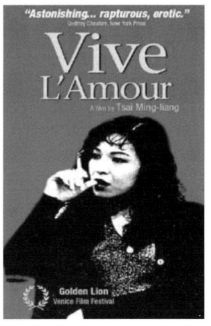

Figure 10.2. *Vive L'Amour. Source:* http:// mongrelmedia.com/films/Vive.html

Figure 10.3. *The River. Source:* http://207.136.67.23/film/DVDReview/the_river.htm

Figure 10.4. *The Hole. Source:* http://www.cse.unsw.edu.au/~peteg/zine/toto/tsai.htm

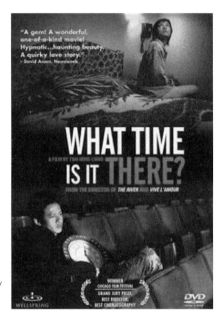

Figure 10.5. *What Time Is It There? Source:* http://www.pegasosfilm.de/programm/film.asp?fMovieID=62

Is It There? (*Ni nabian jidian zhong?*; see figure 10.5), in Taipei and Paris, which also received rave reviews.

Recurrent Themes in Tsai Ming-Liang's Films

By 2001, Tsai had made five interrelated films, using an ensemble cast and revisiting certain characters, locations and themes.[2] They are presented as one film either seen from five different angles, or perceived under the influence of five different moods, or as a sequence of family history. Several recurrent themes appear in these films, which have uniquely become Tsai's special concern. These similarities seem more striking than their differences.

Taipei – An Unspoken Central Character/Setting

Spatial location is pertinent to Tsai's films. His image of Taiwan's contemporary culture of the 1980s and 1990s is elaborated through his portrait of Taipei. In *Rebels*, Tsai's debut, the film is actually encircled in a particular neighbourhood, the Ximending district in southwest Taipei, known to be teeming with teenagers, where young protagonists aimlessly zip along its main avenues on their motorcycles. This particular district holds a significant meaning for Tsai for it was here he observed teenagers and received a thorough introduction to Taipei and world cinema.

In all Tsai's five feature films, Taipei is portrayed as a world of urban dissatisfaction, in which people are physically isolated from each other; their feelings are cut off from one another; they move around like perverse beings in dimly-lit rooms, flooded apartments and murky hotel rooms; they hang out in a noisy video arcade, a coffee house, or a gay sauna, looking for comfort to ease their loneliness and isolation. Tsai Ming-Liang, during an interview, told a reporter:

Everything has its place and its own life. It is an idea very close to Chinese Buddhism, which regards the human body as a place of 'passage', which means that after some decades, the mind will abandon the body. This belief also holds true for a home and a building.' (Rehm et al., 1999, p. 103)

He is clearly targeting his subject on a specific social group. In Tsai's films, because his characters exchange very few words, the place or setting of where the character has chosen to be becomes very important. Under this mindset, informed by his experience, Taipei is a melancholy central character in which delinquency, vandalism, lonely souls, dysfunctional families, and homosexuality all herald. This metropolis also projects a new cultural model personified by Western capitalist ideology that challenges traditional Chinese cultural values by tearing down and reconstructing moral disciplines and social order *vis à vis* the family, the school, and sexual relations (Wu, 2002, pp. 58–64). Tsai's films hone directly into the social conflict and ideological confrontation evidenced in a globalizing Taipei.

Marginal People and Common Problems

All characters in Tsai's films are underclass people, by their own choice on the fringe of urban society, and somewhat socially dysfunctional. Some critics describe Tsai's characters as rather invisible and unnoticeable to other people whose paths they cross. Tsai's aim of portraying these types of character in his films, by unveiling the characters' privacy, is to make them noticeable and become real in the audiences' eyes (Rehm *et al.*, 1999, p. 98). Tsai claims he films these people because they interest him and please him. They are the people with whom he is familiar and feels close to. For example, Lee Kang-Sheng, named Xiao Kang in all his films, and Miao Tian, who portrays Xiao Kang's father in most of his films, are images familiar in his own life. The actresses in his films are also women whom he finds adorable. They all have a motherly, strong-willed side, which reminds him of his own maternal grandmother. What interests Tsai is that those people come from an environment that he is familiar with and has experienced.

In Tsai's first feature film, *Rebels*, Xiao Kang lives in a very typical family in present-day Taiwan. His father, like many other fathers in Taiwan today, is a Mainlander who has retreated to Taiwan from his hometown in China. He has gone through wars and left his family behind in China. He is quiet, diligent, and lives with the traditional obligation of feeding his family. Even though he has lived more than half his lifetime in Taiwan, has married a Taiwanese woman and fathered a son, he still considers himself a Mainlander and not a local Taiwanese. He hopes that some day he will be able to return to China, but most likely he will not be able to do so. This is a typical family which has a built-in identity conflict.

Xiao Kang, another typical product of the second generation of Mainlanders, with a father from the mainland and a Taiwanese mother, was raised in a bilingual environment. He is confused, unmotivated, distracted and bored with his tutorial classes, and rides a motorcycle through the streets of Taipei. He spends his time hanging out in noisy, crowded video arcades, tailing two juvenile delinquents who steal computer chips from the arcade, and finally vandalizes one of the delinquents' motorcycles.

Young people, like Xiao Kang in *Rebels*, riding motorcycles, cruising around on scooters or wandering the city on foot, waiting for something to happen, are common street scenes in Taiwan, especially the Taipei of the 1980s and 1990s. They are lonely, lost, unable to communicate with their parents, and left out of the global economy and society. For Taipei's youth, riding a motorcycle, even if aimlessly and going no where, seems to be the only hope they have to seek escape from an oppressive modern urban culture – the city is desolate, the nights seem endless, and life becomes monotonous.

In the late 1980s, juvenile delinquency was the most visible and serious social problem in Taiwan. Rapid industrialization has decentralized traditional notions of patriarchy as well as disintegrated lines of communication between different generations. Young people, who were born and grew up during the newly developing industrial culture, and the elderly, who belonged to an agrarian culture, found it difficult to communicate with each other. The generation gap, rather alien to traditional Chinese culture, became a thorny social problem. With the ever widening generation gap between parents and children, young people neglected their school work and spent long hours playing video games in crowded video arcades, hanging out in dark coffee houses, and sometimes committing activities of petty thievery (Harrell and Huang, 1994, p. 212). They were ill prepared for participating in the new urban activities and taking advantage of the economic opportunities brought by global modernization.

In Taipei, increasing numbers of delinquents were arrested for crimes – about four times greater than the increase in Taipei's teenage population (Selya, 1995, p. 173). Some studies conclude problems of juvenile delinquency as being caused by rapid population growth and modernization, which complicated family life. Furthermore, some KMT elites blamed the political liberalization, taking place in Taiwan over the past two decades, for contributing to the increase of juvenile delinquency. Others feel that economic development has led to an overall decline in values and morals (Selya, 1995, p. 174). These are the displaced youth portrayed in Tsai Ming-Liang's films.

A Woman's Place is Not at Home

In the 1970s, when economic growth gave rise to new employment opportunities, women in Taiwan began leaving the kitchens and moving into the labour market; however, they were mostly poor, young women, on average 25 years old or younger taking the many low-skill, manual labour, and service jobs. As rising educational opportunities appeared, women gained better employment outside their homes in the 1980s and 1990s. Education became a social mechanism in altering the lives of women, providing a means for them to realize their potential and advance their status in the family and society.

Tsai's films deal with issues of modern women in Taiwan. His female characters are strong-willed. The best representative is Ms. Lin, a real estate agent, in *Vive L'Amour*. She knows that the modern society of Taipei is dominated by buyer-seller relationships. She does not talk much, except when she is trying to persuade her clients to buy properties – when she talks with enthusiasm. Throughout the entire film, she is extremely quiet and indifferent to her surroundings, and shows neither pleasure nor displeasure in her life. She simply moves around the empty apartments and houses she sells. Her emotional response is as empty and cold as those houses, depicted by her abrasive way of talking to her clients and by her ways of dominating her partner during sex without showing any feeling.

Ms. Lin, a working-woman, has completely abandoned her kitchen. In *Vive L'Amour*, she eats at a roadside food stand at the night market and brings home a takeout lunch box. Here, the elimination of a functional kitchen seems to be a way she avoids any domestic duty, setting herself free to be socially independent and able to do her work outside the home. Interestingly, however, this liberation brings no happiness or fulfilment to her. The most unexpected emotional outburst occurs at the end of this film, after she has had sex the previous night. She leaves a luxury apartment and walks into a nearly finished park, Da'an senlin gongyuan

(Ta-an Forest Park) also known as No. 7 Park, sits on an empty bench, and begins to cry. Her crying lasts at least four minutes. Her eyes are empty. Her face is fallen. She appears extremely exhausted. The film ends at the crying scene in the park, seemingly to imply the failure of the city to provide her with any sense of identity and stability. Tsai offers no resolution to her desolation, but an acute social observation and commentary.

Disintegration of the Family and Confronting Sexuality

Tsai's five feature films, thus far, have all centred on the main character Xiao Kang. It is important to view Tsai's films in the order of their release because they are presented as a sequential history of one family. Tsai even admits in his production note for *The River* that the film is a continuation of *Rebels* and *Vive L'Amour* and further expansions of his character. Xiao Kang is no longer an adolescent in *Rebels*. He left home in *Rebels*, searched for his identity in *Vive L'Amour*, and returned to his home in *The River*. However, it is not certain whether the idea of producing all Tsai's films in the same framework, as a sequential family story, was already formed with the filming of *Rebels*.

According to his production note for *The River*, Tsai wanted Xiao Kang to come back to a family or home that he does not really care for, but needs his parents to care for his illness. Xiao Kang's family, in an under-lit apartment, flooded with rainwater in every corner, becomes 'the river' that buries his gay father's unspeakable secret. In Tsai's first two films, *Rebels* and *Vive L'Amour*, he probed into Xiao Kang's search for sexuality in a very hesitant and quiet way – with no attempt to expand this self-exploration further or to offer any resolution to his search. However, in *The River*, the father's hidden secret, like uncontrollable rainwater pervading every corner of the apartment, has come out.

In *The River*, Tsai cries for the disintegration of the traditional Confucian family. Under the stress of modernization, the Confucian familial tradition, considered a source of values for the Chinese people and society, has completely disintegrated. The ideology of multiple generations all residing under the same roof has given way to a modern nuclear family, where family members lack communication; father and son engage in casual promiscuous sex, while the mother has an affair with a sullen, younger video-porn pirate. In addition to deconstructing the father image and family order, Tsai has also exposed issues of incest and homosexuality, a gay father's genuine pain of not being able to come out of the closet and a son's questioning of his own sexuality. The father in *The River* is incapable of making any autonomous decision. In a larger social-cultural context, he is defined as a father who must provide for the family. But, as a secretly gay father, he has very few options in a closed society. It is extremely daring for Tsai to stage a scene in

The River that has the father unknowingly masturbating his son in a gay sauna, and then slapping his son when the lights come on.

According to Tsai, his original plan was to have the father and son just run into each other without having any sexual interaction in the sauna. At the last moment, however, he asked himself why he wanted to shoot this scene; why not have the father and son physically interact in the dark; why hadn't he dared to have thought that until then? Was it because of a fear of shooting such a scene? It is from this process of Tsai's own internal dialogue – without external concern of how an audience would react – that Tsai shot the scene, because it had emerged from the depths within his own self. This scene in *The River* has brought him much hostile criticism. Some people, only remembering the incestuous scene, hated his film. Meanwhile, the homosexual community questioned why he had to show homosexuals in such a sad, dysfunctional, and dark setting. Finally, feminists disliked this film because it shows a world full of men who reject women. Tsai obviously has touched a latent social raw nerve, which seriously concerns Taipei society. He says *The River* is his favourite because it is the richest of his films. However, after shooting and before editing the film, Tsai hid for a month because he was simply terrified of editing that scene (Rehm *et al.*, 1999, p. 98).

Water is Much More Important than Food

One fascinating aspect of Tsai's movies is his conceptualization and reduction of food and eating to a purely practical act of maintaining bodily function. This is completely against the Chinese tradition of enjoying eating. In the Chinese tradition, a kitchen and a dinner table are where family members cook and eat together – and is the symbolic heart of the home. However, in Tsai's films, the kitchen appears as an unused little corner with very few utensils and, at times, even clogged or flooded with water. His characters often eat simple instant-noodles alone in their dimly lit rooms or apartments. Apparently, Tsai has no intention of portraying those pleasurable aspects of eating rituals or family solidarity, because in his films the emptiness of living and the disintegration of family have stripped away all concerns for a so-called 'good life' – good food, extravagant living quarters, and congenial family – which were major concerns of Taiwanese society in the 1990s.

Instead of eating normal food, Tsai constantly shows his characters drinking and applying water to their bodies, and ultimately soaking their entire bodies in the bathtub. Tsai often mentions that water is very important in his films because it symbolizes love. He regards the characters in his films as plants, which are short of water and almost on the verge of dying from lack of water. Therefore, water for Tsai symbolically represents the love that his characters lack and desperately need (Rehm *et al.*, 1999, p. 114).

Water is also a subterranean flow within the characters of Tsai's films. There are unspeakable secret desires and yearning for love. In *The River*, there are several forms of water that appear in the film, including heavy rains outside the apartment or rainwater flooding Miao Tian's room. In this film, water symbolizes a gay father's unspeakable secret of yearning for love. This uncontrollable subterranean flow floods his room. He tries everything he can to stop the water from ruining his room, but fails. Instead, water floods every corner of his apartment. The movie ends with his wife climbing up to the rooftop to do everything she can to cover up the leaking spot.

In Tsai's films, his representation of water is easily detected in scenes of a polluted Tamsui River as well as the non-stop pouring rain, or the recurrence of flood water inside an apartment, and waste-water flowing back into the kitchen. Though Tsai mentions only the relations between water and love in his films, in many instances, all these different forms of water also imply his unspoken concern for Taiwan's social chaos and environmental issues, resulting from changes in familial and social order, economic prosperity, and political climate of the 1980s and 1990s.

It is no coincidence that the polluted water of Tamsui River appears as a main source that caused Xiao Kang's strange illness in *The River*. Tamsui River, located in the northern part of Taipei, was once a scenic river that provided navigation all the way upstream to Taipei and to fishing and recreation grounds. Since the 1950s, some 10,000 shops and factories have been built along the river, fouling it with human and industrial waste. The river has also been used for decades as a garbage dumping ground from the metropolitan area. Even though the Environmental Protection Agency, working with the Department of Environmental Protection in the Taipei City Government, established a 15-year programme in the mid-1980s to clean up the Tamsui, today it is still polluted with raw sewage along the riverbank. The name 'Tamsui,' meaning 'clear water,' thus reflects a rather ironic connotation (Rubinstein, 1994, p. 250).

In Tsai's production note for *The River*, he even mentions that when he was filming one of his TV dramas he had an actor jump into Tamsui River for a scene. Three days after the filming, that actor became sick because he had swallowed its polluted water. As a matter of fact, after Tsai finished filming that movie, there was also news about a dead body discovered floating in the Tamsui River (Jiao, 1997, p. 19). In Tsai's films, water is also symbolic of environmental concerns.

Popular Religion as a Part of Daily Life

As a second generation Mainlander whose mother is Taiwanese, Xiao Kang is raised in the Taiwanese tradition, especially with respect to his religious beliefs. The best example of these beliefs can be seen in *Rebels* and *What Time Is It There?*. In *Rebels*, the mother goes to the temple and finds out from the Daoist priest that the reason Xiao Kang is disaffected and unwilling to concentrate on his studies is because he is the reincarnation of the child rebel god named Nezha, which is the source of the film's title. She requests the priest to give her a talisman for her son. After obtaining one, she returns home, burns it, and mixes the ashes into the dinner dishes so that Xiao Kang may consume the remedy and hopefully resolve his problems. In *The River*, when Xiao Kang is sick with a strange illness on his neck, his mother goes to the temple and prays for him. The father also takes Xiao Kang to see a religious healer, hoping that religious prayers and remedies could heal Xiao Kang's illness. In *What Time Is It There?*, the mother is obsessed with the death of her husband and thinks that his spirit is a white fish in the fish tank in the apartment. She pays for a Daoist priest to perform channelling rituals, she offers food to her dead husband at a special altar and at the dinner table, and she covers the entire house with paper and bed sheets because she thinks her deceased husband would be afraid of light.

These recurrent scenes of religious rituals or practices may appear superstitious or even ridiculous to some viewers, yet, it is Tsai's way of showing how popular religion is still a very common practice among many Taiwanese families in contemporary society. Xiao Kang's parents might seem ignorant in using the ashes of a talisman to prevent him from rebelling against them, or in using a religious healer to cure his strange illness; nonetheless, it is their way of expressing love to him.

Nowadays, even successful Taiwanese politicians use religious practices and ceremonies to build electoral support for their campaigns. In the 1980s, some townships even began their executive campaigns with a rally at the candidate's campaign headquarters and a procession to Mazu's temple and other local temples throughout the town (Rubinstein, 1994, p. 397). Religious practices, including the use of a Daoist priests and the spiritual medium to communicate with the dead, are very common in families, where one of the parents is Taiwanese.

Speech is a Dangerous Thing

In Tsai's films, the characters communicate with each other without much dialogue. He says to reporters that the lack of dialogue in all his films is not deliberate – not as a way of creating a style for himself. Rather, his characters are merely presented in solitary situations, and are unlikely to talk to themselves. For instance, in *Vive L'Amour*, the three main characters, a second-hand real estate agent Ms. Lin, a salesman for ceramic reliquaries Xiao Kang, and a illegal night-stand clothing peddler, A Long, are all isolated individuals, about whom Tsai offers no past information or hints about their future. They are unaware of each other's existence and sometimes hide from each other; therefore, there is hardly any dialogue in *Vive L'Amour*. By cross-cutting three unrelated characters and withholding their background information, Tsai leaves a lot of space for the audience to interpret their relationships and simply trusts his characters to move the audience without dramatized conversation and emotional background music.

As for the scenes in which family members do not have much to say to one another, Tsai explains it is so simply because they are that type of family – a type common in present-day Taiwan. He further explains that since people, in reality, rarely communicate and talk to one another, it is only natural for him to show such social truth through his films. Tsai also believes that the message he wants to convey to the audience, reflecting his long observation in Ximending, should be presented not through superficially constructed dialogue, but through the way his characters would naturally behave, and through how the audience interprets their viewing. In other words, he wants to transmit his message to and communicate with his audience through action, and not, spoken language, through real life characters, and not, artificial ones.

Tsai thinks that often what people say is the reverse of what they do. Under this mindset, he thinks that using too much speech in the film is a dangerous thing. Instead, he considers spoken language as merely one aspect of sound, which is also often lacking in his films. He does not want the dialogue to explain the action taken by characters. He does not want music to enhance artificially the emotion or atmosphere of his films. Tsai wants to reduce his communication of Taipei's social and cultural malaise in the starkest form so that the audience is able to feel the true spirit and atmosphere of his narrative as the film develops. Furthermore, Tsai's scripted silence further corresponds to his objective effort to show that 'every individual is very hard to understand', as he often explains to reporters. Limited dialogue in his films certainly creates a certain mystique of each character. Without much dialogue, his films allow audiences to interpret and judge – unimpeded – any thought or action of Tsai's characters.

Summary and Conclusion

Tsai Ming-Liang, although living in Taiwan for more than 20 years, still considers himself an outsider in Taiwanese society. He claims repeatedly that he is disinterested in understanding Taiwan's past – also asserting, his films do not search for Taiwan's identity. Tsai often emphasizes to reporters, 'I am using the films to document what I think; I only make films that I want to make . . . I care for people who surround me . . . and everything I described (in my films) is related to my life'. From his conversations with reporters and the content of his films, we can see that Tsai's films echo a neo-realist style of filmmaking. A film critic in Taiwan claimed Tsai's *Rebels* is

a story of you (the audience) and I (the reporter) in our youth as we sadly and aimlessly drift in the marginal city area of Ximending feeling empty and discontented. It is a neo-realist film. The setting and background of the film is so real that it could not be anymore real than the real life. It appears that the story reflects our own past experience, but it actually continues to reflect the current life of others . . . 'rebellion, the family, desire, disasters' are the basic rhythm of marginal city life. This is also the basic rhythm of Tsai Ming-Liang's films. (Deng, (2003) http://www.ncu.edu.tw/~eng/FilmCenter/TsaiF.htm)

Indeed, Tsai successfully presents his observations in genuine and true to life documentary-like films. He does not tell fictional stories in his films. At the end of all Tsai's films, he offers no definite answer or resolution to the situations presented in his films. He does not draw verdicts, but presents social reality as he sees it, and draws his audience to confront the social and cultural problems of the marginalized community and individuals.

Tsai distrusts the use of narrative as an artificial structuring device. Absence of conversation prompts his audience to absorb fully his unique and powerful observation, while permitting the audience itself to assess the social condition through its own interpretation of the meaning underlying Tsai's films. He uses 'real people', such as Xiao Kang, who had no formal theatre training before appearing in Tsai's first film *Rebels*, instead of actors. He also made extensive use of locations within Taipei city – for instance, an apartment in a low-income housing project – to produce a grainy and under-lit look, rather than studio shooting. Most importantly, his films deal with social issues and changes affecting the everyday life of the underclass in Taipei. When an official questioned Tsai why he often depicts Taipei as such a dark, dirty and noisy city even though there are many beautiful locations in Taipei, he replied, 'It is so obvious that there are a large group of people who are still living in a rather poor condition and rotten environment; their voices are often neglected by the so-called clean and orderly society, where both sides are unable to communicate with each other' (Huang, 1998; http://lib.tngs.edu/tw/webnote/). Inevitably, Tsai's films prompt their viewers to reflect on the ills of globalization, and the cultural malaise it engenders throughout society.

It is impossible to view Tsai's films in a historical vacuum in spite of his own insistence and proclamations of disinterest in understanding Taiwan's past. Undeniably, Tsai's evocative, if not shocking, filmmaking echoes of social commentary on the effects of modernization as well as a forewarning that those significant recent social, economic and political changes are the determinants of its present and future. True, his films are comparably less loaded with political and historical issues – a radical departure from his fellow directors, Hou Hsiao-Hsien and Edward Yang. Nevertheless, Tsai's films reflect the real, and even troubling, change in recent Taiwan, having both social and historical value. Tsai is able to demonstrate through his films his observation and selection of a nexus of complex human relations intertwined with contemporary social issues – particularly, crises in faith and identity, juvenile delinquency, dysfunctional patriarchy, disintegrating communication, dissolution of the traditional family, homosexuality, and environmental degradation – in the postmodern society of Taipei in the aftermath of the economic miracle.

Paradoxically, Tsai often says to reporters that his films are closely related to Taiwan's economic prosperity and social change. Yet his method of showing this aspect is to move methodically from a commonly portrayed surface to his character's inner life by exploring and revealing the impact that Taiwan's globalization has brought on their lives and behaviour in the urban reaches of Taipei. Tsai reveals the superficiality of Taiwanese life and the psyche of those people who live on the fringes of society, and their emptiness and hopelessness in a vast metropolis. It seems Tsai wants his viewers to re-evaluate the assumption that globalization, modernization, and the 'economic miracle' in Taiwan is 'good and desirable'. Are there negative impacts of modernization and globalization – namely, a deterioration of morale standards and cultural breakdown – plaguing Taiwan society today? Some scholars posited that the Confucian values – of hard work, loyalty, consideration – had enabled the spectacular, recent economic progress of Taiwan. However, it is possible that within the mobile, atomistic, and individualistic society of Taiwan, the effect of economic progress and modernization has been the erosion of those Confucian values – those same ones which are supposed to have brought about the advantage of globalization and modernization in the first place (Harrell and Huang, 1994, p. 9).

Furthermore, Taipei is often presented as an unspoken central character in all Tsai's films, where traditional familial and social order break down and conventional sexual identity collapses. Tsai's stories often unfold in fragmented spaces – a desolate Taipei city park; deserted Taipei streets at night; empty and dingy unsold apartments; and murky hotel rooms – which constitute an important microcosmic representation of parts of Taipei as purposeless, hopeless, and uncertain. The approach of using these spaces for self-indulgent fantasy may be Tsai's way of implying that Taiwan has long been perceived as a transitional stop by many Mainlanders (Deppman, 2001). To many first generation Mainlanders in Taiwan, the island is not a place that is meant to be a final home. Rather, it is merely a temporary sanctuary or shelter, believing they will eventually return to China or they will move onward to America or Europe if returning to China becomes impossible. So the apartment room and hotel are just temporary locales for them to check in – until they are ready to move on to a permanent and better place. The feeling of 'homelessness' and not being able to be accepted as 'a Taiwanese' is a constant worry of Mainlanders, caused in part by the threat of cross-Strait military tension. This deep and unspoken concern is vividly captured in the sojourn of Tsai's characters all of whom have no claim to love or stability.

Besides Tsai's unique style of filming, the stories presented in his works have clearly made him distinguishable from other contemporary directors in Taiwan. Tsai's films have critically exposed the social and cultural phenomena of the marginalized society in Taipei – a subject which has escaped other filmmakers' attention. His films have uncovered the cultural and social displacement evident in Taiwan society, particularly Taipei, where marginalized individuals excruciatingly and meaninglessly subsist on the fringes of society with no hope or dreams, and where every move and action they take seems to run counter to Confucian ideals and Chinese traditions. While other directors use their films to make political statements or seek historical truth, Tsai Ming-Liang uses his films to present his own insight into contemporary life in Taipei. Indeed, Tsai's genuine, true to life and documentary-like films serve as essential and unapologetic social documentation and commentary of Taipei's society today.

Notes

1. The 28 February Incident marks a major conflict between Chiang Kai-Shek's Nationalist forces and local Taiwanese. It was triggered by an incident occurring the day before when a mainland Chinese policeman confiscated the goods of a Taiwanese woman selling smuggled cigarettes. She was beaten mercilessly by the policeman when resisting the arrest. The next day, 28 February, 1947, angry crowds of Taiwanese gathered in the streets of Taipei to protest against the political corruption and economic repression of Chiang's Nationalist regime. As a result, martial law was declared, and thousands of Taiwanese were murdered by Nationalist troops. (http://cinemaspace.berkeley.edu/Papers/CityOfSadness/behind3.html).
2. Tsai made two more films in 2003. *Good Bye Dragon Inn* (Original title: *Bu san*) and *The Sky Walk Is Gone* (Original title: *Tianqiao bu jian le*). Although *Good Bye Dragon Inn* is also centred on Xiao Kang, it is not related to Tsai's first five films.

References

Deng, W.R. (2003) Qingshaonian Nezha (Rebels of the Neon God – Film Review). http://a107.ncu.edu.tw/fsc/act/director/tsai/index.html.

Deppman, H.C. (2001) Recipes for a new Taiwanese identity? Food, space, and sex in the works of Ang Lee, Ming-Liang Tsai, and Tien-Wen Chu. *American Journal of Chinese Studies*, 8(2), pp. 145–168.

Harrell, S. and Huang, C.C. (1994) *Cultural Change in Postwar Taiwan*. Boulder: Westview Press.

Huang, L. (1998) Tsai Ming-liang zhipai ziji xiangpai de dianying (Tsai Ming-Liang only makes films he wants to make). *Mei Li Jia Ren*, December, http://lib.tngs.edu/tw/webnote/.

Jarvie, I.C. (1978) *Movies as Social Criticism: Aspects of Their Social Psychology*. Metuchen, NJ: Scarecrow Press.

Jiao, X.P. (1997) *He liu: Tsai Ming-liang de dianying* (The River: Tsai Ming-liang's Films). Taipei: Huangguan wenxue chuban youxian gongsi.

'Love, Life and Lies. The Films of Tsai Ming-liang in the Context of the New Taiwanese Cinema'. http://www.cs.mu.oz.au/~peteg/zine/toto/tsai.htm (archived copy dated July 6, 2002).

Lu, F.Y. (1998) *Taiwan dianying: zhen zhi, jingji, meixue, 1949–1994* (Taiwanese Cinema: Politics, Economics, Art, 1949–1994). Taipei: Yuanliu chuban gongsi.

Lu, S. (1997) *Transnational Chinese Cinemas: Identity, Nationhood, Gender*. Honolulu: University of Hawaii Press.

Rehm, J.P., Joyard, O. and Rivière, D. (eds.) (1999) *Ts'ai Ming-liang*. Paris: Dis voir.

Rubinstein, M.A. (ed.) (1994) *The Other Taiwan: 1945 to the Present*. New York: M.E. Sharpe.

Selya, R.M. (1995) *Taipei*. New York: Wiley.

Teng, S.F. (1999) Can grants save the Taiwan film industry. *Sinorama*, November, also available also available at http://www.gio.gov.tw/taiwan-website/7-av/anglee/tf_3.htm.

Wu, I.F. (2002) Flowing desire, floating souls: modern cultural landscape in Tsai Ming-Liang's Taipei trilogy. *CineAction*, Winter, pp. 58–64.

Ye, L.Y. (1995) *Guangfu qian hou Gaoxiong Shi de xiyuan yu dianying* (*Theaters and Movies in Gaoxiong City in 1940s and 1950s*). Gaoxiong: Gaoxiong Shi wenxian weiyuanhui.

Postscript

Current Dilemma and Future Uncertainty

Reginald Yin-Wang Kwok

In reviewing the major urban development issues, the previous chapters have analyzed the consequences of Taipei's transformation towards a global city. Taipei's development followed the global path after Taiwan entered into the international economy in the 1960s. In the last two decades, the city has been explicitly pursuing its global city goal. Taiwan's economic development in general and Taipei's urban development in particular have been facilitating global demands and adjusting to the impact of transnational economy. This chapter will examine the prominent features of the current urban condition and its global city prospect, as Taipei embarks on the globalization project.

The Current Condition

In summarizing the key features of Taipei's current conditions and their causal factors, the domestic factors will be emphasized in guiding the analysis. Part I examined Taipei's economic and spatial restructuring to further its position in the global hierarchy. Hsu, Ching and Chou are in general agreement that Taipei has yet to become an advanced global city, and there are serious obstacles in its developmental path.

Given that Taipei has joined the global city race, it has to fulfil the basic requirements for the world's economic command post – that the city should have technological and financial superiority and control over its territorial region. At present, Taipei is a technological transmission space between the United States west coast and coastal China in information technology and computer related production (Chapter 1), targeting the global market. While Taipei is not at the innovation forefront in information technology, it possesses the highest technological knowledge in the region. Through its regional technological superiority, it dominates the production space in coastal China, particularly around Shanghai and the Yangtze Delta. Following the production relocation from Taiwan, entrepreneurs and technological professionals have also emigrated (Chapter 7), as has capital (Chapter 2 and 3). With these economic, human and knowledge outflows, Taipei is unable to transform into a high-tech professional and producer services dominated city – the hallmark of a global city.

The Taipei Metropolis consists of a suburban county dominated by manufacturing, surrounding a relatively low level service urban centre. Within the Asia-Pacific region, Taipei is the regional command post for information technology and computer-related production, functioning as the production middleman in the global context (Chapter 2). To advance and strengthen Taipei's global position, the state has to be able to react and facilitate the transnational production needs (Rodrik, 1997), in particular, opening borders for market integration (Yergin and Stanislaw, 1998). The Taiwan government, committed to localization and influenced by identity politics, has crafted a cross-Strait policy in the opposite direction (Chapter 3), thus hindering Taipei's growth towards a global city (Chapter 2). Current cross-Strait policy restrains Taipei's global city development.

Centre-city politics under the two-party system has directly affected Taipei's major development (Chapter 3 and 6). In the last decade, the central government and the city government have been led by opposing parties. The central state, using its allocation power, distributes resources and activities away from Taipei, to localities led by the same central state party, thus weakening the city's agglomeration economy and advantages (Chapter 3). Often, the two levels of government are at odds with each other in policy formation and resource allocation (Chapter 6). In terms of global competition, decentralization reduces the attraction for transnational corporations and global capital, as they seek urban nodal locations with diverse skills, activities and services. As Taipei progresses towards a global city, concentration of economic activities and cultural events is necessary to propel the city towards its goal. Centre-city politics in Taiwan has been dis-privileging Taipei in the last decade, and is most likely to continue into the near future. Until the central state and the city state are both led by the same party, Taipei's path towards a global city will be continuously impeded.

Contrary to the assumption in the Introduction that by sharing developmental goals and locality, the central and city governments have not made Taipei's development towards a global city frictionless. Instead, Taipei's global development is constantly interrupted by the central government. The cross-Strait politics and party politics, together, are the main obstacles to Taipei's post-industrial development and its globalization ambition.

In Part II, the transformation of the state–society relationship is reviewed. As Taipei moves deeper into the global system, the role of state–society relations is changing, seemingly similar to that of other global cities. Taiwan's rapid development was credited to the successful economic management of the developmental state. The state's active direction and orchestration of development have been the key to its economic growth. In the recent decade, Taiwan's government has reduced its power, as democracy has replaced an authoritarian single-party state. The state is supposed to retreat as a developmental state, and the society expands its domain and influence in policy formation. Taiwan governance appears to have followed this theoretical trend.

Against the position put forward in the Introduction, there are seemingly strong arguments that globalization normally is accompanied by the erosion of the state. Several reasons are given. First, the dominance of the international marketplace replaces state power in economic development (Ohmae, 1995; Yergin and Stanislaw, 1998). Second, transnational economy requires greater political transparency and accountability, social participation and consensus building for effective development (Diamond, 1993). Third, neoliberalism adopted by the West and UN agencies as a principle of economic policy weakens much of the state's control in the economy (Williamson, 1999; Martinez and Garcia, 2000; Watson, 2001). Finally, the parallel rise of non-government organizations and the globalization process further diminishes the power of the state (Boli and Thomas, 1997). These conditions lead to the society's expanding role in polity and policy formation, accompanied by the rise of democracy as the necessary condition for global economic development. To a great extent, these conditions apply well in Taiwan's recent condition.

In spite of the apparent loss of state powers, what follows is that the state is shifting from a direct to an indirect role in managing development. Instead of organizing development, local governmental institutions now have to resolve the social consequences of these new external impacts. Under globalization, the state has to forego its traditional role of economic and social controller. Instead, the state should be the balancer of social concerns, provider of social insurance, and manager of domestic economic reform (Rodrik, 1997). In other words, the roles of the state will have to transform into addressing social inequity by providing social services and welfare, and garnering social acceptance and support for the adoption of the global competitive economy. The change of governance responds to the widening of economic and social polarization, particularly in cities, caused by the transnational production process and international division of labour. The developmental state, though less visible, still exists and functions.

Taiwan and the Taipei government should be prepared for these new social demands. Their performances, however, show different levels of response. In this Part, Huang, Chen and Jou, investigate different sectors of urban development, and find that the state plays multiple roles. At times, the state advocates social participation in policy formation, or leaves the sector entirely to market forces. Other times, it stays as the developmental state and coordinates private capital. Taiwan has adopted democracy for more than a decade. Middle-class politics are particularly active and demonstrative, keeping the state socially responsive (Chapter 4). The multi-party system leads to opposition party politics, which is the cause of the centre-city inter-agency politics, inhibiting Taipei's global growth. The state, both central and city, is aware of the necessity for changing roles, and makes some policy adjustments. Responding to global process and domestic political pressure, the introduction of participatory planning at the neighbourhood level in the mid-1990s allows the middle-class a voice in urban community development and planning projects (Chapter 4). Whereas social participation is practiced at the neighbourhood community level, the same is not true in major citywide development. The most prominent and important urban global project in Taipei is proposed, designed, constructed and managed by a consortium of financial capital, commercial entrepreneur and real estate, engineered by the state, but excludes the local urban communities (Chapter 6). In the Xinyi Planning District development, financial and construction corporations emerge as a major influential political player in urban politics and policy formation. In these major and visible global spatial and infrastructural developments, the state remains as a developmental state. For provision of social services and welfare, in the case of public housing, the state relinquishes practically all developmental responsibilities (Chapter 5). In this sector, the market reigns supreme. In doing so, the state has not intervened on behalf of the underclass, and opts out of its role as the social service provider, allowing social inequity to exist unabated.

As far as adapting into the above mentioned new mode of global governance, Taiwan and Taipei are moving forward unevenly, responding to social pressure in a piecemeal process. The withdrawal of the state has given rise to the emergence of corporate power, which is now a major force in urban development (Chapters 5 and 6). Society, represented by the middle class, has made significant gains in the political arena (Chapter 4), but is less effective in addressing to the widening social inequity. The underclass is still left out of the policy formation process (Chapters 4, 5, and 10). As a result, the state has not been proactive, and has a mixed record in facilitating Taipei's global city project.

In Part III, urban social changes are examined. Urban society has mutated responding to or preparing for globalization. In general theories, social polarization, income inequity and political conflict should occur. Tai and Wu find Taipei's society does not necessarily follow the general trend. Instead of differentiation, urban society initially diversified but now shows a tendency to homogenize.

Globalization generally expands an urban producer service class while polarizing its urban population. Taipei, however, does not follow this general rule. With the emigration of the upper class and immigration of low-skilled labour (who are excluded in official statistics, and isolated from society), the society is dominated by a sizeable middle-income class. Social polarization is, thereby, kept relatively low, and the income gap rises slowly (Chapter 7). The expansion of the middle class leads to its social dominance and reinforces democracy (Hsiao, 1993). The middle class is not only the dominant social and political force, but also the arbiter of consumption. This is the class that is responsive to globalization and tends to be multi-cultural with diverse tastes (Kwok, 2003). Their varied consumption demands the transformation of the retail market structure and keeps this sector in flux. Taipei's food market responds to this social phenomenon and diversifies into several specific markets. Each market provides for specialized goods and services, which suit the changing tastes and demands. The present diversity is, however, gradually moving towards the global market practice and consumption trend (Chapter 8). The movement towards uniform, international, large-scale, one-stop marketing signifies that the society is leaning towards homogeneity.

A single class social dominance and not differentiation, along with movement towards global marketing and consumption, and not diversification, are signs of a society on the move towards global uniformity. Taipei society is beginning to accept the global value and embrace global mentality and behaviour. In general, society is ready and prepared for joining the global community.

In Part IV, cultural changes within the realm of the society are explored. The state normally accepts the dominant cultural norm. The state generally allows the market to dominate and operate, but intervenes when specific institutional requirements appropriate for global development are needed. Wang and Yao explore the cultural conditions of the society in two opposite cases, where, in the former, the state intervenes, and in the latter, it withdraws.

Where the state takes a strong position of maintaining a developmental state is in the Rapid Transit System. In cultural conditioning for globalization, Taipei's government takes a unilateral role in disciplining and regulating its urban citizens through the Rapid Transit System (Chapter 9). This is a collective consumption that most urban citizens consume or encounter on a daily basis. The state seizes the opportunity to condition urban society to assimilate global culture. In this respect, the developmental state is preparing the populace as a conducive and appropriate human resource and consumer for the global capital.

The fact that social polarization is not severe does not mean that globalization reduces inequity to the underclass. The conditions of Taipei's underclass, marginalized by globalization, are hidden but socially problematic. The disillusion, lack of purpose, alienation from family and cultural tradition, and the purposeless survival of this marginalized class pose a major urban social enigma (Chapter 10).

This is a lost class. There is no evidence that the state is taking any major effort to address this serious predicament.

The level of state intervention and market operation, the state–society relations in different sectors of development, and the state's position as social and cultural arbiter are the city's responses to globalization. Together, they are the factors that affect Taipei's path to global development. The city's development, though progressing increasingly deeper into the global network, has encountered some difficulties. The three domestic political issues, cross-Strait policy, identity politics and centre-city inter-agency politics, in combination, pose a major hindrance to the city's globalizing path. These complex and intertwined issues are subject to the international political environment, therefore are unpredictable and susceptible to periodical changes.

Internal to the city, Taipei fares fairly well socially. The developmental effect on the urban society has, so far, shown little impact on social polarization. With the middle class guarding and expanding democracy, keeping state power in check, ameliorating social polarization, the present social structure protects the state from many of the social functions needed for globalization. The relative social stability masks the state's inactivity in providing welfare and services to address income inequity and expansion of the underclass. The plight of the marginalized class is still unattended.

In facilitating Taipei's pursuance of a global city status, the state has made some major changes. By yielding power to some communities, allowing the market to take over selected collective consumption, but retaining the role of the developmental state in major spatial development, the state has taken on a complex set of roles, seemingly inconsistent and hazardous. In general, the developmental state is still in control, paying attention to society only in the realm of economic development, and neglecting the socially marginalized class. In doing so, the state is positive about the global objective but overlooks the negative effects of globalization. There is an obvious irony in the state's attention to global cultural conditioning and its neglect of the urban underclass. As Taipei moves upwards in the global urban hierarchy, the marginalized class will expand, so will social discontent and apathy.

Future Uncertainty

The most immediate question is how Taipei will fare in the future relative to the metropolises in the Asia-Pacific region. Global cities operate within the borderless free market capitalism, and their political economies are volatile and unstable. Given these developmental uncertainties, Taipei's global city project is fluid and unpredictable, subject to the changes in the domestic and international situations. The domestic political economy and its causal factors discussed above are transitory and often contrary to Taipei's global interest. The city's future global position and ranking depends, primarily, on its response to exogenous political and economic changes and intercity competition (Friedmann, 1997). Based on these two points, the following will give a brief projection of Taipei's future from a global perspective.

The exogenous political economy of Taipei is complex. Amongst the many international issues, the most important and outstanding one is the China–Taiwan relationship. Ever since China took its seat in the United Nations in the early 1970s, the international position of the two territories has been reversed. Taiwan has been officially left out of the international political arena. Taiwan's international diplomacy and political agenda have to operate within the confines of the US–China diplomatic negotiations. There are two kinds of international political economies, which ultimately affect Taipei's global development. First is the US–Taiwan relationship. The United States tacitly defines the international position for Taiwan, but vacillates according to the concurrent international situation. Depending on its interests in and exchanges with China, the US. position is subject to change over time. Crisis and conflict occur. In this triangular relationship, the United States has become the broker of the China–Taiwan relationship, maintaining cross-Strait political balance and stability. Constant monitoring and diplomatic dialogue with the US become necessary to maintain or improve Taiwan's international position. Second is the transnational economic tie between China and Taiwan. The growing economic integration and business dynamics between Taiwan and China ameliorate the political tension between the two territories. The present relationship is that both sides accept, albeit reluctantly, the *status quo* as the temporary pragmatic solution, but each side is constantly seeking opportunities to improve its position. The impasse is fragile, as it will alter when the international political context changes. Given these situations, Taipei's global ranking is in flux. The majority of analysts suggest that the most reasonable way to maintain development is through cross-Strait economic cooperation instead of political confrontation (Leifer, 2001; Lin and Lin, 2001; Sutter, 2002; Yang and Hung, 2003). In reality, there is a political impasse, and both sides are not eager to restart negotiations. Without political good-will, cross-Strait economic cooperation is difficult to attain. Political cooperation and economic integration will have to proceed simultaneously. Unless both sides agree to pursue this direction, Taipei's global development is unlikely to be assured.

Intercity competition between candidates for global city status is constant and severe. Cities in the Asia-Pacific region constantly upgrade their infrastructure, investment climate and human resources in order to compete for foreign investment and transnational corporation. The Asia-Pacific nations proactively project their top cities as global consumption space to attract global capital. They are keenly aware of their rival cities' advantages and disadvantages, and perpetually attempt to improve their global position. Cultural activities and international events are the elements in the urban environment important to the knowledge-based labour force. Urban images and aestheticism are articulated to project global appeal. The state has constantly to promote its primary city as a place for global business and production, apart from providing the necessary infrastructure hardware and business institutions. The completion of Taipei 101, a state assisted project (Chapter 6), as the world's tallest building will give a new urban image of a potential global centre, and should attract global capital and transnational corporations. This global image will clearly announce Taipei's commitment to the global city race – a signpost of its invitation for global investment. Other Asia-Pacific cities, however, are also continuously improving their global images by encouraging new and more spectacular built icons. Taipei has improved its position in the race, but has not yet won.

At present, Taiwan stands as the regional leader for the export of computer-related production, specializing and excelling in information technology and semi-conductor production, both of which have a built-in obsolescence. The growth of these key export sectors, in the short term, will continue, since they have adopted the transnational production process by relocating the industries to coastal China, taking advantage of the low production costs. As a highly volatile industry, constant technological innovation is crucial to preserve the leadership position. While the government supports research and development in these sectors (Chapter 1), international competition in technological innovation is intense, and there is no guarantee that Taiwan can maintain its regional superiority in the long term. Other national states in the region, such as South Korea, which has been specializing in electronics, are ready to prepare their labour, training and expertise to mount a challenge. The race within the Asia-Pacific region should put Taiwan on alert, and the state should invest and prepare its capital city for the global challenge. Given the centre-city politics, the reverse is true, making it difficult for the city to sustain or advance its regional position. The state should resolve this political dichotomy in order to provide Taipei with the comparative advantage to compete in the global race.

Within the South China Growth Triangle, there is a concentration of higher education institutions in engineering in Shanghai and Nanjing, and the Yangtze River Delta has been successful in providing abundant computer-related professionals and labour to accommodate Taiwan's relocated information industries. China, one scholar estimates, will catch up with Taiwan in semiconductor technology by 2012 (Klaus, 2003). In time, the Shanghai metropolitan region will upgrade its information technology and knowledge, and enter into the competitive arena. The information technology which crosses the Strait (Leng, 2002) leads to Shanghai emerging as a future chief competitor to Taipei. Taiwan's present technological superiority can only be maintained if it continues to lead in technological innovation. With flexibility in financial and production space, global capital has little constraint in selecting investment and trade locations. If Taipei's competitive edge in the presently fast growing knowledge industry diminishes, its regional supremacy in the information technology industry will be replaced by other locations.

When foreign investment began to penetrate the Asia-Pacific region in the 1970s and China in the 1980s, Hong Kong began to establish itself as the regional financial centre, connecting the global finance from North America and Europe to the Asia-Pacific region. Apart from filtering Taiwan's investment to China, Hong Kong has been the prime foreign investor in and the producer service provider for China. Hong Kong's investment and services permeate into and dominate over not only the adjacent Guangdong Province, but also all parts of China, including Shanghai. However, with the future development of Taipei, this situation is likely to change. Both China and Taiwan have been accepted by the World Trade Organization (China Briefing, 2001). Once their memberships are fully effective, and the WTO rules on trade are applied, direct free trade across the Strait will be enforced. The capital outflow and entrepreneur emigration to coastal China will be relaxed. Taipei's capital, information and trade transactions will flow directly to China, bypassing Hong Kong, providing an opportunity for Taipei's economic diversification. Taipei's producer services are likely to expand. By retrieving Taiwan–China transaction flows, Taipei will diminish Hong Kong's role as the global financial centre.

Taipei's globalization process is progressing, and its economic growth continues to be impressive. At present, the city's global position is at an impasse. Within the global economic system, it cannot compete with Tokyo, Hong Kong or Singapore as a world financial centre. Technically, it is behind the US and Japan in general technical expertise and knowledge development. In production, the transnational network ties it spatially to coastal China. Politically, its globalization plan invariably involves the developmental state. The opposition party politics will continue to be obstructive. Taipei is having a rough climb up the global city rank. Remaining as a global middleman, the city's development is arrested. Whether Taipei will be able to outrank its rival Asia-Pacific cities in providing global financial, trade, infrastructure and institutional services in the future depends on the resolve and readiness of its government to pursue its globalization project.

References

Boli, J. and Thomas, G. (1997) World culture in the world polity: a century of international non-government organization. *American Sociological Review*, **62**(2), pp. 171–190.

China Briefing (2001) WTO. *Far Eastern Economic Review*, **164**(46), p. 34.

Diamond, Larry (1993) The globalization of democracy, in Slater, Robert O., Schultz, Barry M. and Dorr, Steven R (eds.) *Global Transformation and the Third World*. Boulder, CO: Lynn Rienner Publishers, pp. 31–69.

Friedmann, J. (1997) World City Futures: The Role of Urban and Regional Policies in the Asia-Pacific Region. Chinese University of Hong Kong, Hong Kong Institute of Asia-Pacific Studies, Occasional Paper 56.

Hsiao, H.M. (ed.) (1993) *Discovery of the Middle Classes in East Asia*. Taipei: Institute of Ethnology, Academia Sinica.

Klaus, M. (2003) Red chips: implications of semiconductor industry's relocation to China. *Asian Affairs*, **29**(4), pp. 237–253.

Kwok, Reginald Yin-Wang (2003) A paradigm for Asian Pacific urban form: cultural contention of globalization and vernacularization, in Jin-Ho Park, Jin-Ho (ed.) *Creating Livable Communities in Asia Pacific: Value, Relevance and Connectivity*. Honolulu: University of Hawaii, School of Architecture. pp. 65–77.

Leifer, M. (2001) Taiwan and South-East Asia: the limits to pragmatic diplomacy. *The China Quarterly*, No. 165, March, pp. 173–185.

Leng, T.K. (2002) Economic globalization and IT talent flows across the Taiwan Strait: the Taipei/Shanghai/Silicon Valley triangle. *Asian Survey*, **42**(2), pp. 230–250.

Lin, W.L. and Lin, P. (2001) Emergence of the Greater China circle economics: cooperation versus competition. *Journal of Contemporary China*, **10**(29), pp. 695–710.

Martinez, E. and Garcia, A. (2000) What is 'Neo-Liberalism'? available at http://www.globalexchange.org/campaigns/econ101/neoliberalDefined.html.

Ohmae, K. (1995) *The End of the Nation State: The Rise of Regional Economies*. New York: Free Press.

Rodrik, D. (1997) *Has Globalization Gone too Far?* Washington, DC: Institute for International Economics.

Sutter, K.M. (2002) Business dynamism across the Taiwan Strait: the implications for cross-Strait relations. *Asian Survey*, **42**(3), pp. 522–540.

Watson, Iain (2001) Politics, Resistance to neoliberalism and the ambiguities of globalization. *Global Society*, **15**(2), pp. 201–218.

Williamson, J. (1999) What Washington means by policy reform? in Williamson, John (ed.) *Latin American Adjustment: How Much Has Happened?* Washington DC: Institute for International Economics, pp. 7–38.

Yang, C. and Hung, S.W. (2003) Taiwan dilemma across the Strait: lifting the ban on semiconductor investment in China. *Asian Survey*, **42**(4), pp. 681–696.

Yergin, D. and Stanislaw, J. (1998) *The Commanding Heights: The Battle between Government and Marketplace that is Remaking the Modern World*. New York: Simon & Schuster.

Index